The Collins Complete
Woodworker

"Whatever I am working on, I get excited. It does not matter if I have done the same piece many times. I still cannot wait to get out to the shop in the morning."

Sam Maloof, b. 1916, America's most widely
admired contemporary furniture craftsman

From the editors of

**WOODWORKER'S
JOURNAL**

The Collins Complete

Woodworker

Contents

Chapter **1**

A Brief History of Woodworking and Furniture Styles

Chapter **2**

The Nature of Hardwood

Chapter **3**

A Safe and Comfortable Workshop

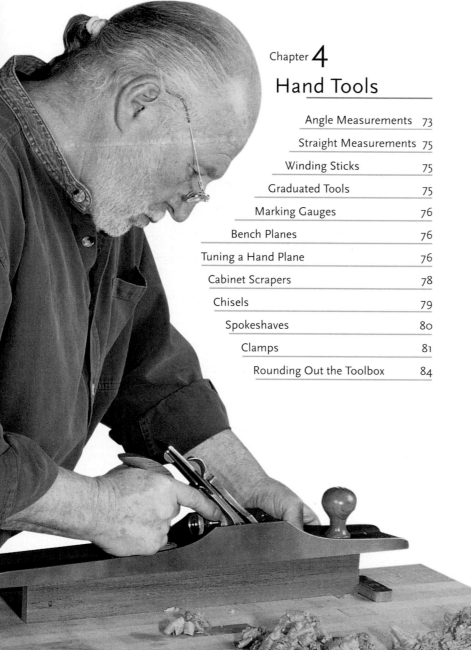

Chapter 4

Hand Tools

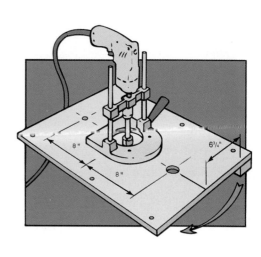

Chapter 5

Portable Power Tools

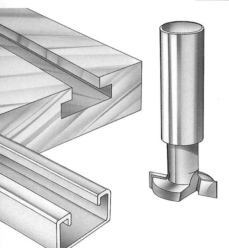

Chapter **14**

Hardware

Chapter **15**

Sanding and Finishing

Chapter **16**

Setting Up Shop

Projects

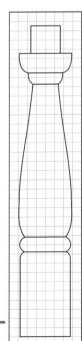

Acknowledgments

Woodworker's Journal:

Publisher Ann Rockler Jackson
Editor-in-Chief Larry N. Stoiaken
Editor Rob Johnstone
Senior Editor Joanna Werch Takes
Art Director Jeff Jacobson
Illustrators John Kelliher, Jeff Jacobson

Hydra Publishing:

Publisher Sean Moore
Publishing Director Karen Prince
Editorial Director Aaron R. Murray
Art Director Brian MacMullen

Senior Editor A.J. Hamler
Senior Designer Patricia Childers
Designer Ken Crossland
Contributing Editors John English,
Lee Gordon, Chris Marshall, Charlie Self
Production Eunho Lee
Copy Editor Glenn Novak

Woodworker's Journal recently celebrated its 30th anniversary—a benchmark few magazines ever reach. Over the years, hundreds of woodworkers—far too many to mention here—have played a role in our contribution to the body of woodworking knowledge. I would, however, be remiss if I didn't acknowledge the 300,000-plus woodworkers who make up our current readership. Obviously, without them, there would be little to tell.

We are also grateful to our sister company, Rockler Woodworking and Hardware (*rockler.com*), which just celebrated its 50th anniversary as the premier supplier to woodworkers everywhere. Rockler provided most of the hardware, wood, and other products you see in this book. Our publishing partner, Hydra Publishing, did a terrific job updating and presenting our material, and we are particularly grateful to Aaron Murray and Patricia Childers for their dedication to the content. Senior editor A.J. Hamler, a writer for our magazine and longtime woodworking editor, pulled together a great team of editors to help him write, rewrite, and edit our stories. And for advice, consultation, and the sharing of their expertise over the years, *Woodworker's Journal* is grateful to Nordy Rockler, Betty Scarpino, Chris Marshall, Michael Dresdner, Sandor Nagyszalanczy, Ian Kirby, Mike McGlynn, Bill Hylton, Bruce Kieffer and Rick White.

Finally, our thanks to Peter Muldoon, Conservator, Castle Collection, Smithsonian Institution; Ellen Nanney with Smithsonian Business Ventures; and to Phil Friedman, publisher at HarperCollins.

Larry N. Stoiaken, Editor-in-Chief

Introduction

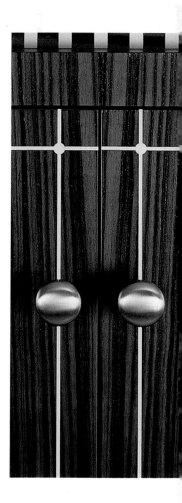

Why woodworking? As master woodworker and *Woodworker's Journal* regular Ian Kirby will tell you, in times past we made things out of wood because we needed them to survive: a bucket to carry the cow's milk, a table on which to work and eat, a cradle to hold the baby, and maybe even a chair for grandmother to sit in. But let's face it, it's been a long time since the prime motivation for our woodworking efforts was truly need-based.

Some woodworkers will tell you their hobby saves them a lot of money. While occasionally true, 20 years of editing a woodworking magazine has given me significant evidence to the contrary. It might be a helpful line for the spouse when you're gearing up to buy that next big tool, but otherwise this theory is a fantasy most of us have long since abandoned. A $600 table saw can be used to make a dining room table easily worth $6,000, but then there is the cost of the jointer, planer, drill press, miter saw, router, belt sander, lathe, disk sander . . . well, you get the picture. (And by the way, the wood itself isn't cheap either, especially considering the two "prototype" tables you gave to relatives because they weren't "quite right" for your home yet.)

(Continued)

"We engage in the craft of woodworking to satisfy our need to create, to have our efforts be appreciated, and to give something significant of ourselves to those we love—to bring both order and beauty into our lives."

Rob Johnstone, Editor, *Woodworker's Journal*

Above: *Ascending Rhythms* **by William Hunter, cocobolo, lathe-turned and carved** *(From the Nordy & Bert Rockler Collection)*

Opposite, from left:

Smoothing plane, by Kerry Pierce

Craftsman professional miter saw

Shaker-inspired drop leaf table, by LiLi Jackson

Why woodworking? It's not a simple question to answer. After all, woodworking is practiced around the world, in nearly every culture and clime. My editor Rob Johnstone and I have batted the question around a lot in recent years, given the rise of ready-made furniture from IKEA and the precipitous decline in woodworking shops in our schools. Rob feels that "we engage in the craft of woodworking to satisfy our need to create, to have our efforts be appreciated, and to give something significant of ourselves to those we love—to bring both order and beauty into our lives." This speaks volumes about the results of our shop efforts, but I've always thought we also engage in the craft because working with wood connects us with a wondrous tradition that has our history knitted intricately into it. "Woodworking," Ian once told me, "is a logical way of doing something. A way of doing something that is rightful, and helps us to understand the world around us."

Of course, if you watch woodworking on the many cable television shows today you might miss this connection to the past. Everything on cable takes exactly half an hour to complete. On TV, you see the before and after; in the shop, woodworkers experience the in-between. In the shop, it's just you, losing yourself for hours at a time to the background music of humming power tools. Woodworking is slowly running your hand along the grain, testing and retesting the fit of a gently sloping tusk tenon. In the shop, the excitement is in the details.

Frank Grant, one of the best woodworkers in Minneapolis, once described for me his rationale for the top of a podium he made for a local church: "I held the center panel proud of the frame by just less than the thickness of the veneer. This helps a person get a fingernail under a piece of sheet music lying on the podium. Not a big deal . . . but it does make the stand more pleasant to use." That brings us right back to Rob's feeling about giving something of ourselves. At the end of a long day in the shop, woodworking is finally taking off your apron, shaking the sawdust out of your hair, and proudly showing off (and describing) your latest project to your family.

People in all circumstances do what they can to add decoration and luster to their existence—and woodworking has forever been a part of that effort. Austere Shakers built furniture that served eminently practical purposes, but what they built was beautiful. Arts and Crafts furniture was created to support a philosophy that rejected ostentatious ornamentation, yet its elegant beauty is impossible to deny. This mantle of beauty with which we surround ourselves also creates an orderly shelter that provides comfort in a disorderly world. While it has been a long time since our survival depended on building the things we use in our daily lives, we still have a human need to do so;

those of us whose daily work does not create things to hold in our hands find this to be especially true.

In these pages our contributors have covered everything from the history and characteristics of the wood we work, to the tools and jigs in our shops, to the hardware and finishing techniques we employ to complete our projects. It's my hope that this updated compilation from the pages of *Woodworker's Journal* will provide a glimpse at the wonderful world of woodworking.

This book is dedicated to woodworkers everywhere who have, through this craft, discovered a connection to the past and are doing their part to pass their skills on to the next generation.

Larry N. Stoiaken
Editor-in-Chief
Woodworker's Journal

CHAPTER 1

A Brief History of Woodworking and Furniture Styles

A Brief History of Woodworking and Furniture Styles

ANCIENT ROOTS

Woodworking as a craft has been with us since the advent of tools, when flint gouges and knives were used to fashion crude weaponry and domestic utensils. The craft became art when it was discovered that metal would hold an edge, which in turn quickly led to joinery. The earliest discovered examples of mechanical joinery are 5,000-year-old dovetails found in the exhumed tombs of royal families in both Egypt and China. Artifacts from Bronze Age excavations in northern Europe include caskets and chairs, while later Iron Age finds are often more artistic and perhaps less utilitarian, such as carvings, statuary, and other ornamentation. Much of what we consider to be modern joinery—butt, lap, and dovetail joints, for example—was at least familiar to the Egyptians and later the Romans, although few examples have survived, due to the biodegradable nature of wood. Early Egyptian hand tools and cutters would most likely have been bronze, as iron didn't become widely available until after 1200 BCE. This corresponds to a similar timeline within a few hundred years across Asia, most particularly in China but also on the Korean peninsula and in Thailand.

As with other aspects of the culture, European woodworking lay virtually somnolent through the Dark Ages. The earliest evidence of what was to become an exquisitely advanced craft can be seen in carved aspects of the rough-hewn and stolid furniture in medieval castles, monasteries, and abbeys. As glorious cathedrals soared to the skies a thousand years ago across northern Europe and the British Isles, highly skilled carpentry became a requisite of their engineering and pattern-making, their intricately trussed roof systems and highly figured panel doors.

By the time Columbus sailed west for the Orient, European furniture had become two things. In the English court and church, the trappings and traceries revealed the influence of a borrowed Gothic past, while the inhabitants of rural villages and farms continued to value the mundane utility of medieval furnishings.

BAROQUE: AN EXUBERANT GRANDEUR (1600–1770)

On the continent, a rebirth in art, architecture, and all manner of craft had newly become the Renaissance. Combining the Christian embodiment of Byzantine art with an enlightened approach to the physical sciences, southern Europe had, after a long stagnation, rediscovered the joys of learning. While ecclesiastical influences were still strong, the sponsorship of secular powers, most notably the courts in France, Germany, Austria, and Russia, would soon bring a similar renaissance to the world of furniture and woodworking. The first instance of this was the Baroque style (beginning around 1600), which embraced grand themes, high drama, and, beneath its curtain of excess, a goal to convey simple ideas most simply. Baroque furniture took its lead from architecture, where massive staircases and sumptuous state apartments framed the lives and homes of the aristocracy, disguising simplicity by surrounding it with distraction. In England, Sir Christopher Wren created his Renaissance masterpiece, St. Paul's Cathedral, and built numerous London churches after the Great Fire. Late Baroque furniture brought two innovations that defined the style. The first of these chronologically was the use

Opposite page: Baroque master André Charles Boulle (1642–1732) created many exquisite pieces for the Sun King, Louis XIV of France. This richly decorated cabinet features many hidden niches and drawers and uses veneers of contrasting woods and other materials cut into tiny pieces and arranged to form a pattern in a technique called marquetry. The cabinet, made between 1670 and 1680 at the Parisian court, is currently on display at the Rijksmuseum in Amsterdam.

of caryatids (female figures acting as corbels or supports), along with scrolled decorative elements in legs, and carved spirals. The second innovation was, in the opinion of many curators, a watershed event that ushered in a rush of later styles—curved fronts on chests, wardrobes, and other large pieces. The leading light of this movement was the Frenchman André Charles Boulle, who created many exquisite pieces for Louis XIV and worked extensively with veneer. As with most European artistry, modern woodworking saw its beginnings in the Renaissance.

**Above:
Daniel Marot**

Right: This carved and gilded limewood table was completed in 1692 for Queen Mary II of England. An inscription on the stretcher is probably in Marot's own hand.

Opposite page: Reeded and inlaid panels of figured birch on this bed's foot posts are typical Federal elements.

DANIEL MAROT (1661–1752)

Daniel Marot was the Frank Lloyd Wright of his day. His designs for furniture, and just about everything else in a house, influenced woodworkers from Holland to England and the American colonies. Born in France, Marot designed clocks for André Charles Boulle, the cabinetmaker for Louis XIV. Marot did apprentice work on furnishings for Versailles. When Louis revoked the Edict of Nantes in 1685, Protestants could no longer worship freely in France, so Marot moved to Holland and worked for the future King William III and Queen Mary II of England.

Marot's experience with the court of Versailles helped his business while he worked for William and Mary in both Holland and England. As he filled their palaces, his own interpretation of the Baroque style continued to gain recognition. He expressed this vision in tall-back chairs with turned legs and elaborately carved back panels. He featured shells and acanthus leaves in his designs, and sometimes carved and pierced the chairs' front stretchers. Some

of Marot's chairs had cabriole legs, which were just beginning a rise to the popularity they would enjoy under Queen Anne. He generally used walnut, the select species of the time.

Marot set the 1690s trend toward great state beds with textile coverings that made their finish unimportant, but his cabinets, tables, and mirror frames featured a wide array of veneers. Oak was popular for the carcasses, but the veneer might be anything—walnut, yew, mulberry, chestnut, olive, holly, beech, or even ivory, sometimes stained green. One Marot set (a side table, candle stand, and mirror) has been described as "figured and festooned with green covers." The mirror was gilded, and the table had a white marble top. That group was designed for a Dutch palace, but it was in England that Marot became known for the new concept of matching furniture, textiles, and other elements to make each room a unified, decorative space.

His influence eventually spread to the American colonies. In the 1690s, wealthy families imported English furniture, and local woodworkers copied the new ideas. Marot's influence shows up in high chests

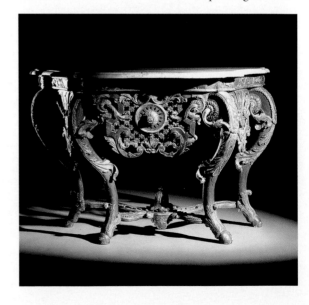

An architect, and the appointed Master of Works to His Majesty, King William III of England, Marot worked extensively on the furniture at Hampton Court Palace.

with multi-arched skirts and legs turned to resemble ancient Roman balusters. Not one to limit himself, Marot also designed outdoor furniture, introducing wooden garden benches with high backs that often featured elaborate carvings based on Greek and Roman mythology. His commitment to unity showed up in this arena as well, since he often laid out the gardens where his benches rested.

Although he is closely associated with William and Mary, Marot never chose to make England his permanent home. He did work for the king's English properties until William's death in 1702, but Marot himself lived in Holland during the 1700s. He died in 1752.

THE FEDERAL PERIOD (1776–1820)

America's founding fathers framed their new republic on classical Greek and Roman concepts. Furniture makers of the day, caught up in the groundswell of change, were of a like mind. Beading, fluting, reeding, and classical motifs like urns, drapery, and cornucopia that appeared on Federal furniture paid homage to a classical heritage, while American patriotic symbols such as Liberty, sheaves of wheat, and eagles expressed the new country's optimism. George Washington himself frequently appeared on Federal furniture, in the form of portraits either created by or surrounded by inlay, a popular Federal adornment.

The first appearance of Federal furniture was in a year with particular significance for the young United States: 1776, when Benjamin Randolph of Philadelphia created a mahogany lap desk with satinwood banding for Thomas Jefferson. For approximately the next 40 years, until around 1820, the delicate lines and fine ornamentation of Federal furniture were a visual manifestation of these ideals. As President James Madison furnished the White House in 1808, architect Benjamin Latrobe even designed furniture for the president's mansion in the "new Greek style."

In 1776, Randolph built

BENJAMIN RANDOLPH
(1721–91)

Born into a Quaker family, Benjamin Randolph owned a New Jersey sawmill with his brother Daniel: a handy resource for a budding young woodworker. He also served as an apprentice to Philadelphia joiner John Jones, or at least paid him rent in 1763. By the next year, he was buying 18th-century status symbols like a horse and bridle, a cow, and guns, and receiving deliveries of cedar boards.

At first, Randolph seems to have concentrated on house joinery and other carpentry work. The cabinetmaking enterprise developed as he slowly got acquainted with the right crowd. Like John Jones, Randolph was a member of St. Paul's Episcopal Church. So was Plunket Fleeson, an upholsterer who was the City of Brotherly Love's first promoter of the easy chair.

Randolph opened his doors at a new Chestnut Street location in 1767, the same year he started calling himself a cabinetmaker. He had already been working out of other locations for a couple of years, becoming a shop foreman overseeing apprentices and carvers. Randolph had access to Thomas Chippendale's *Gentleman and Cabinet Maker's Director*. The pieces referred to in his advertisements for "all sorts of cabinet and chair work" during the 1760s and '70s were, for the most part, in the "Philadelphia Chippendale" style. This American version of the Chippendale style mixed elements from the *Director* with those portions of earlier English styles that American woodworkers (and their customers) liked. Randolph and his colleagues also added

Top right: *Portrait of Benjamin Randolph*, by Charles Peale (Philadelphia Museum of Art: Gift of Mr. and Mrs. Timothy Johnes Westbrook, 1990)

Above, and right: Randolph's Philadelphia Chippendale style combined cabriole legs with rail and splat carvings that emphasized curves.

the first piece of Federal furniture, a lap desk for Thomas Jefferson,
which he subsequently used to write the Declaration of Independence.

ornamentation in the Chippendale rococo style: free-flowing, asymmetrical items, often from nature. Generally, these "extras" showed up in carvings.

Sometimes, he put carvings of swans on his furniture, incorporating two important stylistic trends of the day: the free-flowing rococo ideal from Chippendale and the "line of beauty" curve from the Queen Anne style. He also was partial to carved finials in the shape of flames, urns, and busts of 18th-century heroes like Benjamin Franklin. Most of Randolph's pieces had carved ball-and-claw feet, with the claws modeled after talons on American birds of prey.

When the Continental Congress met in Philadelphia, Thomas Jefferson was a houseguest of Randolph's. In May 1776, he paid for the construction of a lap desk. The wood, mahogany, was typical of Randolph's earlier pieces. The style was new: The desk is the first documented example of American neoclassical furniture. Its simple, delicate lines introduced American woodworkers to what became known as Federal style. Instead of curves, it emphasized straight lines. Ornaments weren't bold, like the carving on Chippendale-style pieces; they were in a fine scale, like the satinwood inlay banding around the desk's front drawer.

Randolph's desk ended up playing an important role in the fight for freedom: Jefferson used it to write the Declaration of Independence. As for Randolph himself, he played host to Jefferson and to George and Martha Washington while they traveled to army camps, before signing up himself. During the war, Randolph served as a dispatch carrier for Washington. When peace came, he

sold his shop and retired to New Jersey, where he had bought his brother out at their sawmill. He died in 1791 and was buried in Philadelphia.

For Randolph, pattern books were a way to supply his well-to-do Philadelphia clients with pieces in the latest London styles. By supplying American-made versions, he could simultaneously satisfy the sensibilities of his own patriotism and his customers' desires.

DUNCAN PHYFE (1768–1854)

No story of woodworking in the 19th century would be complete without mentioning Duncan Phyfe. His work in New York City from the 1790s to the 1840s spanned several styles, including the neoclassical work for which he is best known. Unfortunately, few documented Phyfe pieces survive, and recent research indicates that some furniture previously attributed to him was actually the work of other New York cabinetmakers.

Nevertheless, Phyfe deserves his fame: Letters from his day include comments like "Mr. Phyfe is so much the rage" and his cabinet shop "[is] the largest and most fashionable [such] establishment in the country." Like John Henry Belter (see page 13), Phyfe was an immigrant, arriving from Loch Fannich, Scotland, with his family in 1783. The 15-year-old Duncan served an apprenticeship in Albany, then moved to New York City. He opened a shop on Broad Street around 1792 and in 1806 relocated to Partition (later Fulton) Street. The

Above: Descendants of Randolph's wife kept this carved, upholstered easy chair, which features a mask on the apron. Jefferson's lap desk (above, left) is mahogany with satinwood inlay banding around the drawer.

Eighteenth-century English furniture makers Hepplewhite, Sheraton, and Chippendale influenced later styles with their cabinetmakers' pattern books.

Almost all of the furniture above is attributed to Phyfe, whose shop employed over 100 people.

CABINETMAKERS' PATTERN BOOKS (1788–94)

One method by which furniture designs traveled from country to country was through the dissemination of popular pattern books, including George Hepplewhite's *Cabinetmaker's and Upholsterer's Guide*, published posthumously by his widow Alice in 1788; Thomas Sheraton's *The Cabinetmaker & Upholsterer's Drawing Book*, published in several parts between 1791 and 1794; and Thomas Shearer's *Cabinet-Makers' London Book of Price and Designs of Cabinet Work*, first printed in 1788. These books had such a strong influence that the Federal furniture era has

historical judgment has been that Phyfe's earlier work was better than his later pieces. Described as Federal or Sheraton, his furniture from the 18th and early 19th centuries drew heavily on popular Greek, Roman, and Egyptian influences. Throughout his career, even when styles shifted and he applied Gothic or rococo ornament to classic forms, Phyfe worked with high-quality mahogany veneers. He would pay $1,000 a piece for lumber that West Indian harvesters referred to as "Duncan Phyfe logs."

Phyfe could afford those prices: In 1816, he charged $265 for a table. By the time he auctioned off the business in 1847, Phyfe was ready for a nice retirement, building doll furniture on his backyard workbench. He died in 1854, with an estate worth nearly $500,000.

sometimes been called Sheraton and Hepplewhite. Customers and cabinetmakers alike used the books as inspiration for reproducing designs, or for mixing and matching different elements. Although the names Sheraton and Hepplewhite have each come to be associated with a particular style of chair, both of these designers showed several stylistic options in their books—including the ones that now bear the other's name.

Sheraton (1751–1806), in particular, offered other suggestions, telling the wealthy that the more elegant their parlor was, the more it showed respect for visitors. He also suggested hanging green silk behind glass doors, to conceal the contents of bookcases. Sheraton was working on an encyclopedia for cabinetmakers but got only to the letter "C" before he died.

The oval back and the square, tapered front legs of this Hepplewhite chair (below, right) are indicative of his style. The three smaller chairs are, left to right, a striped green Hepplewhite-style drawing room chair from Philadelphia; a very typical square-backed Sheraton version with turned front legs; and a truly American piece of furniture, the Martha Washington high-backed armchair, which was named for the new nation's First Lady (see page 11).

Eagles are the theme for both the finial and the inlay on this very representative Federal secretary. Sheraton advised hanging green silk behind the glass, to conceal the contents.

Brave workers in wood, as you work for the ladies, your work must be good."

Benjamin Franklin, as quoted by the Federal Society of Cabinetmakers, 1788

POPULAR 18TH AND 19TH CENTURY SPECIES

Woodworkers in coastal towns, with access to the shipping lanes, tended to use mahogany as their primary wood, while woodworkers with inland locations were more likely to choose walnut. Cherry was also popular as a primary wood, particularly in the Connecticut River valley and western Massachusetts. Northern New Englanders sometimes used species like birch or maple. White pine was prevalent everywhere as a secondary wood, and other choices included chestnut and tulip in Connecticut and Rhode Island, and holly and satinwood further south. Frequently, the lighter-colored woods were applied as veneer or inlay to contrast with the dark mahogany or cherry.

Boston's most famous Federal cabinetmakers, John and Thomas Seymour, were fond of such contrasts. They were associated with tambour desks, which were frequently inlaid with bellflowers. Another popular desk form of the day was the secretary, which was particularly popular in Salem. Other common elements in Massachusetts Federal furniture were figured birch panels, chevron stringing, and ebony spade feet. Baltimore's woodworkers developed a style that was the closest to England's interpretation of neoclassical furniture. It was often painted, and sometimes incorporated *verre églomisé*, glass panels with biblical or mythological scenes painted on the reverse side.

New York had already become the nation's center of culture and fashion by the early 1800s. Its most prominent woodworker was Duncan Phyfe, a Scottish immigrant whose early work for John Jacob Astor cemented his place in the fashionable world. New York woodworkers tended toward solid wood, usually carved or reeded mahogany, rather than the light and dark contrasts other regions achieved with inlay. Chairs with back splats carved as urns, fans or feathers were associated with New York and with Phyfe, as were pedestal-base dining tables with curved legs and brass claw feet.

New York shared with Philadelphia a preference for the design element of inlaid, astragal-ended satinwood rectangles with dark elliptical centers. Philadelphians also had a predilection for chairs with heart or fan-shaped backs (a John Aitken advertised them in 1790 as a pattern "entirely new, never before seen in this city"); square-back chairs with turned columns; and ladder-back chairs with pierced and carved slats, tapered legs, and rounded shoulders.

Perhaps the most symbolic furniture development of the Federal era was the "Martha Washington chair." The design for this tall armchair does not appear anywhere in Hepplewhite, Sheraton, or Shearer, but was instead an American adaptation of a similar, outdated style illustrated in Thomas Chippendale's *Director*. With its high back and tapered or occasionally turned and reeded legs, and its name derived from the young country's First Lady, the Martha Washington chair was a truly American idea.

Development of the Grecian or Klismos chair (left), with its scrolled back, cross-bars, and saberlike legs, occurred around 1805 in the New York area.

Pieces like the lady's cabinet and writing table shown at far left reflect a new emphasis during the Federal era on women's education. The panels on this mahogany piece with satinwood inlay use Baltimore's *"verre églomisé"* painted glass technique.

Work tables (above) were a new form of furniture in the Federal period. Some incorporated a fabric pouch to hold a lady's sewing.

WINDS OF CHANGE (1790–1812)

Woodworkers of the Federal era were experiencing other historical changes as well—like the beginnings of the Industrial Revolution. Already, they were more likely to be specialists than generalists. Carvers, turners, gilders, inlay makers, cabinetmakers, chair makers, and upholsterers sometimes had individual shops and purchased elements from each other. In this system, an inlay maker might produce several copies of a design for sale to cabinetmakers. He would make the copies of his design by pricking through his original drawing onto other sheets of paper and pasting those papers to one thin slice of wood, with other species pinned to the workpiece. After clamping his layers into a vise and sawing out his design, the inlay maker discarded the unnecessary pieces from each layer. The cabinetmaker who purchased this inlay would place it onto an area of dried glue and clamp it with a heated wooden caul to remelt the glue.

"Machinery for Sawing Arabesque Chairs" was the first patent that Belter received on July 31, 1847

After the War of 1812, the fashionable ideal gradually shifted to French culture. Heavier, bolder pieces of furniture with marble tabletops and columnar supports started replacing delicate Federal furniture, as it gave way to the French Empire style.

The most well known name from the era is probably Thomas Chippendale (1718–1779). Recent research suggests, however, that Chippendale himself merely published designs created by his employees, and didn't build furniture, either. His book, *The Gentleman and Cabinet-Maker's Director of 1754*, was a compilation of stylistic influences popular at the time: the free-flowing rococo that had begun in France, where it took its name from rock gardens; the Oriental influence British traders brought back from China, along with the tea that sparked the idea for tea tables; and the pointed Gothic arches that were the 18th-century romantics' idea of what the Middle Ages should have looked like.

JOHN HENRY BELTER (1804–63)

Best known as the leading maker of Victorian rococo-revival furniture, Belter also would have understood how close to the heart today's woodworkers hold their jigs and shop tricks: He received four different patents for them in his lifetime. Born in Ulm, Germany, in 1804, Belter served an apprenticeship in the province of Württemberg before emigrating to the United States in the early 1840s. Records of his life in Germany are sketchy, but it was obvious he was well-trained and ready to set up shop as soon as he stepped foot into the New World. He did have his own shop at 401 Chatham Square by 1844, when his name first appears in the New York City directory.

Belter didn't waste any time filing patent applications, either. He received his first patent, for "Machinery for Sawing Arabesque Chairs," on July 31, 1847. The vise and jigsaw apparatus held and cut chair backs with openwork designs. The saw was adjustable to allow for curving chair backs.

Modern familiarity with Belter's work generally comes from parlor sets, because that is what survived the years, but his own advertisements say he made "all kinds of furniture." The style he worked in was Victorian rococo revival. The inspiration came from the 18th-century movement of the same name, but the rococo revival of the Victorian age wasn't an exact copy. Furniture manufactured in the 19th century, for example, tended to be larger in both weight and height. Belter and his contemporaries got ideas from the past but adapted them to fit their own time. They used naturalistic carvings, as the original rococo artists did, but made them bigger and truer to life. Belter's favorite subjects included grapes, pomegranates, roses, and morning glories. Throughout his career, he produced pieces with both simple and complex carvings incorporating these elements.

Belter popularized laminating wood as a means of giving it the strength to support intricate carvings and piercings. Generally working with rosewood, he layered between three and sixteen thicknesses together (the usual number was six to eight) with the grain in every layer running at a 90° angle to the one before. Each sheet of wood was about 1.6 mm thick. After gluing and pressing the layers together, Belter placed them into an iron mold, which created bends and curves, and then steamed the laminations. He became so well known for this process that people referred to carved, laminated rococo-revival pieces as "Belter furniture," no matter who made it. He died of tuberculosis in 1863.

Opposite page: Federal sofas had a soft outline, frequently embellished with delicate carvings. The carving on this piece has been attributed to Samuel McIntire of Salem, Massachusetts.

Left: Belter was known for his carved, pierced works, such as this armchair, which incorporates rosewood, rosewood veneer, pine, and chestnut.

SHAKER FURNITURE SINCE 1774

Shaker woodworkers built furniture that was simple, functional, and (most of the time) adhered to their religious rules. (Above) Drawers were made to fit the items stored in them, not to follow some principle of design.

"Plain and simple" sums up the popular image of Shaker furniture, according to Smithsonian curator Jeremy Adamson. But woodworkers need to remember other influencing factors, too.

"We look at the period 1820 to 1840 as the heyday of Shaker design. Shakers didn't see it that way," Adamson explained. Instead, they believed in striving for perfection. An 1824 tool chest might be "perfect" for its time, but the design was open to later improvements.

Shaker founder Ann Lee was born in Manchester, England, in 1736 and worshiped with the Quakers there. Due to the movements in their form of worship, she and some others became known as "shaking Quakers," which became Shakers. Fleeing religious persecution, she and a small group of followers emigrated to America in 1774, where the pacifist group faced imprisonment as suspected British sympathizers during the Revolutionary War. Despite such setbacks, they managed to acquire property in Niskayuna (now Watervliet), New York, that became the home base for the society they were founding. The imprisonment of "Mother" Ann actually enhanced her saintly standing among her followers and other 18th-century spiritual seekers. The most prominent of these was Joseph Meacham, a Baptist minister who joined the Shakers after New England's "Dark Day" of 1780, when the sun didn't appear to rise.

For the Shakers, another spiritual turning point had already occurred. Early members thought that Mother Ann was the second coming of Christ, a female form of God on earth. Her life, they believed, ushered in a millennium of peace—which is why they needed to build furniture that could last a thousand years. Mother Ann's comment, "Work as if you had a thousand years to live, and as if you knew you would die tomorrow," encouraged this practice.

Officially known as the United Society of Believers in Christ's Second Appearing, they practiced communal property ownership, regular confession, and celibacy. At the height of the Shaker movement, 18 communities existed. During the period of 1820–60, when a Shaker religious revival led to increased isolation from the world, Shaker woodworkers built within a simplified neoclassical style. Plain, tapered legs and simple tops were easy to produce in quantity, a necessity for a community that lived in large groups, and something that fitted in well with their philosophy. They pushed the rectilinear and oval units to a uniform simplicity, took off unnecessary ornaments like tall bedposts, and emphasized rectangular and horizontal shapes. Although they liked to use the concept of the Golden Mean when possible, they didn't hesitate to violate it, creating both long, low counters and high, thin cupboards. Practicality was the basis of their projects, with drawers and compartments designed to fit the items they would store. An 18th-century statement summarized their design philosophy: "Regularity is beautiful. There is great beauty in harmony. Beauty rests on utility."

Since the Shaker communities were scattered from Maine to Kentucky, the woods they used varied, including pine, maple, walnut, and others. The pieces were trestle tables, oval boxes, ladder-back chairs, and other useful items. They placed trestle table stretchers directly under the tabletop, to make

". . . religion produced good chairs"

Shaker sister

sweeping easier; employed bevel-edged swallowtails to let their oval boxes expand and contract with humidity; and put a slight angle in the back of the chairs so they would be comfortable to sit in. Features that helped maintain cleanliness, one of the communal values, were very popular. After 1820, for example, their raised panels flattened out, with a ¼-inch round thumbnail around the frame: They were easier to dust that way. They invented the circular saw and the chair tilter, while believing that patents were monopolistic and un-Christian. Shaker archives mention Tabitha Babbitt of the Harvard community developing a circular saw blade and water-powered machine in 1813, three years before others filed for the U.S. patent on a circular saw. Shaker woodworkers regarded their tasks as a form of worship.

Craftspeople sometimes found their designs disallowed. The Millennial Laws of 1845 clearly stated what kind of furniture Shakers could possess and, by extension, make. Frequent rationales for embellishments that violated the rules of simplicity were that they stopped splintering, cushioned heads against sharp corners, or protected the furniture against feet and brooms. Crafters sometimes even used hidden dovetails, which were forbidden because they violated the principle of openly displaying an object's features. In 1872 the Mount Lebanon, New York, community opened a commercial chair factory. Competitors who tried to sell their own ladder-back chairs as Shaker-made forced the believers to bend to the ways of the world and develop a trademark between 1874 and 1875. The last Shaker man to make chairs, William Perkins, died in 1934, and the last woman chair builder, Lillian Barlow, passed in 1942. Shakers, however, still live at Sabbathday Lake in Maine.

Included in the Smithsonian's collections are typical Shaker objects such as the baskets at left, which were constructed between 1830 and 1880.

In 1876, the Philadelphia Centennial Exhibition awarded a medal which recognized Shaker seating as having "strength, sprightliness and modest beauty."

According to a Shaker sister, "religion produced good chairs" like this rocker, circa 1840.

Art Deco is "characterized by the restrained stylized use of ornament, simple furniture shapes, an emphasis on fine craftsmanship, and

Charles Boyce, from the *Dictionary of Furniture*, as quoted by Robert J. Orr. *Smithsonian Preservation Quarterly*, summer 1994 edition

JACQUES-EMILE RUHLMANN (1879–1933)

No name is more thoroughly identified with a school of thought than Jacques-Emile Ruhlmann and the Art Deco movement. Ruhlmann was nothing less than the high priest and foremost practitioner of Art Deco. From 1919 until his death, Ruhlmann's name and Art Deco were virtually synonymous.

There is no doubt that Ruhlmann was a brilliant, original designer, and that he pushed his highly talented craftsmen to staggering levels of fit and finish, but he also had one other small detail working in his favor. At the age of 27, after the death of his father, Ruhlmann took over his family's business, Société Ruhlmann, a highly successful commercial painting and wallpapering firm. The success of the company allowed him to run his interior design firm, Ruhlmann et Laurent, essentially as a money-losing business. In his notebooks, he freely admits to losing money on almost everything his firm turned out. Making an elaborate piece of furniture is much easier if you don't have to worry about making a profit. That's not to say his pieces weren't expensive. There was, for example, a so-called "slipper bed" that sold for 19,000 francs in the mid 1920s, sufficient at the time to buy a nice house in Paris. The bed took 1,200 hours to build.

Ruhlmann employed the very finest craftsmen. Over 60 woodworkers, finishers, and specialists were paid up to half again as much as comparable workers of the day. The veneer and inlay work they completed is breathtaking, with striking details like a 1⁄32" band of ivory inlay at the corner of each facet of an eight-sided, curved, torpedo-shaped leg veneered in Amboina burl. Ruhlmann noted that a highly skilled craftsman needed 40 hours to make one of these legs.

The materials used in a Ruhlmann piece were the richest available. Many were veneered in either Macassar ebony or Amboina burl veneer. Oftentimes, writing or interior surfaces were covered in shagreen (sharkskin) or doeskin. Several of his cabinets feature elaborate metal lock plates created by either Foucault or Janniot, who were well-known metal sculptors of the day. And, in addition to furniture pieces, Ruhlmann designed a wide variety of lighting fixtures, fabrics, rugs, and other decorative items.

THE BAUHAUS (1919–33)

The Bauhaus was primarily an architectural school, which was centered on a single building in Dessau, Germany, after 1925. It was founded six years earlier in Weimer by Walter Gropius, a dedicated teacher with a belief that art was born of craft. Gropius insisted that his students learn how to work with their hands. He even scheduled classes with team teachers, one a fine arts specialist and the other an accomplished craftsperson. His innovative approach was perhaps mistimed. It was difficult to sculpt ancient crafts into a modern industrial economy. Nevertheless, for most of its brief existence, the Bauhaus created extraordinarily beautiful and useful prototypes designed for mass production. By the mid '20s, the movement was using the slogan "Art and technology—a new unity." Like Frank Lloyd Wright and the Greene brothers, the masters of the Bauhaus believed that they should design a house and everything in it. Their campus was a lively forum, which inevitably turned toward politics

an opulent use of precious and exotic materials."

Jacques-Emile Ruhlmann, considered the "high priest" of the Art Deco movement, designed some of the most complex and finely crafted furniture of the early 20th century (below, and inset). Much of his work has survived in wonderful condition.

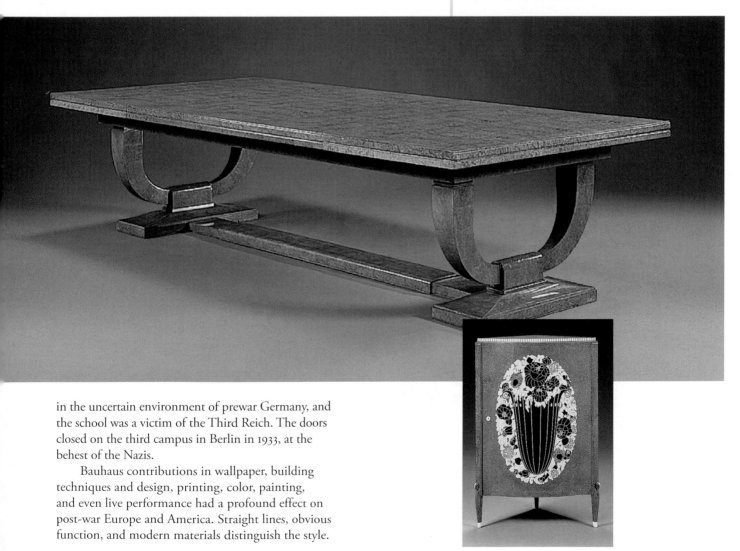

in the uncertain environment of prewar Germany, and the school was a victim of the Third Reich. The doors closed on the third campus in Berlin in 1933, at the behest of the Nazis.

Bauhaus contributions in wallpaper, building techniques and design, printing, color, painting, and even live performance had a profound effect on post-war Europe and America. Straight lines, obvious function, and modern materials distinguish the style.

"Have nothing in your houses that

William Morris (1834–96)

WILLIAM MORRIS AND THE ARTS AND CRAFTS MOVEMENT

The Arts and Crafts movement of the late 1800s developed as a rejection of Victorian values and decorating tastes. In Britain, movement leaders like John Ruskin and his disciple William Morris struggled to improve oppressive factory conditions and railed against the ornate, poorly made goods they produced. As an alternative, they advocated the revival of medieval guilds made up of skilled artisans turning out high-quality, functional objects for use by the middle class. Morris, an architect, poet, and prolific designer of fabric, wallpaper, and furniture, emphasized the wise use of machinery in combination with handwork, an idea that was very appealing to a young American woodworker named Gustav Stickley (see page 20).

Working from Morris's model, Stickley began building "sensible" furniture for the common man. His simple designs relied on the beauty of the wood and exposed joinery for adornment. Despite the short-lived success of his businesses, this approach to furniture making continues to be Stickley's legacy.

More than a style, Arts and Crafts is an attitude, with high value placed on traditional technique. Elements of Gothic and medieval design, and occasional folk art decorations, reflect the movement's reverence for history and for designs accessible to the masses. Some Arts and Crafts designers even explored Japanese and Italian Renaissance influences. What all of them had in common was a view of their work as art, not mass production. They created furniture, textiles, stained glass, and other objects with this concept in mind. To carry that message to the world,

you do not know to be useful, or believe to be beautiful."

Morris named his 1880s organization the Arts and Crafts Exhibition Society.

"The aim," as *Hobby Horse* magazine stated in 1884, "is to render all branches of Art the sphere, no longer of the tradesman, but of the artist." England's Arts and Crafts artists supported each other with publications, a network of guilds, and even a number of communal societies. Later, when the movement reached American shores in the 1890s, all these aspects went with it.

THE MISSION STYLE

Among those preaching the Arts and Crafts gospel of good design in the United States were the Mission furniture makers. That is not the name the designers would have chosen, but it caught on after New York salesman J. P. McHugh used it to sell a line of furniture patterned after a California chair. McHugh encouraged stories that the original chair had come from an old Spanish mission. Despite disliking the name, American designers did view themselves as missionaries of a sort. Elbert Hubbard, founder of the Roycroft crafters' community, asked people to call him "Fra Elbertus" and published *An American Bible* to dispense his brand of practical wisdom. Gustav Stickley, the best-known Mission designer, used his *Craftsman* magazine as a pulpit. The lack of excessive ornaments and the exposed construction details, like tenons, dovetails, and butterfly joints, were supposed to make the furniture more "honest." Straight lines and solid vertical and horizontal members were also characteristic of the style. Stickley noted that oak, the style's wood of choice, adapted

well to Mission's simplicity, showing off the natural character of the tree. In making their furniture and crafts, several Mission designers did use machines. They still paid homage to the Arts and Crafts idealization of handmade items, though, by courting at least a handmade appearance for any hardware or ornaments, like hammered-copper drawer pulls.

Although Mission is most closely identified with furniture, some of the designers tried to extend these concepts to the houses that would hold the furniture. Stickley, for example, published Craftsman home plans that employed materials indigenous to their location: pine, oak, and limestone in the Midwest, for example, and redwood in California.

"Better art, better work,

Gustav Stickley, *The Craftsman* magazine, 1906

Frank Lloyd Wright designed entire environments, including homes and everything in them. The side chair (top) was created for the Larkin Administration Building, and the arm-chair (bottom) was for the Evans House.

THE PRAIRIE STYLE

The Prairie style's strength is architecture. Prairie architects designed homes to fit into their natural surroundings— low, horizontal houses that conformed to the flatness of the prairie. Blueprints provided interaction with nature through porches and patios, and rooms flowed into one another to encourage informal gatherings. Most important, however, was the concept of unity: between the exterior and the interior, between the interior and the furniture. "The whole must always be considered as an integral unit," wrote noted architect Frank Lloyd Wright. To create this unity, Prairie architects sometimes became Prairie furniture makers. Their creations were usually specific designs for specific houses, and they often incorporated Japanese influences.

Although Prairie furniture generally had a rectilinear, geometric base, it frequently displayed rhythmically repeated slats, radiated stretchers, mullioned case pieces, and an Oriental "cloud" shape in bracings. When brothers Charles and Henry Greene revealed the structure of their Prairie furniture, they did so in a delicate manner that owed more to Japanese aesthetics than the brash aspect of Mission's exposed construction.

GUSTAV STICKLEY (1858–1942)

Born on a Wisconsin farm, Stickley supported the family after his father abandoned them, and learned early that he loved working with wood.

"I began to study [wood's] beauty more carefully, to note its varied grains and textures, the way it lent itself to sturdy forms and soft finishes, and these things filled me with enthusiasm," he said.

From his early work in a chair factory near the home of his Pennsylvania uncle, furniture became and remained an important part of Stickley's career. His exploits as a young man included making chairs with his brothers and, one rumor says, designing New York's electric chair while director of manufacturing operations at a state prison. Perhaps the defining moment of his life, however, came as Stickley entered his middle years. In 1898, at age 40, he sailed to England on a pilgrimage to meet the still-living founders of the Arts and Crafts movement. Returning home with examples of Charles Voysey's furniture and textiles, Stickley also brought with him a conviction to Arts and Crafts ideals: honesty, morality, and simplicity. As the new century began, Stickley unveiled a line of furniture patterned after these ideals at the 1900 Grand Rapids Furniture Exposition. The exposed joinery recalled medieval times, an idyllic period for Arts and Crafts aficionados. Over the next few years, he saw many

and a better and more reasonable way of living."

imitators of what came to be called Mission furniture. In contrast to their nails and screws and decorative mortises and tenons, Stickley employed dowels and functional mortises. He also paid attention to details other manufacturers overlooked, like running his desk drawers on hardwood guides. Stickley's furniture reflected his philosophy.

"The constructive features must be plainly visible and declare the purpose and use of the work," he said. Structural components were important elements in his design. At first, Stickley also vehemently opposed any ornamentation that wasn't part of the construction. Hiring Harvey Ellis in 1903, however, introduced some lighter construction methods and delicate inlays to the company, elements that continued to influence Stickley even after Ellis's sudden death in 1904.

Color was important to Stickley. Autumn hues were his favorites. His chairs might have brown, green, or red leather seats, and he offered some of his early furniture with gunmetal gray or Tyrolean green finishes. He was particularly fond of "a rich nut brown" produced by fuming oak with ammonia.

Gustav Stickley's version of the Morris chair featured an adjustable back and removable cushions.

Natural materials gave a warm look to Stickley pieces, including the fumed quartersawn white oak sideboard above, with its copper pulls. The same effect was achieved with leather upholstery on the settle at left.

Stickley's family home at Craftsman Farms (above, left) rested on 600 productive acres in Morris Plains, New Jersey, where he also opened a school for boys.

"The lyf so short, the craft so long to lerne."

Gustav Stickley, from the copper fireplace at Craftsman Farms

Operating under the motto "Als Ik Kan" (All I Can), which he had adapted from Flemish painter Jan van Eyck, Stickley spread the Arts and Crafts ideals through social activities as well as furniture. As early as the late 1890s, he tried to establish a national union of chair manufacturers. That effort failed, but when he set up his own company in 1901 as United Crafts, it was an early profit-sharing enterprise: Both the workers and the managers benefited. In 1904, the business reorganized to a more traditional configuration, and Stickley changed the name to Craftsman Workshops. At heart, however, he had a generous nature: On New Year's Day 1902, Stickley distributed $2,000 in gold coins to his employees.

He also wanted to share his philosophy with as wide an audience as possible, so in 1901 Stickley started publishing *The Craftsman* magazine. He wrote over 200 articles for the periodical, addressing subjects that ranged from cabinetmaking and home-building to dance, dress, family, and national issues. *Craftsman* readers learned woodworking techniques, and, beginning in 1903, they could order house plans from the magazine. For a short while, Stickley even owned a construction company that built Craftsman homes in New York and New Jersey. His empire had expanded to include a factory in Eastwood, New York, a family home in Morris Plains, New Jersey, and, in 1913, a 12-story building in New York City that housed the Craftsman showrooms, offices, and restaurant.

By 1915, however, a changing market and some bad decisions led Stickley to declare bankruptcy. He was briefly hospitalized for a nervous breakdown and then lived out his days in an apartment at his daughter's Syracuse home. As a younger man, Stickley had probably designed the home and its furniture. In his retirement, he experimented with furniture finishes in the apartment sink. Stickley died on April 21, 1942.

The wide slats, square legs, ample proportions, and sturdy construction of this upholstered chair (above) evoke the medieval nature of craft that Stickley so admired.

"No artist owes less to tradition than does Mackintosh; as an originator, he is supreme."

The Studio magazine, 1907

CHARLES RENNIE MACKINTOSH (1868–1928)

Celebrated today as one of the greatest architect-designers of his generation, Charles Rennie Mackintosh was impoverished and forgotten when he died in London at age 60. His story is one of acclaim in Europe and unfulfilled dreams in his native Scotland. Most of Mackintosh's astonishing work was created in Glasgow between 1896 and 1910, where much of it survives today, including his finest achievement, the Glasgow School of Art. He combined Scottish vernacular structures, the flourish of Art Nouveau, and the simplicity of Japanese forms into original buildings, interiors, and furniture of breathtaking beauty. He designed more than 300 pieces of furniture and produced superb watercolors, graphics, stained glass, and textile designs.

Charles Rennie Mackintosh combined the influence of a Scottish background, Japanese architecture, the Arts and Crafts movement, and the tenets and traits of Art Nouveau to create buildings, interiors, and furniture of breathtaking beauty, such as the two chairs below.

GREENE & GREENE (1868–1957)

Architects who truly excel at both architectural and furniture design are rare talents. Such were Charles and Henry Greene. Both boys attended the manual training high school in St. Louis, graduating with honors. Next, they graduated from the Architecture School at the Massachusetts Institute of Technology (MIT). This technical education greatly influenced their architectural and furniture designs. One of the major influences on their architectural style was a visit to the World Columbian Exposition in Chicago in 1893. The Japanese booth at the expo featured a timber-framed temple built so that the structure of the building was key to its aesthetics. Thus was planted the seed of the design concepts that were later evident in the Greenes' signature houses and furniture.

In 1893 the boys joined their parents in Pasadena, California, where they set up their own practice. Early in the partnership, the brothers designed in many different styles, doing whatever it took to get the business off the ground. Around the turn of the

century they began to show traces of the style that was yet to come, particularly in the Culbertson house, with its exposed rafter tails and large amounts of stonewash.

From 1903 though 1907, there was a rapid transformation in the Greenes' style. Structural elements were visually softened and the level of detail in their projects became much finer. These changes led to the Tichenor house, their first "total design," including much of the furniture. During this time the Greenes formed one of their most valuable business relationships, with carpenters John and Peter Hall. There was an almost instant recognition that the Halls' skills and abilities were a perfect match for the Greenes' designs. For the next seven years or so, the Halls built nearly all of the furniture and houses the Greenes designed.

Between 1907 and 1909 the Greenes designed a series of five houses that became known as the "Ultimate Bungalows" and today are considered to be the brothers' masterpieces. The owners of these houses were quite wealthy and generally allowed the Greenes total control over the design. The results, in both level of detail and finish, are astounding. Every item, from the structural timbers to the kitchen cabinets—even the outlet plates—are designed and finished like the finest furniture. Photographs don't do the houses justice. A visit to one of the preserved Greene & Greene houses is a real pleasure, and the furniture produced for those houses is amazing in its own right.

Ironically, the Greenes' success at the "Ultimate Bungalows" may have contributed to the eventual failure of their business. Their taste of building "with cost as no object" led them to be demanding and uncompromising with regard to their vision. This, coupled with the fall from grace of the Arts and Crafts style in general, led to the rapid decline of their architectural practice. There is one striking exception to this decline, the James House in Carmel, California.

While designers and architects have long celebrated the brothers' work, much of the recent renaissance of the Greene & Greene style among woodworkers, and

especially advanced hobbyists, has been generated by master furniture builder Michael McGlynn. A Las Vegas resident, McGlynn specializes in both Prairie School and Arts and Crafts pieces, many of which have been published in *Woodworker's Journal* magazine. It is the linear aspects of these early 20th-century designs that appeal to him, along with their solidity.

"I like to take new lumber and turn it into a nice, aesthetically pleasing piece," says McGlynn. He is interested in looking beyond the obvious, as well. While most woodworkers associated with the Prairie or Arts and Crafts schools concentrate on Frank Lloyd Wright and Gustav Stickley, McGlynn points out there were lots of other architects and designers involved. He particularly appreciates the works of Purcell & Elmslie and the Greene brothers. Pieces from Greene & Greene, he explains, were both beautifully made and wonderfully engineered. McGlynn works in other styles, too—he has made boats, guitars, and a 20-foot-long mahogany conference table with a burl veneer top.

Master furniture builder Mike McGlynn creates magnificent museum-quality reproductions of Arts and Crafts pieces, such as the Purcell & Elmslie oak chair above. His favorite practitioners were Charles and Henry Greene, who designed and built the staircase shown at left for their 1908 Gamble House in Pasadena, California.

CONTEMPORARY MASTERS

Around the world, woodworking is thriving as both a profession and a hobby. In particular, this oldest of crafts has reached the hearts and hands of American audiences, where the availability of fine tools and superior materials has fueled tremendous growth over the past half century. A select group of master woodworkers has added the third ingredient of success: knowledge.

As many of these masters would be quick to point out, woodworking is a journey, not a destination. Continually learning about tools, technique, materials, design, and finish generates at least as much joy for the crafter as the presentation of a completed project. These few masters mentioned here are just a vanguard of the incredibly talented teachers, designers, and woodworkers who may invite your curiosity and guide you along the way.

Sam Maloof's signature rocking chairs have inspired three generations of craftsmen. (Photo: Maloof, 1997.88 © 1980 Sam Maloof)

SAM MALOOF

Since 1948, California furniture builder Sam Maloof has crafted some of the world's most beautiful and comfortable furniture. He has built custom chairs for three U.S. presidents and has been a benevolent patron of woodworking, generating large grants, gifts, and scholarships through the Anderson Ranch Arts Center in Colorado and the Sam and Alfreda Maloof Foundation for Arts and Crafts (malooffoundation.org). A gifted teacher and designer, Mr. Maloof has been officially designated a state treasure by the California legislature. His work has appeared in every major woodworking publication and in galleries and museums around the world.

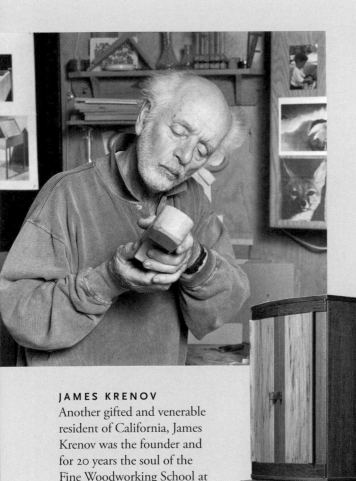

JAMES KRENOV

Another gifted and venerable resident of California, James Krenov was the founder and for 20 years the soul of the Fine Woodworking School at College of the Redwoods. His unique cabinetry is instantly recognizable and highly prized, and his books are essential guides for anybody who is serious about woodworking. Mr. Krenov retired from the college in 2002 and now concentrates on building. His work is represented in museums in Europe, Asia, and North America.

James Krenov's free-standing cabinets are known for the particular attention paid to using the grain patterns themselves as a design element.

JERE OSGOOD

Born in 1936, Jere Osgood has taught master classes in woodworking at Boston University, San Diego State, and dozens of places in between. A two-time recipient of National Endowment for the Arts grants, Mr. Osgood was made a Fellow of the American Craft Council in 1993.

Jere Osgood's *Cylinder-Front Desk* is made up of exotic woods and Indonesian water buffalo calfskin leather. (Photo: Osgood, 1990.53©1989 Jere Osgood)

CHAPTER 2

The Nature of Hardwood

The Nature
of Hardwood

Woodworking owes much to the construction industry, where the requirements of framing lumber have set many standards. The most obvious benefit has been a ready supply of softwood at lumberyards and home centers. New woodworkers generally take advantage of this abundance and start out working with pine, spruce, fir, and hemlock. These species are generally stocked together and sold under such generic names as pine, deal, or whitewood. They are somewhat easy to work but don't stain well or hold an edge, and they lack endurance. After a few basic projects, most woodworkers are ready to move on to hardwoods.

Widely available, hardwoods are quite affordable and easily worked with standard equipment. They come from deciduous trees (as opposed to the evergreen softwoods), and include both domestic timber such as oak, maple, walnut, and cherry, and exotic species like rosewood and ebony. In general, hardwoods are stronger than softwoods, so they lend themselves to lighter, more graceful designs. They also are dense, so they take a higher polish while resisting dents and scratches. Perhaps their best feature is that they occur in a kaleidoscopic range of natural colors and figures that can be put to visual advantage in your projects.

The average lumberyard or home center usually carries only a few common hardwood species, intended mainly for finish carpentry and do-it-yourself projects. They are provided in standard lengths and widths, planed on four sides (S4S means "surfaced four sides"), and sold by the running foot. All that machining costs money, so this isn't the best way to buy more than a minimum quantity of hardwood.

Sourcing a wider range of domestic species involves asking local cabinet shops and woodworking club or guild members where they buy stock. When something special is required, small local sawmills may be the best bet, as they will often cut wood to specifications at a very reasonable price. Dealers in imported or exotic species tend to be located near large cities, and they can be found online, in the commercial section of the phone directory, or in the marketplace section of many woodworking magazines.

HARDWOOD GRADING

Hardwoods are graded to standards set by the National Hardwood Lumber Association (NHLA). The highest domestic grade is "FAS" (firsts and seconds), which has 83% clear wood, without any knots or defects. Next comes "selects," which are at least 83% clear on one face. Other grades include #1, #2, and #3 common. A woodworker can save some money by buying the lowest grade that will yield the pieces needed. FAS delivers long, clear pieces that will be seen on both faces. However, if the need is just for small pieces, cutting around the knots in #1 or #2 common lumber may prove to be far more economical. Some dealers will allow customers to pick through the inventory, but there is usually an extra charge for this, so ask in advance. Experienced woodworkers like to take along a block plane when shopping for rough-sawn hardwoods. Scrubbing some material off the end grain or face of a board tells a lot about its color and grain pattern.

Opposite page: A worker uses a gasoline-powered band saw mill to cut boards.

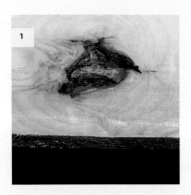

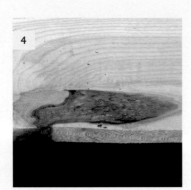

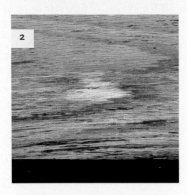

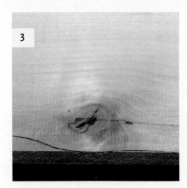

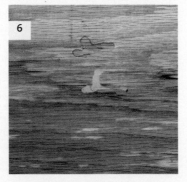

1. Decay
2. Water damage
3. Tight knot and split

4. Large loose knot
5. Wane (bark edge)
6. Insect or worm damage

When buying, there are several things to keep in mind regarding quality. The first is that boards should be as straight and flat as possible. Sight along the edge of each board, keeping the nearest corner about a foot from your eye. This simple method will reveal warps (where the board is flat but veers to the right or left), bows (where it veers up or down somewhere along its length), and twists (where it warps and bows simultaneously).

Beyond these linear deviations, lumber can display an impressive array of other flaws. Some of these are desirable when they add character to a project, as when a turned bowl reveals water or mineral damage. Others are not very desirable because they may weaken a part or present a poor appearance.

Among the most common defects to watch for are areas of pitch or decayed matter, usually forming where a large branch left the trunk (photo 1). Water damage is common (photo 2), where the lumber has begun to rot. This is often accompanied by mineral streaks. One can often work around tight knots (photo 3), but splits are essentially irreversible. They need to be completely removed, or they will begin to run again. Large, loose knots (photo 4) are usually removed, but some woodworkers like to fill them with black epoxy or exotic materials like a ground turquoise resin and create an eye-catching feature. Lumber bought as straight-line ripped (one edge straightened) often comes with bark along the other edge (photo 5). This can have a severe impact on the waste factor, and thus the cost of lumber. However, some designers like to create tabletops, bowls, and other objects with a natural edge, so wane, as it is called, is often quite prized. Trees play host to many avian and other species, and the piece of oak shown in photo 6 shows evidence of worm damage. Discoloration of the lower half of this board also indicates severe water damage, so this tree may have been dead some time before being harvested.

HARDWOOD DIMENSIONS

When it comes to measurements, hardwoods have a terminology all their own. For instance, furniture-grade hardwoods are usually sold "in the rough" (not surfaced), although most dealers will plane stock to a specified thickness for a modest fee. Rough-sawn lumber is specified according to its thickness in ¼" increments before planing. The term 4/4 ("four-quarter" or "four-four") refers to rough lumber that is 1" thick. Six-quarter lumber is 1½" thick. Figure on losing about ¼" of thickness to the plane, no matter what the dimensions are. Planed four-quarter stock will be ¾" thick, or at best ¹³⁄₁₆". Eight-quarter planed is about 1¾" thick. Experienced, regular customers can often convince the mill to "skip" a board—run it through the planer just enough to reveal its character. They then reduce it to final thickness themselves back at the workshop.

Thickness is the only dimension that is fairly uniform when buying hardwoods outside a chain store. The lumber is rarely cut to exact widths or lengths. Boards are often sold with one straight edge and one natural one (straight-lined stock), which can save a lot of shop time later. Some suppliers will cut boards to length and sell them in 2' increments (6', 8' etc.),

but generally the customer must buy the whole board. The least expensive way to buy is to accept several boards in random widths and lengths. If the customer doesn't specify either dimension, there is less labor for the dealer.

Add a generous waste factor when working with randomly sized stock.

PREPARING HARDWOOD LUMBER

A suspicion shared by many novices is that hardwoods are more difficult to work than softwoods. Actually, all of the hand tools and machines used to cut and shape softwoods can be used for hardwoods as well, though the techniques may vary slightly. Since the lumber is likely to be rough-sawn, access to a jointer and planer is necessary, as shown in the set of illustrations below.

Carbide-tipped blades and cutters are a good choice when working hardwoods, especially exotic species. Carbide tooling is more expensive, but it lasts longer and does a cleaner job. For hand tools such as chisels and planes, you'll find that a slightly steeper bevel angle (around 30°, as opposed to a standard 25°)

Hardwood lumber is often sold as S2S (surfaced two sides), where the wide faces are planed. In addition, one edge may be ripped (straight-lined).

Clean up the ends of your rough stock (cut it just a bit long).

Flatten one side of your stock on the jointer (keep the guard on the tool).

With the flattened surface down, start to plane your board smooth.

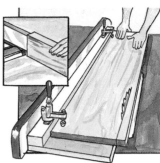

To get a straight edge, turn to the jointer or use a simple shooting-board jig.

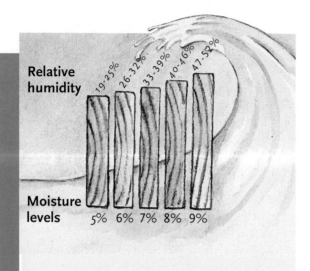

Relative humidity   19-25%   26-32%   33-39%   40-46%   47-52%

Moisture levels   5%   6%   7%   8%   9%

WOOD MOISTURE AT VARIOUS HUMIDITY LEVELS

The following is an example of how to read the chart. A piece of wood stored in a room that has a constant relative humidity of 36% will, according to Eugene Wengert, eventually end up with a moisture level of 7%. His recommendation is that you use wood at a moisture level within two percentage points of the equilibrium level of the place where your project will spend most of its life. In this example, stock with a moisture content of between 5% and 9% should have no problems if fashioned into a project that will be kept in a room with humidity around 36%. Shown in the diagram opposite, top right, growth rings have two distinct zones. Earlywood (spring) cells have thin walls and large cavities, which allow sap to move when the leaves start to bud. Latewood (summer) cells have thicker walls and small cavities. These are what people traditionally refer to as growth rings, although technically each ring is the combination of both early and latewood.

will cut better and last longer in hard or dense wood. One hand tool that you'll find particularly useful for hardwoods is the cabinet scraper. And, when sanding hardwoods, it pays to work your way up through the grits, to eliminate the scratches left by coarser grits. Hardwoods are less forgiving than softwoods in this respect.

UNDERSTANDING MOISTURE

Wobbly chairs, wavy floors, and sticky drawers are often the result of wood changing dimension. That is because the moisture in wood has a natural tendency to move to the level of saturation (humidity) in the surrounding atmosphere. This movement is called seeking equilibrium.

Because humidity in a home changes with the season, the ideal moisture level for wooden items in that home also changes.

The moisture content of wood is measured in terms of weight: the weight of the water versus the weight of the wood. On average, the ideal level will be in the neighborhood of 7% when the wood is used. That is, the moisture in the wood should weigh 7% of what the wood weighs. Freshly cut green wood, on the other hand, can have a moisture content as high as 200%: in this case, the moisture weighs twice what the wood alone weighs.

Eugene Wengert of the University of Wisconsin has completed detailed studies of the relationship between humidity and wood moisture levels. His results are shown in the simple chart to the left.

As a board dries, the large earlywood cells shrink more than the compact latewood cells, which is why a board of the most common cut, plain sawn, moves far more in width than in thickness. A board of the second most popular cut, quartersawn, has very short growth rings running parallel to its edges, so it is much more stable and is often a better choice for the exacting demands of fine furniture building. The grain on a quartersawn board is close, straight, and

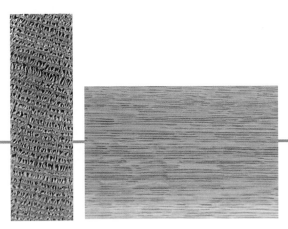

End grain   Face grain
QUARTERSAWN OAK

End grain   Face grain
PLAIN SAWN OAK

Earlywood cells are the lighter colored growth rings from spring.

Plain sawn

Rift sawn

Quartersawn

Latewood cells are the darker colored growth rings from late summer.

In these end views of two boards (above left), the quartersawn stock at left displays very short growth rings running almost parallel to the edges, while the plain sawn board at right features long growth rings running almost parallel to the wider faces of the stock.

The kiln shown at left, located at Timbergreen Farms in Wisconsin, uses a forced-air solar collector to dry lumber.

ideal for legs, cabinet frames, and other long parts. Rift-sawn stock is an architectural grade, close to quartersawn in character and rarely offered.

DRYING TECHNIQUES AND PROBLEMS

There are two ways to dry lumber: by air, and by mechanical means (that is, in a kiln). Air drying is obviously the less expensive way to go, but it has one major disadvantage. It's impossible to control ambient (natural) moisture levels. Wood will eventually reach a moisture level that is about ⅓ that of the surrounding air. The ambient outdoor humidity across most of the U.S. is in the neighborhood of 60%. Lumber dried this way will reach equilibrium at a minimum of 10% or 11% moisture content, and higher in many regions. Unfortunately, most of us use mechanical means to keep

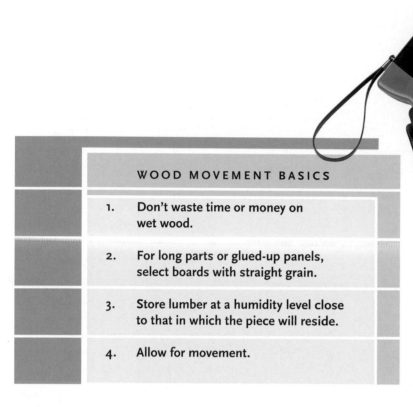

WOOD MOVEMENT BASICS

1. **Don't waste time or money on wet wood.**

2. **For long parts or glued-up panels, select boards with straight grain.**

3. **Store lumber at a humidity level close to that in which the piece will reside.**

4. **Allow for movement.**

Pin moisture meters (above right) use an electronic signal between two metal pins to measure ambient moisture in a board.

our homes at about 35% humidity, which means any new project will stabilize at about 7% moisture once it is brought indoors—shrinking another 3% or so.

One solution for this situation is to bring air-dried stock indoors and allow it to acclimate until it achieves equilibrium, before using it. (Keep in mind that basement humidity levels are typically higher than main floor levels.)

A better solution is to let kiln-dried lumber acclimate. This is lumber dried in a controlled oven that is fueled by fossil fuel, solar gain, or electricity. In fact, the only disadvantages to kiln drying (aside from cost) are those related to the operator. If he or she is in too much of a hurry and turns the heat up too high, the lumber will crack internally. If wet lumber is exposed to overly dry air, the result is case-hardening, where the outside (or case) is dry and the inside is still wet. The result is a honeycomb of exploded cells inside the board, or external surface checking when the outside of a board shrinks faster than the inside, or large cracks if the board subsequently endures freezing temperatures. How lumber is stacked in a kiln can also affect its ultimate quality. When just

one face is exposed to the air as a result of inadequate stickering (the slats between the boards that separate them from each other), the board will cup.

MOISTURE METERING

For woodworkers who live in an area that has large humidity swings, moisture metering (at the lumberyard as well as in the shop) is pretty much essential for quality work. While the best lumberyards will loan you a meter to check stock before you buy, investing in one of your own will help avert disasters in the shop. There are two main types of handheld moisture meters. Pin meters, which often come with a variety of interchangeable pins (up to 3" in length), measure the moisture between a pair of pins inserted in the wood. Pinless meters employ electromagnetic technology to measure moisture, typically from ½" to 1" in depth, without making holes in fine hardwood.

MAN-MADE LUMBER

Casework, the building of cabinets, has evolved dramatically over the past half century with advances in plywood and other manufactured substrates. A substrate is the core, or underlying material, on sheet goods, to which the outside veneers are applied. The most familiar of these is plywood, a layered product where each lamination lies atop the previous one at a 90° angle. Plywood always has an uneven number of laminations, so that the grain in the top and bottom layers always runs the length of the sheet. A major advance in plywood technology was the development of multi-ply, which has become familiar to many woodworkers under the brand name Baltic Birch. The individual laminations in multi-ply products are quite thin (usually about 25 layers to the inch), and the sheets are generally void-free. This means that a cut edge can be sanded and finished, rather than having to be covered with veneer or trim.

POPULAR WOOD SPECIES

ALDER, RED

Alnus rubra

From Alaska to California, red alder is the most common commercial hardwood. This cousin of birch and aspen generally prefers wet climates and usually grows in groves along stream banks or on moist hillsides. Red alder grows like a weed, doing especially well on logged-out or burned land. It often overtakes the efforts of foresters trying to replant softwood species like fir and spruce. Alder's ability to resist the ravages of forest fires also has contributed to its abundance. It could be called a chameleon wood, for it is widely used to imitate some mighty pricey competition including walnut, mahogany, and cherry. Its ruddy coloring and indistinct grain pattern allow a creative finisher to mimic the hues of these other species, and its hardness makes it a suitable wood for furniture and millwork. Also popular with turners, particularly mass production shops, it requires little sanding and has a uniform grain pattern, which reduces tear-out on the lathe.

USES
The top choice of clog-makers for hundreds of years, alder has left a unique footprint on history, and its role can still be described as pedestrian. Alder often makes up the core material in high-quality plywood like Baltic Birch and is widely used for industrial purposes like pallets, broom handles, and commercially made toys.

AMERICAN CHESTNUT

Castanea dentata

Henry Wadsworth Longfellow's classic poem "The Village Blacksmith" immortalized this tree. Around the turn of the century, it was commonplace to find chestnuts towering 90' tall with trunk diameters of 6'. Tragically, it is now near extinction, due to a catastrophic blight first noticed in the Bronx Zoo in 1904. A shipment of chestnut trees imported from China and Japan came with an unfortunate stowaway, a fungus that cuts off the flow of sap, causing the tree to die above ground. Ironically, the fungus can't live in soil, so initially the root systems of chestnuts often survived, sending up shoots that lasted only a few years until they were stricken by the blight themselves. A cross-breeding effort at restoration, with some promising results, is being led by the American Chestnut Foundation located in Bennington, Vermont.

USES
Chestnut timber has myriad uses, from fences to fine furniture. Its high-quality timber and flavorful nuts were important commercial resources. Lighter than oak, it is very strong, with an attractive golden-brown color and open grain. Woodworkers prize it for excellent machining, finishing, and gluing properties. As a testament to their exceptional decay resistance, chestnut trees are still harvested decades after their death. Most newly harvested chestnut wood is riddled with wormholes, which are now considered character marks.

ASH

Fraxinus americana

The most common species of ash used for
woodworking is generally referred to as white
ash, a species that has assumed a legendary role in
major league baseball parks. When a batter takes
his swings at home plate, he is usually relying on
a bat made from white ash. It's a superior choice
for bats because of long fibers, which bend a little
upon impact with the ball. These same long fibers
make ash an excellent choice for woodworkers who
are planning projects that will involve bending
and laminating. Although quite hard and strong,
ash offers excellent working properties in the shop.
When using properly sharpened cutting tools, ash is
rather easy to plane, saw, drill, and chisel. However,
its tendency to splinter when dull tools are being
used is less forgiving than with many species.
Ash also offers outstanding staining and finishing
qualities. The wood is comparable to oak in many
respects, particularly appearance. The open grain
texture shared by both species often fools the casual
observer. Furthermore, oak and ash have almost
identical hardness ratings.

USES

An excellent choice for cabinets and fine furniture,
ash is one of the most available domestic woods
and rarely warps or twists. Because it has low
resistance to decay, it should be used only for indoor
applications . . . unless your surname is Ruth.

BEECH

Fagus grandifolia

The beech is a unique-looking tree with grayish
bark that is remarkably smooth from its twigs to
its trunk, giving romantics a palette to carve their
names. Rebecca Rupp, in her book of tree folklore
titled *Red Oaks and Black Birches*, mentions the
Presidents' tree of Takoma Park, Maryland, which
is, in fact, a beech. The wood is distinguishable by
its evenly distributed tiny red-brown flecks. Even-
textured with small, consistently spaced pores,
it has superb machining qualities. Beech accepts
finishes well and polishes to a nice sheen. Steam
bending and laminating both work wonderfully,
making it a top choice for bent chair parts. It has
poor decay resistance. It is quite difficult to dry
and prone to significant shrinkage and warping
during the process. Once dry, however, the wood is
relatively stable, if not subjected to extreme swings
in humidity.

USES

A national beer brewer boasts that its flagship brand
is "beech wood aged." The irony is that what beech
offers for this purpose is really what it lacks, a strong
taste or odor that might taint the flavor of foods
and drinks. While other species like walnut, cherry,
and oak grab the limelight for their looks, beech (a
relatively plain wood with a reddish hue) often is
employed for hidden structural parts in furniture.
It also is a favorite for hand tools, workbench tops,
flooring, desktops, and counters, since it resists wear
as well as nicks and dings.

BIRCH

Betula alleghaniensis

Birch is a species of contradiction. The white bark boldly stands out from all other trees in the forest, but in the shop the species has one of the subtlest appearances. Complementing its whitish color, a faint pattern sweeps across this closed-grained, evenly textured wood—a desirable characteristic when the project's design needs to dominate the wood's appearance. In the shop, birch works well with both hand and power tools, particularly for a wood that falls between oak (harder) and cherry (softer) in hardness. It saws, planes, and turns well, with relatively little tearing and splintering. Birch experiences significant shrinkage while drying, but once properly seasoned it offers good stability and resists warping and twisting. It is unequaled when it comes to accepting a clear varnish or polyurethane finish but is much less suitable for staining because of its tendency to become blotchy.

USES

Birch is a suitable choice for structurally critical parts in furniture because it compares to oak and maple in strength and beats both of those species quite significantly when it comes to shock resistance. For use in a bending project, birch offers excellent elasticity, somewhat similar to ash. However, keep in mind that outdoor applications are simply out of the question for this species because it is highly susceptible to decay.

BUTTERNUT

Juglans cinerea

Butternut is overshadowed by the highly popular black walnut, its closest relative. Yet this is a quality wood worthy of attention in its own right. Known also as white walnut, a term describing the creamy tan color of the wood, this is a relatively soft species with a hardness rating about half that of its cousin. Figuratively speaking, butternut cuts like butter for sawing, planing, and routing. Even though the wood is easy to cut, butternut's long fibers and softness require that blades be exceptionally sharp to prevent tearing and splintering, especially for turning. A thin application of sanding sealer can help quite a lot when eliminating butternut "hair," which is composed of fibers that are difficult to sand. Carvers will find that the wood is easy to work and holds its shape, for excellent results. The open grain accepts glue, stains, and finishes well. Adhesives deeply penetrate this ring-porous wood for strong bonds, and the texture and natural oils in butternut combine to create a rich lustrous appearance when it is stained or finished.

USES

Since it is in the same weight class as basswood, some woodworkers turn to butternut when trying to reduce the weight of large pieces. However, because of its strength limitations, butternut is not recommended for structurally critical components under stress. In addition, lack of decay resistance makes butternut suitable for indoor applications only.

CATALPA

CEDAR, PORT ORFORD WHITE

Catalpa speciosa

When explorers first passed through the Ohio and Mississippi river valleys, they found trees unlike any they had seen before, with large heart-shaped leaves, a shower of white, springtime flowers, and long beanlike seeds in the fall and winter. Cherokee Indians called them catalpa. The wood's low density contributes to exceptionally small rates of shrinkage and warping. Catalpa also resists cracking. A cross-section of a catalpa log is virtually all heartwood. It's relatively soft and lightweight, comparable to butternut in these respects, and a poor choice for projects that will see a lot of use, or as structural components. But for applications where extra durability isn't critical, catalpa, with its wavy open grain and subtle tan coloring, can be quite attractive.

USES

Carvers love catalpa because it's easy to cut and shape, and it holds details well. Its outstanding decay resistance makes it the perfect choice for outdoor sculpture, and it can attain diameters and heights large enough to carve full-size human figures. The wood is ring-porous, and the variations in ring hardness makes sanding tricky. It's possible to sand away the softer, porous rings if care is not taken, creating an uneven surface. Staining and finishing catalpa produces excellent results, thanks in part to the wood's porous open grain.

Chamaecyparis lawsoniana

A beautiful medium-grained and close-pored softwood, this cedar is actually a member of the "false cypresses." In fact, one of its common names is Lawson cypress, after the Scot who introduced the species to Britain. The lumber has working characteristics that are similar to pine, but it is somewhat harder and takes finishes without the same blotching tendencies. It also releases a pungent fragrance during machining that may be objectionable to woodworkers with allergies to other cedars. The tree grows up to 180' high along the Pacific coast in northern California and Oregon, and can reach a diameter as wide as a man is tall. The cones are small, at less than ½" across. Due to several factors, including a Japanese fungus that has attacked the trees of late, plus juniper scales and spruce mites, supplies of Port Orford white cedar are currently quite limited.

USES

Once prized for building Japanese Buddhist temples, Port Orford white cedar's current uses are in boatbuilding, caskets in the Orient, arrows, outdoor furniture, cabinetry, and the making of musical instruments. It seasons with predictable and acceptable shrinkage and has an even, workable grain that reacts well to sharp hand tools and carbide cutters. It also takes a polish beautifully. Most of the prime heartwood is now exported to Japan.

CEDAR, SPANISH

Cedrela huberi

Making its home on the islands and coast of the Caribbean, Spanish cedar also is known as cedrela. This deciduous tree (unlike other cedars, which are coniferous) grows particularly well in areas of rich, well-drained soil. Cedrela can reach heights of 100' or more, given the right conditions. For perhaps half of that height the trunk is straight and true, with diameters up to 6'. It is somewhat resistant to decay and insect damage, and very resistant to the harmful effects of weather. The heartwood has a fragrant scent due to secreted oils, which appear as small pockets of sticky resin. This fragrance augments the natural flavor and aroma of fine cigars. The sapwood is pale pink or beige, while the heartwood warms to a pink or reddish brown when fresh. At times it is remarkably similar in appearance to mahogany. As it ages, the color mutes to a dull reddish brown with hints of purple.

USES

Spanish cedar is used in boatbuilding, xylophones, fine cigar humidors, and even millwork. It takes adhesives well, especially polyurethane glues in outdoor applications, and as such it can be used in curved work that uses thin, built-up laminations. It is valued as a carving species and also in marine applications. Because of its aromatic qualities and resistance to decay, it is an important element in wardrobes, chests, and other cabinets that are used for storing fabrics.

CEDAR, WESTERN RED

Thuja plicata

This tall cedar likes company. It grows with other species such as spruce and fir in a range from Canada and the northern Rockies to Alaska and the Pacific coast. At heights of almost 200', a single tree can yield an impressive number of board feet. Its heartwood is pink and brown, while the thin layer of sapwood is very light, almost white. After aging outdoors, the heartwood develops a silver-gray color that can be quite attractive in uses such as wall shakes and roof shingles. Western red cedar is very resistant to decay. The key is found deep in the wood cells, where fungi spores cause decay in other species. This species has unique extractives in its heartwood that are capable of repelling or even killing fungi. Sapwood is generally more prone to decay, even in circumstances less favorable to fungi growth, so the high ratio of heartwood to sapwood in this cedar is an obvious advantage.

USES

Some of the best decay-resistant furniture lumber (teak, mahogany, and even white oak) is somewhat expensive and often difficult to find. While not as structurally solid as these hardwoods, western red cedar can compete favorably with them in outdoor applications. Beyond patio furniture, it is used extensively in fences, siding, exterior trim, and as sills in frame structures, where wood meets a concrete foundation.

CHERRY

Prunus serotina

A member of the rose family, cherry is an attractive wood with distinctive characteristics and excellent working properties. A relative of the small orchard variety, the tree that produces most commercially available cherry wood is a native American species reaching a mature height of 60' to 90'. The tan color of freshly cut cherry sometimes has a hint of pink. However, cherry quickly develops a warm reddish-brown patina. All wood develops a patina with age, but Christian Becksvoort, the author of *In Harmony with Wood*, claims that cherry develops it faster than any other native species. This attractive patina makes cherry an excellent choice for clear finishing. Cherry is popular in the workshop, too, because of its outstanding workability. The moderate hardness and weight of cherry is similar to black walnut. In fact, hand tool enthusiasts often adopt cherry as a favorite because of its easy working qualities. Once a cherry project is completed, expect it to last for generations. This is one of the most stable woods to be found, and it rarely warps or twists.

USES

Cherry enjoys the distinction of being perhaps the most popular choice among cabinetmakers and furniture builders. Its moderate hardness makes cherry a suitable choice for furniture and cabinets, while being considered one of the easiest woods to machine.

COCOBOLO

Dalbergia retusa

When a cocobolo log is freshly cut, it reveals a rainbow of purples, reds, oranges, and yellows. The colors eventually mellow to a rich reddish orange, accented by waves of crimson and black, making cocobolo one of the greatest treasures in woodworking today. The tree grows along Central America's Pacific seaboard, where it is harvested for both local use and export. Cocobolo is part of the rosewood family, but its unique colors set this wood apart from other family members. For a highly dense and hard wood, cocobolo is relatively easy to work with both hand and power tools. Care is required when handling the sawdust as, like many tropical woods, it contains toxins that can produce allergic reactions. Dust masks should definitely be worn. The oiliness of the wood presents a gluing challenge, but using an epoxy or a polyurethane adhesive will improve your rate of success.

USES

Due to a combination of heaviness and high value, cocobolo is generally used only for small applications. An unlikely choice for large projects, it can add a distinctive touch when used as an accent. The wood is generally featured in small, highly polished items like brush and cutlery handles, music boxes, carvings, and turnings. It is possible to sand and finish cocobolo as smooth as polished stone, which makes it perfect for use as jewelry.

EBONY

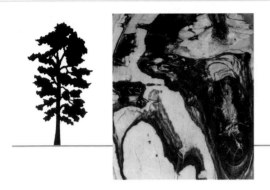  

Diospyros celebica

Only reaching the lower levels of the rain forest canopy, ebony trees are relatively small. Yet specimens that yield black wood have given it a larger-than-life reputation. Ebony comes from a variety of species growing in the tropics of India, Africa, Malaysia, and Indonesia. While the most valuable wood has the characteristic solid black color, much ebony lumber is brown, tan, red, or gray, often with stripes and bands creating variations in color. Persimmon, a domestic wood sometimes called white ebony, is a member of the same family. Two characteristics of ebony are its extreme hardness and brittleness, which make the wood difficult to work with both power and hand tools. Cutting edges are likely to experience severe blunting, and chipping is a problem. Pre-boring for screws or nails is essential to avoid splitting. Because it is so dense, gluing generally calls for epoxy or polyurethane adhesives.

USES

Because the trees are so small, ebony lumber is generally available only in very small dimensions. Since ebony is becoming rarer, use of the wood is limited to accent pieces and small projects, which works out just fine, since its weight and lack of structural strength makes ebony inappropriate for most larger applications anyway. Ebony is a good candidate for any project requiring accents with a highly polished luster.

ELM

Ulmus americana

A favorite of western settlers for their wheel hubs and rims, this shock-resistant species has a wildly twisting and interlocking grain pattern. Elm resists splitting better than any other common domestic species, which makes it a poor choice for firewood. However, elm is an excellent choice when another wood member is being pounded into it, such as when back spindles are pounded into a Windsor chair seat made from elm (a very popular choice for this application). Dutch elm disease, a fungus carried by bark-boring beetles accidentally introduced from Europe, has ravaged nearly the entire range of elms in the United States. Supplies of elm lumber and veneer are still widely available, but this disease will undoubtedly make elm much more scarce in the future.

USES

The reddish-tan color of elm makes it an attractive choice for furniture, accessories, and trim. Carvers and turners find it to be relatively friendly, but chiseling often results in uncontrolled splintering. Elm poses no special problems for straight-line cuts made with power tools. When storing elm, be sure to protect your wood from humidity and moisture because it is highly susceptible to distortion. Like most species with a coarse, open-grained texture, elm glues, stains, and finishes exceptionally well.

HICKORY

Carya ovata

Andrew Jackson earned the nickname "Old Hickory" for his exceptional toughness as a general during the War of 1812. The name was quite fitting because hickory is one of the toughest and strongest woods among our domestic species. It exceeds ash, oak, and maple in both strength and hardness and has more than twice the shock resistance of those species. Among domestic species, hickory can't be beaten for bending properties. Before the introduction of synthetic materials, hickory was commonly used for skis and toboggans. Today, craftsmen employ hickory when a design calls for bent pieces in chair backs. On the down side, hickory's hardness and density do create some workability problems. Cutting is a slow process and blades tend to dull quickly. It is not a good turning wood because of its coarse and splintery texture.

USES

Exceptional elasticity has made hickory the wood of choice for hammer, ax, and other tool handles that experience harsh and sudden impacts. In the early days of baseball, hickory was used for bats, but its use declined because of excessive weight. It continues to find broad applications as structural members in lightweight projects like Windsor chairs, but the weight factor makes it less suitable for larger furniture assemblies.

KOA

Acacia koa

Shortly after reaching the Hawaiian islands in the late 1800s, Portuguese sailors discovered koa, a wood with high resonance qualities that was perfect for making four-stringed ukuleles. In addition, its beautiful grain could be sanded to a glassy smoothness and finished to a lustrous sheen, making it a modern luthier's favorite, too. The most highly figured wood comes from Hawaii's mountains, growing to about 70' with trunk diameters from 5' to 8'. Koa is an evergreen with yellow springtime flowers. The heartwood is golden brown with wavy streaks of red, orange, black, or yellow. An interlocking grain is responsible for much of koa's dramatic figure (often a fiddleback pattern), and contributes to the wood's high shock resistance and good bending characteristics. These qualities make koa a favorite for gunstocks. The Hawaiian name Koa-ka (valiant soldier) aptly describes this extremely decay-resistant wood. Screwing or nailing into koa yields excellent results, with very little splitting or splintering.

USES

Beyond musical instruments, koa is a fine wood for carving and turning, making it popular for jewelry and art objects. Working with koa reminds many people of walnut. The wood is slightly open-grained, even textured, and has a moderate weight. It's one of the easiest woods to dry by kiln or air, and once it is dry, koa is quite stable and exhibits relatively little movement.

LACEWOOD

Cardwellia sublimis

The term lacewood has long been applied to the quartersawn wood of American sycamore, London plane, and most specifically Australian silky oak (the scientific name given above). The first two are related, while the third is not a true oak at all. Sycamore, also called buttonwood (its seeds were used by early settlers as crude buttons), has held only a minor role in domestic woodworking, even though it grows over much of the eastern half of the United States. A reputation for significant shrinkage and warping is one reason for its infrequent use, but this is only deserved by plain sawn sycamore. Quartersawn stock offers average to good stability. Generally good working properties are typical with lacewood, but be sure to use very sharp cutting edges to minimize binding. To really highlight the figure, try finishing lacewood with a few coats of oil and then follow with a coat of wax. When ordering any of these species, make sure the wood has been quartersawn, or you won't be getting lacewood.

USES

Sycamore should only be used indoors since the wood has little decay resistance. London plane has similar properties, but it is slightly darker and heavier than sycamore. Australian silky oak is a considerably more expensive version of lacewood, with a dramatic appearance, and is probably best saved for small projects, or as an accent wood on larger pieces.

LYPTUS®

Eucalyptus grandis et urophylla

The name Lyptus is a registered copyright of the Weyerhaeuser company, which developed this premium Brazilian plantation-grown hardwood. The wood is a natural hybrid of two species of eucalyptus and exhibits many desirable woodshop characteristics, including exceptional workability and machining properties, sound density, good finish tolerance, and overall strength. Lyptus is produced in a sustainable and environmentally responsible manner, interspersed with indigenous trees to preserve natural habitat. It can be harvested in about 15 years, much sooner then other premium hardwoods grown in colder climates. Lyptus is reversing the loss of tropical forests as it is grown on previously barren land in a mosaic pattern interspersed with reintroduced indigenous trees to preserve native ecosystems and create biodiversity.

USES

Lyptus it well suited to furniture building, cabinetmaking, flooring, and architectural millwork. Weyerhaeuser Building Materials offers the species as high-grade hardwood in dimensional lumber sizes, and also as plywood and flooring. It is used where the beauty and appearance of mahogany or cherry is desired. With natural figure similar to quartersawn oak, it oxidizes similarly to cherry and will develop a beautiful patina in a very short time.

MAHOGANY, CROTCH VENEER

Swietenia macrophylla

According to legend, pirates of the high seas buried their treasures on Caribbean islands. What they couldn't know was that another treasure lay hidden right before them, a small amount of beautifully figured wood hidden deep in the crotch of mahogany trees. Mahogany, although not the only tree that produces a desirable crotch grain pattern, offers some of the most spectacular results. Nearly all harvested crotch wood is sliced into exceptionally thin veneer in order to stretch the rare material to its absolute limits. While each specimen is unique, names like plume, flame, feather, and rooster tail generally apply to this kind of grain pattern. Crotch veneer is cut perpendicular to the V created by the spreading branches in the log. Each slice has a wild grain pattern going in all directions, much like burl veneer does. Of course, this usually means that no matter how you glue it to a core material, eventually the veneer will crack and split.

USES

Its primary use is as a decorative veneer on casework, boxes, humidors, furniture panels, and clocks. Due to its irregular grain patterns, crotch veneer is often wrinkly, making it necessary to flatten it prior to gluing. Planing is almost impossible, and crotch veneer has random areas of exposed end grain that absorb stains and finishes unevenly. Mahogany crotch veneer is relatively expensive, fetching five times the price of plain sliced veneer.

MAHOGANY, HONDURAS

Swietenia macrophylla

When New World explorers landed on the shores of Central America in search of bounty for their homelands, they discovered an unexpected treasure. By the early 1700s, shiploads of mahogany were being sent to the old countries, where it had caught the fancy of Europe's royalty and governing classes. Central American–grown mahogany, which consists of several species commonly referred to as Honduras mahogany, is still an excellent wood for today's woodworker to discover. The grain, which can grow in a straight, interlocked, or irregular pattern, offers some attractive surprises. Mahogany is a friendly wood to use in the shop. It cuts, planes, and turns with ease and resists shrinking and warping. Turners also claim that mahogany holds its shape better than many species. It is similar to cherry in weight and hardness, and its strength exceeds hard maple and oak.

USES

Because of its premium value, mahogany is generally reserved for fine furniture applications today, but in past centuries this wood was used for shipbuilding because of its excellent resistance to decay. Woodworkers often use a clear finish on mahogany to preserve its characteristic reddish hue. While it polishes beautifully, resins in the wood have been known to react with glues and cause an undesirable staining effect.

MAPLE, HARD

Acer saccharum

Also known as sweet, rock, and black maple, this durable and abundant species was a popular choice among woodworkers during colonial days. True to form, many of their projects can now be found in antique shops, little worse for the wear and featuring the rich patina of age. Working with hard maple requires very sharp, well-tuned tools. Nothing beats a planed maple surface, and stain will take to it easily. When sanding maple, it is recommended to stop at 150 grit. Any finer sanding will polish the wood to a point where it won't accept stain very well, especially oil stains. Water-based aniline dye stains are the most effective colorants for maple. Hard maple parts may crack to relieve the stress of a tight joint. Due to the wood's hardness, it is all too easy to break a brass screw driven into a pilot hole. To reduce this, find a steel screw that matches the brass screw in size and thread count and drive it into the hole first (after dragging it over a block of beeswax). After withdrawing the steel screw, safely drive the brass screw into the threaded hole.

USES

In addition to furniture, hard maple has been (and still is) used for farm equipment, shoe lasts, tool handles, and other items that needed to withstand a great deal of wear. It turns well, can be carved, and is a good choice for workbench tops, as it withstands impacts.

MAPLE, SOFT

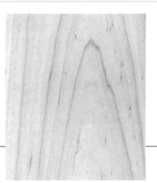

Acer rubrum

Like most families, the maples have their tougher, hardscrabble members (sugar and black), which are 25% to 40% harder than their mellower cousins. Soft maple trees grow faster than hard maples, making them easier to saw, shape, plane, and drill. Generally, soft maple is about as hard and as light as cherry. One feature common to all maples is their low resistance to decay, making them appropriate for indoor use only. The bluish-gray streaks commonly found on soft maple lumber (called spalting) occur when impurities enter the tree through wormholes or other injuries. The streaks don't affect the mechanical properties of the wood but do give it an unusual appearance. Curly figure also is common to soft maple and looks similar to that found on harder maples. Sometimes difficult to glue, it works well with resin adhesives like yellow and white glues, Resorcinol, and urea resin. For an economical wood with a light color that is as easy to work as cherry, soft maple is an attractive alternative worth exploring.

USES

Popular for cabinets and furniture, soft maple also is fairly easy to carve, and its even, closed-grained texture holds small details and under-cuttings superbly. Since the grain of maple is subtle, it never dominates the details of the carving, and the wood can be polished to a lustrous shine, which is why it is favored by many carvers for their best sculptures.

OAK, RED

Quercus rubra

Having an open grain, red oak accepts stains well, although nowadays more people are using clear finishes to preserve its natural color. Moving outdoors, however, where decay resistance is a concern, red oak is not a good choice. White oak is much better suited to facing the elements. To distinguish red oak from white, look for color, pore distribution, and the presence of tyloses, which is a bubblelike cell structure that fills the pores of white oak, giving it an ability to retain and keep out water. A magnifying lens will reveal that the pores of red oak are empty. While looking for tyloses, one may also note that red oak has larger but fewer pores than white oak. Of course, the most recognizable characteristic of red oak is its pinkish hue. For a fairly hard wood falling between sugar maple (harder) and walnut (softer), red oak machines quite easily, and hand tool enthusiasts appreciate how well it planes. Turners, however, report that red oak tends to tear on the lathe. It has excellent bonding properties, but its tannic acid content can cause unsightly black stains when iron clamps contact glue lines.

USES

Red oak is legendary as a fine furniture wood. It also makes excellent flooring, paneling, and moldings, and is extensively used by the domestic kitchen cabinet industry as dimensional stock and as veneers on sheet stock, milled for casework.

OAK, WHITE

Quercus alba

Whenever the old song "Roll Out the Barrel" is heard, white oak should come to mind. In days of old, most of those barrels were made from this sturdy species. That's because the pores of white oak are filled with tyloses, a substance that gives the wood watertight and water-resistance properties. The name refers to numerous species with similar characteristics, all of which are woods worth singing about, especially when considering their natural beauty and good working properties. Oak once had a reputation for dulling tools quickly, but modern power tools and machinery make it an easy wood to work today. Generally speaking, white oak offers somewhat less dimensional stability than red oak, but it is a relatively minor problem for both. Quartersawn white oak offers more stability than plain sawn lumber, a factor that played a huge part in its selection by Gustav Stickley for his Arts and Crafts furniture. However, quartersawn white oak is limited in availability and generally more expensive.

USES

Beyond barrels, white oak is used extensively in fine furniture. Tannic acids, which protect the wood from insect and fungi attacks, make white oak a good choice for outdoor applications, too, where decay resistance is essential. Its hardness, strength, durability, and easy-to-finish nature have made it an enduring favorite of woodworkers.

OSAGE ORANGE

Maclura pomifera

Woodworkers have long looked to the tropics for exotic woods that add unique colors and textures to their work. However, today's concerns about rain forest resources have sparked an interest in finding unusual temperate-climate woods. Osage orange, a novel species with a bright yellowish-orange heartwood, is one of the finest examples of an exotic domestic, one that may actually grow in your own backyard. Osage orange was native to a small area of drought-ridden, windswept prairie in Texas and Arkansas. Today its range extends throughout much of the southern United States. Osage Indians, the wood's namesake, often carried hunting bows and clubs made from this species, which was an excellent choice given its outstanding bending strength and shock resistance. It is more than twice as hard as hard maple, offers better stability than black walnut, and weighs more than hickory and teak. Extreme hardness and density make the wood challenging to machine and glue, but sharp blades and epoxy resin overcome potential problems.

USES

Like tropical exotics, Osage orange is often used for smaller projects and as an accent wood. It exceeds the bending strength and shock resistance of most other species. Settlers found its decay resistance was unequaled, especially as lumber for fence posts.

PADAUK

Pterocarpus dalbergioides

Native to Africa and the Andaman Islands, padauk is known as vermillion for its unique reddish-orange color. When exposed to sunlight, it develops a dark, reddish patina as it ages. For an exotic, padauk offers relatively good stability and machining properties, with an exceptionally low shrinkage rating. With a degree of hardness that falls between hard maple (softer) and hickory (harder), padauk saws, planes, turns, and machines well. The strength of this wood exceeds all commonly used domestic species. When the wood is machined or sanded, toxins are released into the air, possibly causing skin, eye, or breathing irritation to those in the shop. Padauk has oils that can inhibit the penetration of yellow and hide glues. Being somewhat coarse textured, padauk accepts finishes well and can be polished to a high luster. Most oils will darken the wood, changing it from orange to red. Ironically, staining padauk is usually the only way to maintain its distinctive orange color for years to come.

USES

In the past, padauk was a favorite wood for boatbuilding, including structural elements, because of its superb decay resistance, luxurious appearance, and durability. Today, padauk is generally reserved for small projects and as an accent wood because of its high cost and also out of respect for rain forest preservation efforts.

PINE

Pinus familia

Christopher Columbus described the pines of the New World as "trees stretching to the stars with leaves that never shed." What a spectacular sight it must have been to see seemingly limitless forests reaching beyond the horizon. Being so plentiful, pine became one of the woods that early settlers depended on most for furniture and house building. A number of firms are now salvaging southern yellow pine from old buildings about to be razed. Beams, joists, and other timbers are milled into trim, moldings, flooring, and cabinet stock. Pines are softwoods, meaning they are coniferous trees. However, there are hard and soft subcategories. A few pines are actually harder than some deciduous trees. To distinguish hard pines from soft pines, look at their needle formations. On hard pines the needles are usually grouped two or three in a bunch, while soft pines have bundles of five.

USES

Eastern white pine is one of the most widely used soft pines for carpentry and construction. Southern yellow is a term used to describe several hard pine species (shortleaf, slash, and loblolly) sharing similar characteristics. The wood from these species is relatively heavy, hard, strong, stiff, and shock resistant. Southern yellow pines shrink quite a bit while drying, but the wood is quite stable once it has been seasoned.

POPLAR

Liriodendron tulipifera

Known by several names, including tulip poplar and yellow poplar, this staple of the modern wood shop is one of the least expensive and most readily available hardwoods. In fact, it's one of the few hardwoods carried by nearly every large home center (the other two being maple and red oak). Poplar trees grow very quickly, sporting tuliplike flowers in the spring, and when harvested dry easily by kiln or air-drying methods with very little shrinkage or warping. Among the lighter, softer hardwoods, poplar is straight-grained with a medium to fine texture and very few knots. It works extremely well with both machine and hand tools, glues well, and resists splitting when nailed or screwed. Poplar is light in color, with a slight yellow or greenish cast and occasional streaks of purple. Because of these color variations, and because it is extremely prone to blotching when colored with a pigment-based stain, poplar used for visible components is often painted. Durable and shock-resistant, poplar is highly stable.

USES

Poplar is an excellent choice as a secondary wood for drawer boxes, cabinets, and furniture components, and for molding and millwork that will be painted. Because of its fine texture and lack of knots, it's also a favorite for carving, turning, and wood sculptures.

PURPLEHEART

Peltogyne paniculata

Native to Central and South America, this is a very strong, heavy wood without annual rings, rays, or grain. The color is usually a uniform purple, but some pieces have vivid white streaks. In the shop, there are four primary problems with purpleheart: splintering, its effect on tools, color changes, and toxicity. Purpleheart is a very hard, somewhat brittle wood. Going too fast when ripping or crosscutting will cause it to splinter. Routing the wood can also cause splintering. This usually occurs at the beginning or end of the cut. One way to prevent this is to butt two pieces of wood against the edges of the board you are routing, to provide a continuation of the cut. Purpleheart will change color for several reasons, including excessive heat. When pressure accrues on a spot while sanding or routing too slowly, it darkens, as though a deep purple ink had been spilled on it. After purpleheart is finished, it may turn a dark reddish brown from the ultraviolet rays in sunlight. A sealing finish like spar varnish or tung oil is a good choice, and purpleheart refinishes beautifully.

USES

Used primarily as an accent in fine furniture and casework, purpleheart is quite beautiful and can remain that way, but it is definitely an indoor wood. A piece of this species that is exposed to the elements will, unfortunately, turn black.

REDWOOD

Sequoia sempervirens

Redwood is ideal for outdoor projects because its heartwood is naturally resistant to attack by decay-causing fungi and wood-destroying insects. This species grows only in the fog belt of extreme southwestern Oregon down into central California, along the coast. In most areas of the country it is not available at local home improvement centers but can be found or ordered at larger lumberyards. A mature redwood can grow to 325', with a trunk diameter of up to 15'. The heartwood varies in color from light cherry red to dark reddish brown. Sapwood is almost white or pale yellow. Redwood, like most softwoods, cuts easily, but one should always drill pilot holes before nailing or screwing. Redwood splinters easily, but this can be remedied by gluing the splinters in place before sanding, to prevent catching. Redwood is rated good for planing, turning, boring, mortising, and routing, although it is a good idea to make several passes with a router to reduce tear-out and splintering. Though it holds screws and nails poorly, its gluing characteristics have been rated excellent.

USES

Heart redwood is used extensively in construction as sill material where a frame construction meets its foundation. It is a popular wood for outdoor furniture, siding, fences, decks, porches, and other architectural elements that will be subjected to the vagaries of weather.

ROSEWOOD

Dalbergia familia

The name rosewood applies to a group of trees spread over the world's tropical regions, each having its own characteristics and all of them rich in appearance. In the West, rosewood's popularity dates to the 1700s when affluent Europeans imported it to adorn their opulent homes. Beginning in the 1800s, some species were overharvested. Most notable was Brazilian rosewood (*Dalbergia nigra*), a species that now is quite scarce and extremely expensive. Honduras rosewood (*Dalbergia stevensonii*) has a lighter color than Brazilian and is the most commonly available species today. Due to hardness it is a difficult wood to machine. Another rosewood (*Dalbergia latifolia*) comes with forenames like Indian, Indonesian, and East Indian. It is exceptionally hard, and the interlocking grain can cause tear-out when planing. This species has good bending qualities, takes finishes well, and offers excellent dimensional stability. Because of its oiliness, rosewood can be difficult to glue, making epoxy the best adhesive choice, and all species contain irritants that can cause allergic reactions.

USES

Rosewood is generally reserved for small projects and special accents. Veneer is its most cost-effective use. High prices and limited availability have inspired man-made substitutes using common domestic veneers that are compressed and dyed to look like rosewood and machine and finish well.

SASSAFRAS

Sassafras albidum

Due to limited growth, sassafras generally is not used in large volumes, especially by the furniture or cabinet industries. The largest stands today are in the southern states of Missouri and Arkansas. The wood is very similar to ash in grain appearance. It works more easily than ash but is not as strong. Sassafras is usually light yellow, tending toward reddish brown, but some trees yield a greenish-yellow color. It bears an aromatic herblike odor, which is substantially reduced in kiln drying. Some questions as to carcinogenic properties have been raised in recent years but not proven. As with all wood dust, protection is a good idea. Sassafras is priced in the same range as ash but more limited in availability. Traditionally, the wood was used in the manufacture of juvenile furniture, especially from 1880 through the 1920s. This was perhaps motivated by folklore that claimed the scent was a deterrent to childish nightmares. Since then the wood has been chiefly used as drawer siding in dressers. Sassafras is a great wood for chip carving and turning.

USES

The roots and underlying bark of sassafras are used to distill oil that is used in flavoring candy, as a scent in soap, and for folk medicines. In some parts of the United States, tea made from sassafras bark and roots has been used as a substitute for imported tea for years.

WALNUT, BLACK

Juglans nigra

Some old, abandoned barns provide interesting surprises in the form of black walnut that has been hiding under years of weather-beaten exposure. Although hard to comprehend today, black walnut was commonly used for barn construction generations ago because of its exceptional decay resistance and abundant supply. Today the law of supply and demand has made black walnut one of the most expensive of all domestic species. The chocolaty brown color of this species brings a warm, comfortable look to any room, while its strength and durability ensure that assemblies are likely to last for generations. The hardness of black walnut falls between cherry (softer) and oak (harder). In the workshop, black walnut works quite easily with both power and hand tools, and its outstanding stability prevents woodworkers from getting bent out of shape with frustration. It planes, carves, and turns beautifully, with very infrequent tearing and ripping. While it has excellent gluing properties, allergies are common. The rich color is perfect for clear finishing, and it polishes beautifully.

USES

Woodworkers are willing to pay a premium price for black walnut to complete their finest projects. Considering the price, it is generally reserved for fine indoor applications nowadays such as architectural millwork, cabinetry, and fine furniture.

YEW

Taxus brevifolia

For centuries, the yew tree has symbolized life and death. Early Egyptians honored it as the tree of life, while the Greeks associated it with Hecate, queen of the underworld. In England, yews guard cemeteries as symbols of everlasting life, and researchers are finding that the bark of yew contains a substance that may prove effective in the fight against cancer. For woodworkers, yew is one of the most desirable softwoods. Its orange-brown coloring with reddish-brown bands makes a striking appearance. It is one of the hardest and densest softwoods, exceeding many hardwoods. The close grain stains fairly well and polishes to a highly lustrous sheen. Yews are cone-bearing evergreens, with deeply fluted trunks that contain many knots, reducing the amount of usable timber. Working with yew can be a little tricky, for irregularly grained pieces are difficult to plane and frequently tear. Because yew is so hard, preboring nail and screw holes is a must. In addition, yew's slightly oily character can cause occasional gluing difficulties.

USES

Yew steam-bends well, making it a favorite choice for the hoop backs of Windsor chairs. Figured yew, with wavy grain that is dotted by little black knots, is highly prized by carvers and turners. It makes good outdoor furniture, exterior trim, and fences. Historically, yew was preferred for archery bows, because it is so elastic.

CHAPTER 3

A Safe and Comfortable Workshop

A Safe and
Comfortable Workshop

Woodworking is a surprisingly safe hobby, in large part because it actually is work for some people. The woodworking industry has developed safety standards that are excellent guidelines for hobbyists who wish to maintain a safe and comfortable workshop. In an environment that involves machines, cutters, dust, finishes, and fumes, accidents can happen, and long-term health risks exist. Limiting their impact is mostly a matter of common sense.

AVOIDING BACK INJURIES

From the day that first machine arrives on the shop doorstep, lifting is part and parcel of the joy of woodworking. Industry guidelines here are pretty straightforward, and they center on the fact that leg muscles are strong and back muscles are weak. Heavy loads should be lifted vertically, using the legs instead of the back. Reaching and turning or twisting can cause serious lower-back injuries and tear at arm and shoulder muscles. If a load feels off-balance, its center of gravity is too far from the person who is doing the lifting. On a centered load, the strain should be felt in the backs of the thighs and calves, and never in the lower back. Most shipping companies forbid their young, fit employees to lift loads in excess of 70 pounds. When deciding how much to lift alone, a good rule of thumb is to limit loads to one quarter of one's body weight. This is a rough, unscientific, anecdotal guideline for fit, strong adults. People with previous back trouble, problems related to the cardiovascular system, or other

medical concerns should consult their doctor. To summarize, never stoop over to pick up an object. Bend the knees, and this will soon become a habit. Pressing the chin toward the chest helps force the back into a straighter (not necessarily vertical) posture. Spread the feet to about shoulder width, acquire a solid stance, and keep elbows tucked in.

STAYING SHARP

Dull tools require a woodworker to force a chisel or knife through stock. When a slip occurs, a person's weight and momentum carry him forward, causing a lack of control. Sharp tools and cutters reduce the effort required by hands and machines, reduce friction on the cutter, and reduce burn on the workpiece. Most of all, they reduce accidents. There's an old saying in woodworking that the most dangerous tool in the shop is the dullest one. On the other hand, sharp tools are a joy to use and greatly enhance the wood-shop experience.

Beyond sharpening, there are several small steps that a woodworker can take to reduce hazards and create a safe and comfortable workshop environment. Extension cords are a nuisance and can be hazardous. They present a fire danger when an overloaded circuit hosts several cords. Long or undersize extension cords create electrical resistance, and this can cause problems in motors (especially air compressors). Cords can trip a woodworker when they are draped willy-nilly across the shop floor.

Another aspect of wiring, shop lighting, is worth noting. OSHA guidelines make a distinction between travel/access lighting and task lighting. The former means that there should be plenty of light where people walk, while the latter refers to

Ear and eye protection (shown at left) are essential in the modern mechanized woodshop. Sharp tools are safer tools (below), and learning to lift correctly can virtually eliminate back injuries (bottom left).

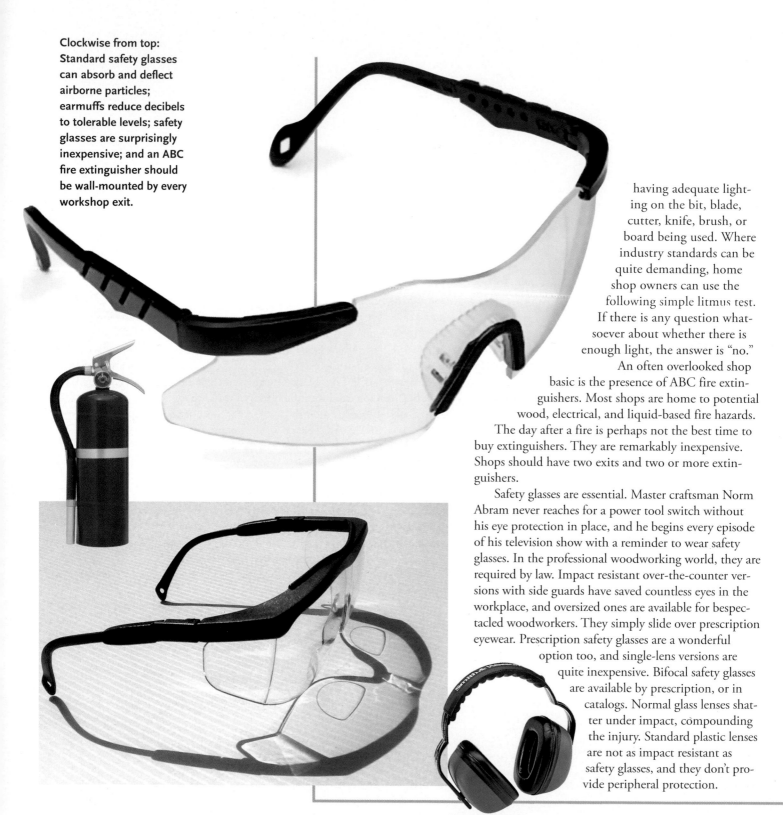

Clockwise from top: Standard safety glasses can absorb and deflect airborne particles; earmuffs reduce decibels to tolerable levels; safety glasses are surprisingly inexpensive; and an ABC fire extinguisher should be wall-mounted by every workshop exit.

having adequate lighting on the bit, blade, cutter, knife, brush, or board being used. Where industry standards can be quite demanding, home shop owners can use the following simple litmus test. If there is any question whatsoever about whether there is enough light, the answer is "no."

An often overlooked shop basic is the presence of ABC fire extinguishers. Most shops are home to potential wood, electrical, and liquid-based fire hazards. The day after a fire is perhaps not the best time to buy extinguishers. They are remarkably inexpensive. Shops should have two exits and two or more extinguishers.

Safety glasses are essential. Master craftsman Norm Abram never reaches for a power tool switch without his eye protection in place, and he begins every episode of his television show with a reminder to wear safety glasses. In the professional woodworking world, they are required by law. Impact resistant over-the-counter versions with side guards have saved countless eyes in the workplace, and oversized ones are available for bespectacled woodworkers. They simply slide over prescription eyewear. Prescription safety glasses are a wonderful option too, and single-lens versions are quite inexpensive. Bifocal safety glasses are available by prescription, or in catalogs. Normal glass lenses shatter under impact, compounding the injury. Standard plastic lenses are not as impact resistant as safety glasses, and they don't provide peripheral protection.

When it comes to noise, earmuffs such as the ones pictured here are recommended by doctors over earplugs, as the latter may carry bacterial infections. Headphones without built-in radio reception are a much wiser choice than those with speakers. It pays to be able to hear when a machine has been left running, or a motor is complaining under stress. The muffs in the photograph actually muffle loud noises electronically.

Pulmonary protective devices (dust masks) are discussed in some detail below.

The final basic concept, and the most important, is that children love to turn on machines. If locking the shop isn't feasible, then locking individual machines is an option. Many come with removable keys. Home stores sell clear plastic lockboxes for thermostats, which work wonderfully for machine switches, too. If wiring is accessible, a single switch can control an entire circuit if the woodworker must leave for a while. When children are in the vicinity, loose materials left on a saw or drill press table are an accident waiting to happen. And, of course, hand tools, finishes, bleach, and other toxins must be stored beyond the reach of wee woodworkers.

TABLE SAW SAFETY TECHNIQUES

As a centerpiece in almost every workshop, the table saw is the most-used machine in woodworking. When ripping plywood, first reduce the sheet to manageable pieces with a handsaw, jigsaw, or circular saw. Always use the splitter and top guard when sawing sheet goods. With pieces 12" or wider, push sticks aren't necessary, as long as the operator's hands are kept at the outer edges of the sheet. The right hand should be on the trailing edge of the workpiece, and the left hand on its left edge. Both hands help support the sheet so that it remains flat on the table.

When crosscutting on a table saw, never trap the stock between the fence and the blade. In the absence of a sliding fence, clamp a small block to the stationary fence at the front of the table and butt the workpiece against this block, if the fence is being used to establish the location of a cut. As the miter gauge slides forward toward the blade, the workpiece slides away from this block and can't be trapped against the fence. Use whichever miter gauge slot gives more control of the workpiece and the waste. A simple shop-made sled attached to the miter gauge adds a great deal of safety when making crosscuts in small pieces.

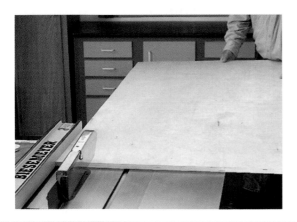

Large sheets should be reduced to manageable sizes with a portable circular saw, before being trimmed to final dimensions on the table saw. The cut begins with the woodworker standing at the far left corner, and ends with the woodworker standing squarely behind the sheet.

The table saw is a great way to cut accurate miters. It is essentially the same process as crosscutting, with the miter gauge set at an angle other than 90º. Use the fence to register the cut, and then remove the fence from the equation by sliding it away from the blade, so that the workpiece can't be trapped. Always leave the splitter and guard in place, if possible, unless a jig prevents their use. Hearing, breathing, and eye protection are highly recommended, and the splitter should never be removed from the saw unless a dado head, a stopped cut, or a tall workpiece require it. If at all possible, push sticks should be used when hands come anywhere close to the blade. The simple pattern shown on the opposite page can be cut from ¾" plywood scraps.

AVOIDING KICKBACK AND BINDING

Kickback means that the workpiece is driven back toward the operator at great speed. When woodworkers hear the term, they think of a ripping operation coming to a sudden and dramatic stop. There are two interrelated causes for this: an underpowered saw, and incorrect blade height. Forensic scientists have long known that a bullet causes its greatest damage as its velocity decreases (small entry, large exit). The same is true with kickback, which occurs when a saw blade is slowing down. If the saw has enough power to keep driving, it won't kick back. Not only does the sheer power of the saw come into play here, but the physical weight does too: If the motor, saw arbor, and blade are heavy enough, their momentum should keep the blade spinning during a sharp impact.

The second cause of this type of kickback (and many other problems, too) is a blade that is set too low: The teeth are cutting more horizontally than vertically. When they catch, they're traveling at the top of the blade's rotation. If the blade is set high, the teeth are traveling downward, forcing the workpiece onto the table, instead of back toward the operator. A low blade also causes motor drag: The number of teeth in

contact with the wood is greater. With a ¾" board and ¼" of blade protrusion on a 10" blade, the teeth must cut through a full 1⅝" of material. This heats up the teeth and the wood, increases drag on the motor, and reduces the feed rate. Not only does heat cause metal fatigue, but as many species of wood heat up, they expel oils that gum up the blade, further reducing its life. Since the blade is already being slowed, and the motor is operating closer to its stall rate than necessary, kickbacks are far more likely.

Over-the-top kickback is the most dangerous type because the wood is thrown at the operator at close to blade speed (about 52 mph). The workpiece catches the rear teeth of the blade and gets lifted off the table. As the saw teeth travel up and forward, they drive the wood toward the operator. With the workpiece no longer on the table, the blade is now free of resistance and its speed increases. The teeth are no longer cutting, so they dig in like baseball cleats, get a good grip on the wood, and hurl it at the saw operator.

The best method for ripping a long board is to stand at the back left side of the board and walk it into the saw. This will result in a smooth, continuous rip.

During crosscuts, a workpiece can become trapped between the blade and fence. Note in the photograph above that the sliding fence has been moved back, to avoid this problem.

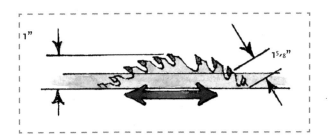

1"

1⁵⁄₈"

2¹⁄₂"

7/8"

A blade set too low (left) causes the teeth to cut more horizontally than vertically, which increases the chance of kickback.

When a blade is set high (lower left), the teeth are traveling downward as they enter the workpiece, forcing it safely toward the table.

An underpowered saw and an incorrect blade height are two main causes of kickback.

Below:
Push sticks, cut from 3/4"-thick stock to the pattern shown here, keep fingers away from rotating blades.

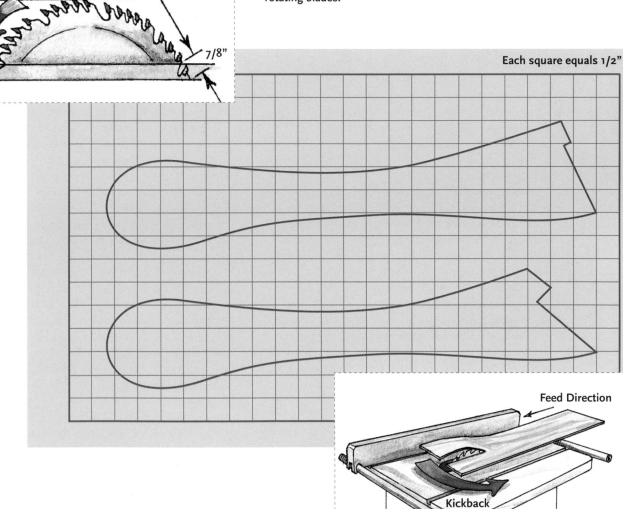

Each square equals 1/2"

Feed Direction

Kickback

Respiratory protection, such as the filtered mask shown above, is just one weapon in the battle against dust. A grounded, properly sized dust collection system and adequate shop ventilation are essential, too.

Keeping the left hand fairly far forward during this operation helps push the edge of the board safely toward the fence. To begin such a cut, hold the sheet very slightly crooked with only the front corner touching the fence. While slowly easing the sheet forward, listen for the blade to make its first contact. Then immediately straighten the sheet, moving it tight against the fence. This ensures that the rip is started with the front of the sheet tight to the fence. As the sheet is straightened, the blade holds the front in place. Exert pressure with the left hand to keep the rest of the workpiece against the fence.

Crosscut binding occurs when the workpiece twists in relation to the fence. Crosscutting short pieces is one of those operations where things can go wrong very quickly. Woodworkers should use a sliding cutoff jig here. It is a good idea to keep the table well waxed when using any jig.

No matter how rough things get, or how probable a kickback will be, don't ever let go of the wood. Nobody is fast enough to get out of the way of a 50 mph projectile. More often than not, by holding fast the operator will actually prevent the kickback. Over the years, one can train the reflexes not to panic and jump away but to hold on tighter than ever and even drive the piece forward if possible, depending on the circumstances.

DUST, THE INVISIBLE ENEMY

Wood dust is related to many health conditions, including irritation of the eyes, nose, and throat; skin rashes; asthma; allergies; and some serious lung diseases. It has even been linked to a rare form of nasal cancer. The impact for occasional woodworkers is far lower than for professional, full-time woodworkers, but age, other medical conditions, and poor dust control make this a serious issue for hobbyists, too. In addition to risks regarding asthma and emphysema, over 140 varieties of wood have some type of adverse effect on health. Some contain irritant chemicals, either naturally present or in treatments. White oak, walnut, and mahogany may cause bronchitis, while many types of exotic wood can cause skin problems. Even pine has been linked to nasal irritation and a decrease in lung function.

Although it is difficult to remove all the dust from a workshop, one essential strategy is to vacuum the shop regularly. Sweeping or blowing dust merely moves it around, while vacuuming removes it.

Lowering and controlling dust levels should begin at the point of generation, with the tools that generate the most dust. Handheld power tools such as orbital sanders and routers are among the worst offenders. Small dust-collection bags connected to these tools are usually not very effective. For sanding and routing operations, a downdraft table, a sanding booth, or even a vacuum-assisted power sander are highly recommended. While shop vacuums are popular among woodworkers, they may not be the best solution for systematic dust control. Along with their noisy demeanor, they have small capacities and filters that usually don't trap the tiny particles that aggravate allergies and irritate the respiratory system. For most shops, a complete dust collection system is the best choice. For many hobbyists, such systems seem a luxury, the last tool to buy. But the workshop machinery industry doesn't share that view. Almost all new tools feature either built-in dust collection ports or innovative in-tool collection devices.

CENTRAL DUST COLLECTORS

Central dust collection systems are generally measured in CFMs (cubic feet per minute). A 1 hp model generates 650 CFM of volume. That means it sucks 650 cubic feet of air through its intake port every minute it is turned on, and expels the same amount after filtering it. How big is 650 cubic feet? It's all the air in an 8' x 10' room. Most table saws require about 300 CFM of vacuum, while a jointer or a radial arm saw will usually be rated around 350 CFM. Planers and band saws need a little more volume (about 400 CFM). While most power tools have a dust collection port, it may not be large enough to control all the dust generated. Jointers and table saws may need a second collection port,

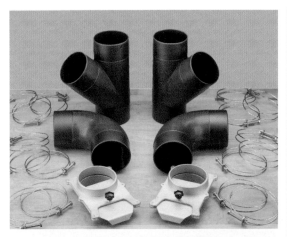

A central dust collection system consists of a collector, hoses, and specialty fittings such as the blast gates, clamps, and connectors shown here. Hoses must be grounded, as fine dust in suspension is an explosive hazard.

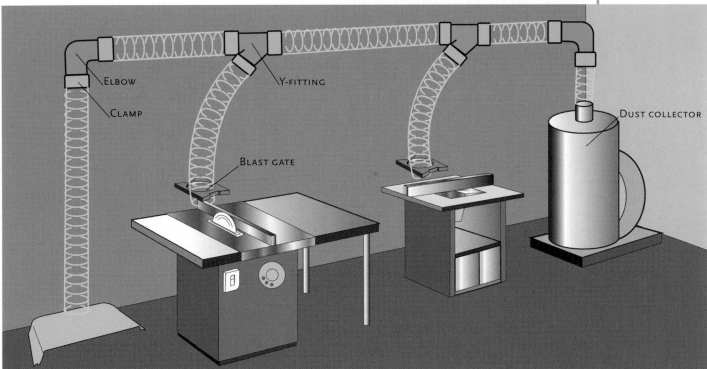

ELBOW

CLAMP

Y-FITTING

BLAST GATE

DUST COLLECTOR

because dust falls down and builds up inside. Both of these tools also project a significant amount of dust from their saw blade or knives. The second part of the sizing decision involves static pressure. Most domestic dust collectors are rated on the same scale, so CFMs are the main key to power ratings. But an understanding of static pressure may help clarify choices while sizing hoses or dealing with imports.

At sea level, the air is pressed down at 14.7 pounds per square inch (psi) by all the air above it in the atmosphere. The higher one goes, the lower this pressure becomes. But for most purposes, manufacturers use the 14.7 psi measurement (known to engineers as "one atmosphere" and to

Small cyclone collectors like Oneida's Gorilla 2 hp unit are surprisingly affordable and very powerful.

This Rockler downdraft sanding table, available in kit form, scrubs the air using a series of filters.

the industry in general as standard cubic feet per minute, or SCFM) as their baseline when rating a vacuum. So, if a room at sea level is 650 cubic feet, and a dust collector can empty that much air in one minute, the collector can be rated at 650 CFM at one atmosphere. At higher altitudes, the air pressure will drop: There will actually be a little less air in the same 650 cubic foot room. So a 650 CFM vacuum will run slightly less air through its filters.

The final element in sizing your dust collector is the nature and size of its filter. A filter increases resistance, reducing the number of CFMs. The more efficient the filter is, the less air a given vacuum will move through it. This resistance is called static pressure loss. That 650 CFM rating? It's for a collector with absolutely clean filters. They come in all shapes and sizes. For most shop vacuums, they are simple accordion-shaped paper prefilters, or cloth bags secured by rubber straps. Low-end dust collectors generally employ large cloth bags, while units at the top of the market have an elaborate series of cloth, paper, wire, electronically charged, or fiber filters. Most shop air cleaners (the type that hang from the ceiling) are equipped with two or three filters of varying quality. They are rated by the size of particle they can trap, which in turn is measured in microns.

HOW BIG IS A MICRON?

Air filters are rated by the size of dust particle they can capture and the amount of air they can treat. The smaller the particle, the better (and more expensive) the filter. The unit of measurement for dust particles is the micron, which is 1/25,400". The human eye can only see dust particles bigger than 10 microns. Most of the dust you see in a beam of sunlight is on the order of 100 microns. Here's a discomforting fact: 99% of all dust in the woodshop is less than 1 micron in size. The dust collector's filter alone is generally not up to the job

Air scrubbers such as JET's Air Filtration System contain a fan and two or three filters in sequence. The first filter removes the largest particles, while the ensuing ones remove sequentially smaller contaminants.

of removing submicron particles. Instead, a separate air filtration system (most of which are designed to remove particles down to 0.3 microns or less) is the safest way to deal with these contaminants.

Air filtration systems contain a fan and two or three filters in sequence. The first filter removes the largest particles, while the ensuing ones remove sequentially smaller contaminants. The most recent innovation in air filtration technology is to add electrostatic fibers to the final filter in the sequence. For example, 3M's Filtrete series of home furnace filters employs this technology to remove microparticles of smoke, viruses, bacteria, and fine dust at efficiency rates up to 25 times more effective than ordinary fiberglass filters.

AUTOMATIC BLAST GATES

Every woodworker has forgotten to turn on the central collector when taking a cut or two on the table saw, or failed to open a blast gate for some piece of shop equipment. These lapses can be avoided by controlling the central collector with an automatic blast gate system. The Ecogate system (shown on page 68) employs special solenoid-operated blast gates that automatically open and close when the machine at that gate is turned on or off. A small contact pickup mounted to the machine's motor

SPARKS AND GROUNDING

Dust is a notorious fire hazard, so central dust collection systems require two types of grounding to avoid sparks. Motor housings must be sealed and rated spark-free. The second type of grounding applies to static electricity buildup in the ductwork. Metal ducts are most often grounded automatically when they are hooked up to a collector (see the documentation that comes with your machine). Plastic ductwork is a little more difficult to ground. The most common strategy is to run an exposed metal wire through the duct and then attach one end of it to a ground outside the building.

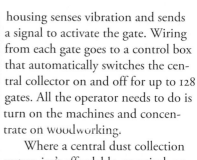

housing senses vibration and sends a signal to activate the gate. Wiring from each gate goes to a control box that automatically switches the central collector on and off for up to 128 gates. All the operator needs to do is turn on the machines and concentrate on woodworking.

Where a central dust collection system isn't affordable, practical, or functioning effectively, dust masks and breathing devices can protect a woodworker. These are most efficient in sanding and turning situations. Various versions are available, from simple masks with changeable filters to helmets that incorporate electronic filters. The version shown below is a Trend Airshield, which is a lightweight battery-powered face shield that circulates air while protecting the eyes and face from small debris such as wood particles and shavings.

SINGLE AND TWO-STAGE DUST COLLECTION

A single-stage collector is a big impeller that pushes dust and chips into a plastic bag, while forcing clean air out through a large filter. Shop vacuums are low-powered single-stage collectors, so they're not a realistic choice for large stationary machines. A two-stage collector has an additional collection device to trap the largest particles before they hit the impeller. This cuts down on wear and tear and is generally offered in larger systems (2 hp and up), but can be added to a single-stage collector in kit form. Both systems require constant monitoring. The more waste that accumulates in either the plastic bag or the drum, the less efficient the collector will be. This is also true of dust stuck to the inside of a filter bag: By plugging the filter holes it reduces the static pressure.

Professional shops generally employ a large cyclone type dust collector that can cope with a huge volume of dust. Some downsized versions of the cyclone system are now available in the home-shop market. They are more efficient than a stock two-stage and cost about the same as the better contractor table saws.

SAFETY TIPS FOR WOODTURNERS

The wood lathe is a reasonably safe tool, but it will bite if care isn't taken. Each turning session should begin with the removal of rings and watches, tying back long hair, and getting shirtsleeves out of the way. Anything that can wrap up in a lathe will do so, sooner or later. A face shield and dust mask are essential equipment. Inspect all turning stock carefully for hidden flaws and cracks. Having a knot or a checked spindle or bowl blank suddenly let go at high speed is not pleasant. Check the rotation of any workpiece before starting the lathe, and always check the lathe's speed setting before flipping the switch. Improper initial speeds and work hitting the tool-rest account for a lot of accidents. Also double-check the mounting job before trusting a bowl blank. Use the tailstock whenever possible to help keep work secure. When using a chuck to remount work, be sure the new mounting is aligned concentric to the old axis, and slow the lathe's speed before starting newly mounted pieces.

Be wary of intentionally out-of-round or out-of-balance work. Many fascinating effects of turning are achieved by doing off-center or multi-axis turning, but these are techniques that demand extra attention to

safety. Irregular pieces are more dangerous and deserve respect.

Fingers must stay behind the tool-rest. Many turning injuries are the result of a finger caught between the turning and the rest. Natural edges can be especially dangerous this way, as they are irregular, can drag stray fingers into the gap, and then act like a saw blade.

Sanding is another danger spot. Lots of jammed fingers and twisted wrists happen while sanding inside a bowl. Be sure that letting go quickly is an option, if the paper catches. Keep the tool-rest completely out of the way when sanding. Try using a foam-rubber finger to hold abrasives in bad spots.

Chisels must be sharp. A clean cutting edge creates less drag and leaves a better surface. It is also less likely to catch and cause an accident. Use the right chisel for the job. An ANSI rated impact visor should be a regular part of a turner's gear.

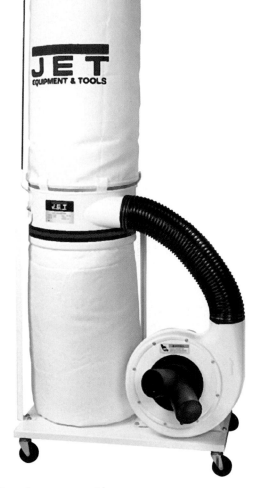

Automatic blast gates, opposite page, top, built into a dust collection system open and close as machines are used, and the collector runs only when woodworking equipment is turned on. Full-face powered respirators (opposite page, bottom) are ideal for turners because they protect the eyes and the lungs. Dedicated dust collectors such as the JET model shown above can handle debris from two or three machines.

CHAPTER 4

Hand Tools

Hand tools, evocative of traditional woodworking skills, have largely been replaced by powered equipment. There is still a vital role for measuring and marking tools, chisels, scrapers, and smoothing planes, but the vast majority of woodworkers will now use an electric router rather than a manual router plane to profile an edge. While tradition would suggest that we retain hand tools and their accordant skills, common sense and a combination of new materials and techniques have made it more expedient to reach for the router. There is sweet satisfaction in running a perfectly tuned plane across a board or along an edge and watching a uniform ribbon appear in its throat. However, the harsh truth is that a jointer and belt sander can usually do a better, faster job, especially for a novice. Most hand tools have a learning curve. If one has the time to acquire the skills, there is no greater reward in woodworking.

The oldest and perhaps the simplest hand tools are those used to measure and lay out cuts. Woodworkers need to be able to quantify four things: angles, straightness, twist, and length. The measuring tools used to determine angles fall into three subgroups: try squares, which measure 90° angles; miter squares, which measure 45° angles; and sliding bevels, which measure variable angles.

ANGLE MEASUREMENTS
The try square

A try square is two pieces of wood, metal, or a combination of the two, fastened together at right angles. The part that is held by the hand is called the stock, and the part at right angles to it is called the blade. A major difficulty with an all-wood try square is the tendency to slice the blade when using a knife to mark a line. The answer is a striking knife, beveled on one side only, with the flat side being held against the try square blade. Factory-made try squares are generally a mixture of wood and metal. The wooden stock is often fortified on the inside edge with a brass strip, a clear nod to superior aesthetics and quality. The hard blue steel blade, held in place by three studs, clearly states this is a sound, workmanlike tool, built to last.

An all-steel square, shaped the same as wooden ones, is made for metalworkers. Its standard of accuracy is very high, and its economical price makes it a very worthwhile purchase. Plastic squares are useful in rough carpentry. They are inexpensive, lightweight, durable, and resilient. For marking out boards when harvesting parts or marking out a crosscut, they can be quite handy.

Opposite page: Master woodworker and author Ian Kirby looks for twist in a board using two winding sticks.

Below: A basic square can measure both outside and inside corners and allows for accurately marking stock square for cutting.

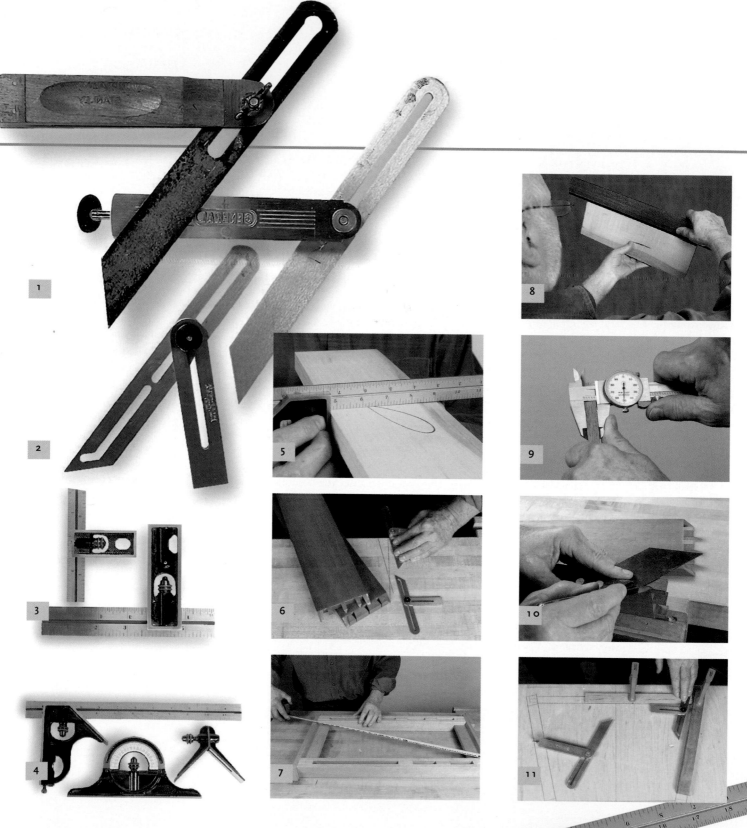

"A good, sharp hand tool is a joy to use. It gives the woodworker a strong sense that he or she is working wood, rather than simply machining it."

Larry Heinonen

The combination square

The combination square's design has two features not associated with a try square. First, the blade is graduated, so that it works also as a rule. Second, the blade slides. Blades are interchangeable and can be any length up to 36". They can have a revolving head or a 45° head attached to them, instead of the usual 90° one.

Miter squares

A miter square is used for measuring and marking corner miter joints. The Japanese version of the miter square is an excellent choice. To use one, locate the point of a marking knife on the face of the workpiece, slide the miter square up to it, and knife the miter line.

Sliding bevels

Three types of sliding bevels are available, and the all-metal model has a useful feature. Its curved end is separated from the straight edge by a small step, so the bevel can be positioned accurately when there is only a small area to land on. Sliding bevels are essential when laying out hand-cut dovetails. The angle of pins and tails on a dovetail joint is expressed as the slope: the ratio of width to length.

To set a sliding bevel to mark out a beveled shoulder line on a tenon, a full-size working drawing is required. A piece of wood is clamped on top of the drawing, and the bevel is set against this.

STRAIGHT MEASUREMENTS

Experienced woodworkers often make their own wooden straightedges, which are elegantly thin with an inlay of ebony along one edge, which will extend the life of the tool and better resist knocks. Steel straightedges were originally made for machinists. They come in different lengths, with square or chamfered edges.

WINDING STICKS

A twist in a board, often missed with the naked eye, can be seen dramatically with winding sticks. These are usually a pair of parallel-sided straight pieces of wood of the same dimension, and are shop-made. Honduras mahogany or any clear, straight-grained, quartersawn, and dry material works. They must be parallel, perfectly straight, and identical. A center mark on each is essential to sight along the work. Suggested dimensions are ⅜" x 2¼" x 14¼". The maple strips on the tops of the winding sticks shown on page 72 taper from ⁷⁄₁₆" down to ³⁄₁₆" at the top edge. As a woodworker sights across the closer strip, the other one is moved along the board to reveal any twist.

GRADUATED TOOLS

A graduated tool is one that has incremental measurements stamped, printed, or engraved on it. The most common is the metal tape measure. In furniture making, 12" and 24" straightedge rules are the most useful for setting gauges, calipers, and sliding bevels, and for taking measurements.

Another graduated tool, the vernier caliper, is an excellent gauge for measuring the depths of grooves, stopped holes, or stopped mortises. The jaws can measure inside or outside dimensions of grooves or tenons.

1, 2. **Sliding bevel gauges**

3, 4. **Combination squares**

5. **Using a combination square to check edge squareness**

6. **Setting a bevel gauge**

7. **Checking a frame for squareness using a tape measure**

8. **A good straightedge is essential for checking workpieces.**

9. **Vernier calipers can measure to exacting tolerances.**

10. **Marking dovetailed corner with a miter square**

11. **Bevel gauges can be used for elaborate layouts.**

MARKING GAUGES

Used to mark lines on boards, marking gauges have three major parts: the fence, the stock, and the marker, which will be either a pencil, knife, or spur.

A spur (steel pin) is designed to mark with the grain, while a knife is designed to cut across the grain. Steel spurs are sharpened like the point of a pencil with a small sharpening stone. To adjust the spur, clamp its blunt end in a machinist's vise and tap the gauge up or down. A cutting gauge has a small steel knife, which is held in a mortise by a wedge of cast brass. The knife usually comes with a sharp point, but it works better rounded.

A variation on the marking gauge is the mortise gauge, which has a fixed top spur and a moving bottom spur. Some mortise gauges have a third spur on the back side of the stock. The idea is that by using this spur like a regular marking gauge, one buys two tools for the price of one.

BENCH PLANES

Set coarsely, a bench plane will hog off shavings ⅛" thick. But with a fine setting, it will remove a shaving that is just one-thousandth of an inch thick. Bench planes come in different sizes and widths, but practically all flat furniture parts can be planed using only two tools, a No. 4½ and a No. 7. The No. 4½ is 10" long, and the No. 7 is 22" long. They are both 2⅜" wide, so the blades are interchangeable.

To work successfully, the plane's blade must be sharp, and the set (amount and angle of the blade protruding through the base) must be correct. The face of a workpiece is planed flat on the bench with the aid of a bench stop, while long edges and ends are planed when the wood is held in a vise.

To make a plane stroke, grip the handle with the right hand. Press the index finger against the cast frog. Apply firm left-hand pressure on the toe of the plane at the beginning of the stroke. By midstroke, apply pressure with both hands. Apply right-hand pressure at the end of the stroke. Four feet is about the maximum length one can plane without taking steps. The most common mistake is to exaggerate arm movement. In the early stages of the stroke, only lower body and leg movement propel the plane forward. In the beginning stance, the feet are about 18" apart and the back foot more at right angles than a walking step to enable a strong push-off. Lubricate the operation by rubbing a little paraffin wax onto the sole of the plane.

TUNING A HAND PLANE

The equipment required for a tune-up includes a lapping plate, which is a totally flat surface. Quarter-inch-thick plate glass works well. A machinist's square or straightedge is helpful, as are files: A mill bastard file is best for the preliminary coarse work, and a mill smooth file handles the fine adjustments.

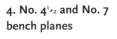

Set the sole of the plane on the lapping plate to see how flat the sole is. Use automotive feeler gauges to discover if it's dished around the mouth, or lifts up at the ends. The sole prevents the shaving from splitting and tearing, so pay special attention to the portion of the sole in front of the plane's mouth.

The lapping plate should be two or three times the length of the plane. Use spray adhesive to glue emery cloth or silicon carbide sandpaper to one of its surfaces (seams in the paper are OK). If there is a lot of metal to remove, start with coarse emery cloth or 60-grit paper and change it regularly. Corrugated soles go faster than flat ones. Check the progress carefully with a straightedge.

The two-part iron is the heart of any plane. The cutting iron (blade) must have a flat back and a bevel sharpened at about 30° right to its tip. Begin flattening the back on the lapping plate, then move on to fine honing stones. Make a comfortable wooden block to fit around the iron and protect hands, then concentrate on the first ½" or so of the iron: Eventually this should become highly polished.

To create the bevel on the front of the iron, use a honing guide. It's quick and easy, and it won't round over the bevel. Start with a coarse (800 grit) water stone and work until a burr is raised. Then remove

1. Checking the sole of a bench plane for flatness with a feeler gauge

2. Marking gauge

3. Setting the marking spurs on a mortise gauge

4. No. 4½ and No. 7 bench planes

5. A proper bench plane stroke

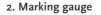

1. Bench chisels

2. Burnishing a cabinet scraper

3. A cabinet scraper should always be used with both hands.

4. Planes work more smoothly if the sole is lubricated with paraffin wax.

5. A plane's cap iron fits atop the cutting iron to curl shavings up and out of the plane.

6. Sharpening a cutting iron with a honing guide

7. Using a bench grinder to create the bevel on a cutting iron

the burr by honing the back side of the iron on a polishing stone. Next, raise another burr on a medium (1200 grit) water stone, and then hone both sides on the polishing stone. A highly polished edge will stay sharp longer. After a few honings, regrind the bevel to a 27° to 28° angle at a bench grinder. This secondary bevel means less honing. For this, use a white aluminum oxide wheel and maintain it with a diamond point wheel dresser.

A plane will jam up if shavings get caught between the cutting and cap irons. The cap iron creates the curl in a shaving by levering it up right at the cutting edge, in effect constantly breaking it. This levering prevents the shaving from splitting out ahead of the iron, minimizing tear-out. The front edge of the cap iron should be lapped to form a straight, sharp edge. Pinch the two irons together and sight toward a bright light to achieve a tight fit. Form and smooth the rounded top of the cap iron next, as shavings must glide up here. This won't happen if the curve is too perpendicular to the cutter, so file a smooth curve on the top that leans into the cutter. Finish up with very fine sandpaper.

A plane's cutting iron has a shape that corresponds to the type of job it is designed to do. A plane for coarse work has an iron with a noticeable curve, while one for shooting fitted edges, like a jointer, will have an iron that is straight across. On a smoothing plane, or one used to level a surface, the iron is a bit of a hybrid. Its corners are slightly rounded so they don't dig in. Between them, the majority of the iron is straight, but it should trail off to a very slight rounding at each side. This creates very shallow scallops with ridges that are easily sanded off. One can create this profile when honing by twisting the honing jig every other pass or so.

The plane's mouth must be open enough to admit a plane shaving, but the smaller the opening, the less tear-out there will be. So, a plane set for

curly woods should have a very small mouth opening, with the cap iron barely set back from the cutting edge. Widen both for normal wood.

Lubricate the sole often during use with a few light strokes of paraffin wax. This is sold as canning wax in grocery stores, but it's not really a wax at all. It's a petroleum derivative related to mineral spirits, so it won't contaminate the wood or prevent a finish from adhering to newly planed wood.

CABINET SCRAPERS

A cabinet scraper is a flat rectangle of steel, and it is used to shave very fine ribbons of wood, producing a clean surface that is ready for finish. The key to sharpening a scraper is to file the edges perpendicular to the face. It makes sense to sharpen all four edges at once. A mill file and a series of sharpening stones will accomplish this. Once the edges are square, it's time to reach for a burnisher. This requires a fair amount of force while stropping the burnisher back and forth at about a 5° angle on the flat side of the scraper, about 15 or 20 times. The goal here is to push the edge out from the flat plane of the scraper. In the final set of passes, angle the burnisher to about 85°. Even though the effect is invisible, this will curl the edge over to create the scraper's cutting edge. Give all four edges the same treatment. The burnisher shown here has a triangular profile, but some woodworkers get good results from a round profile. The key is that the tool needs to be made from a very hard steel to successfully push the scraper edge. It's also important for the burnisher to be smooth, without any nicks or dings that would potentially catch on the scraper.

In use, a scraper is held with two thumbs in the middle of the back. Bend the steel slightly so that only part of the scraper is in contact with the wood. As it is pushed forward, fine shavings come off the tool. A scraper can also be used on shaped parts. It can be pulled or pushed. It can be used to clean up interior corners.

CHISELS

A sharp bench chisel can be used to chop a mortise, trim dovetails, pare a tenon, square the end of a routed dado, and a thousand other tasks. These flat tools come from two distinctly different traditions, Western and Japanese. The important difference is in the blades. Western chisel blades are made from a single piece of steel, of which the last 1½" or more is tempered to a hardness of 59 to 62 on the Rockwell scale. Japanese chisels, on the other hand, have bimetal blades. A thin layer of hard steel is welded to a thicker, supportive layer of soft steel, and the lamination is then tempered to a greater Rockwell hardness of 64 to 66. The harder a piece of steel, the sharper edge it will take, but it also becomes more brittle and prone to nicking.

Both types are generally ground to a bevel angle of 25° to 30°, but where Western chisels are often hollow-ground, Japanese chisels are flat-ground to give their brittle cutting edges a little extra support. With either style of chisel, when the cutting edge begins to fracture it often means the bevel is ground too acutely.

Chisel blades are secured to their handles with either a tang or a socket. Both types of construction are durable. A tang chisel is recognizable because of its brass or other metal ferrule, and the handle is

usually wood. On a tang chisel a bolster, ferrule, and leather washer protect the handle from splitting when it is struck with a mallet. These features aren't needed on socket chisels, which are most often equipped with a plastic handle, as the force of each mallet blow is directed into the cone-shaped socket. Plastic-handled bench chisels are versatile, inexpensive, tough, and a good place to start a chisel collection. An adequate initial set includes ¼", ⅜", ½", ¾", and 1" chisels. Eventually, a set of mortising chisels is a sound addition. These are essentially very large versions of bench chisels. There are specialized chisels for carving and turning (see chapters 11 and 12).

SPOKESHAVES

Once among the most common tools in the workshop, spokeshaves were used by wheelwrights to shape spokes and felloes, by coach builders to create curved fenders and mudguards, by chair makers to fashion spindles, and by farmers who needed to shave a new ax or shovel handle for a perfect fit. Although most traditional spokeshaves sported a flat sole, there were some, called travishers, which were curved for specific uses like shaping the saddle in a chair seat. In the modern shop a spokeshave works well for shaping and roughing out stock, and it is absolutely ideal for trimming hardwood edging applied to plywood.

TUNING A SPOKESHAVE

Prepare the blade by removing large nicks with a file, keeping the bevel intact. Then smooth the cutting edge by moving through a series of sharpening stones, from medium coarse to very fine (left drawing). Hone both faces in a figure-eight pattern to keep the cutting surfaces smooth.

Reinstall the blade, keeping in mind the distance that its edge protrudes beyond the sole is critical (middle drawing). As with a block plane, start by setting the blade past the sole the thickness of a hair. Test your set-up on a piece of dense-grained maple, adjusting the blade and your hand positions until you feel comfortable pushing your spokeshave. Many craftspeople feel more comfortable pulling a spokeshave, but the tool was actually designed to be used with a pushing action (right).

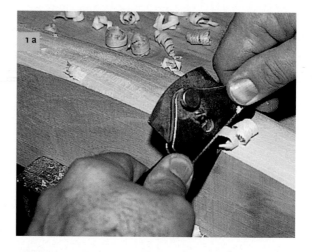

1a

1b

Spokeshaves have transitioned from wood to metal bodies, with knurled knobs for blade adjustment. Old wooden spokeshaves typically had their cutter set at a very slight angle, making them great for edge-grain work as well as end-grain shaving. Unfortunately, the new iron-bodied spokeshaves have a blade set at about 45°, making them suitable only for edge-grain work.

CLAMPS

Pipe clamps

Perhaps the most obvious use of clamps in the wood shop is for creating panels. The basic panel clamp is the pipe version, available for ½" and ¾" black iron pipe that has been threaded on at least one end. In addition to standard clamps, they are also available in a model that holds the panel in the center, and another with deep-reach jaws. Other accessories include slip-on pads to protect projects from the evils of metal jaws, and saddles, which hold the pipes off the bench top to make clamping somewhat easier.

If the pipe isn't long enough, it can be replaced, or two lengths can be joined with a coupling. Black iron is preferred over galvanized (silver) pipe because the surface is rougher and less likely to slip. It also costs a little less.

1a & b. Spokeshaves are excellent for shaping curved workpieces.

2. Bar clamps used with a Rockler Clamp-It™

3. Bar clamp

4. Corner clamp

5. Pipe clamp

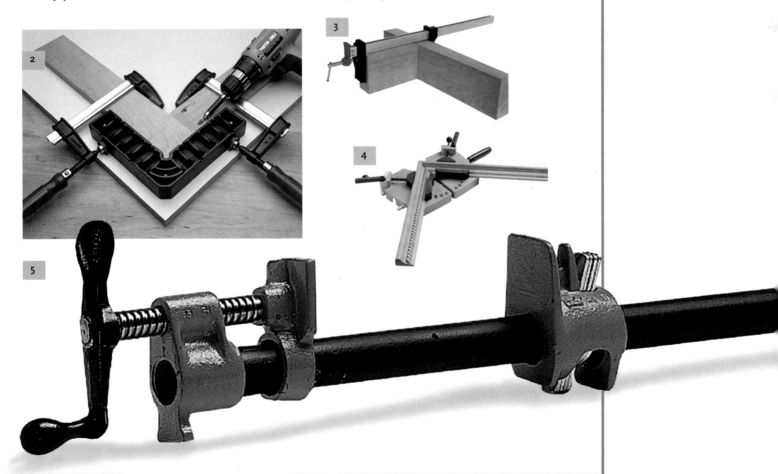

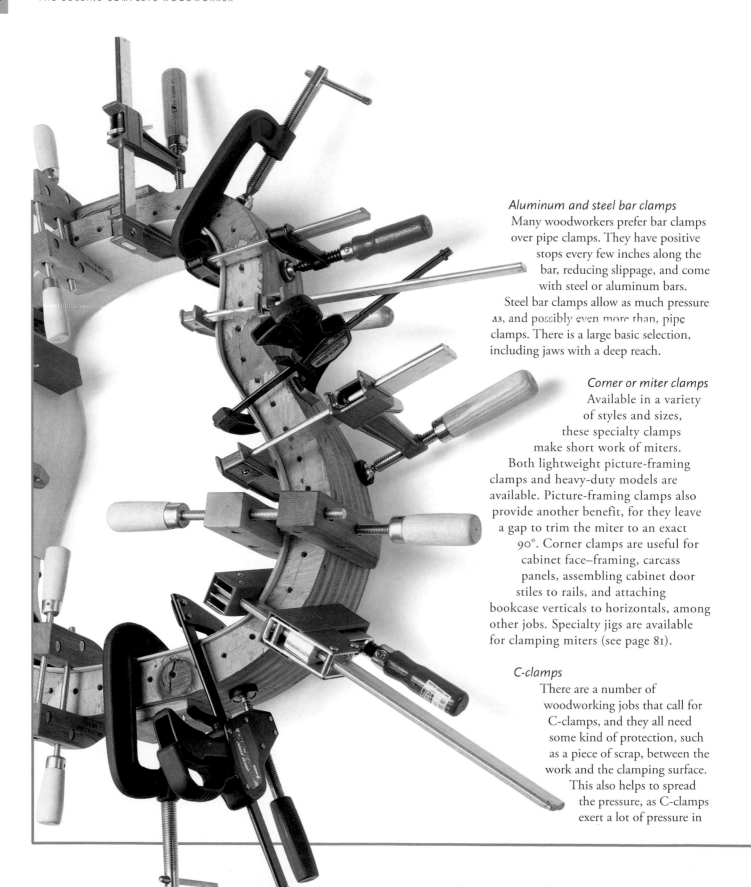

Aluminum and steel bar clamps

Many woodworkers prefer bar clamps over pipe clamps. They have positive stops every few inches along the bar, reducing slippage, and come with steel or aluminum bars. Steel bar clamps allow as much pressure as, and possibly even more than, pipe clamps. There is a large basic selection, including jaws with a deep reach.

Corner or miter clamps

Available in a variety of styles and sizes, these specialty clamps make short work of miters. Both lightweight picture-framing clamps and heavy-duty models are available. Picture-framing clamps also provide another benefit, for they leave a gap to trim the miter to an exact 90°. Corner clamps are useful for cabinet face–framing, carcass panels, assembling cabinet door stiles to rails, and attaching bookcase verticals to horizontals, among other jobs. Specialty jigs are available for clamping miters (see page 81).

C-clamps

There are a number of woodworking jobs that call for C-clamps, and they all need some kind of protection, such as a piece of scrap, between the work and the clamping surface. This also helps to spread the pressure, as C-clamps exert a lot of pressure in a very small footprint. Possibly the best of the edge-clamp designs is an adaptation of the C-clamp: It comes with a center post that screws into place after the clamp is tightened down to the panel surface. C-clamps are inexpensive, so having plenty on hand is not a hardship. Round protective pads are available that can be hot-melt glued onto the jaws, to avoid small depressions in wood.

Hand screws

Hand screws are among the oldest, most versatile, and most underused woodworking clamps. The wooden jaws and steel threads allow work at different angles, so these clamps are wonderful for tackling nonparallel surfaces and objects. Sizes vary from about the 4" to 14" range, but larger models are available up to 24". Rotating the handles adjusts the jaws. Using the front screw for initial sizing works quickly, while final pressure is applied with the rear screw. Jaws must be kept clean and free of glue drippings, as hardened glue will indent a workpiece and fresh glue may even attach the wooden jaws to a project. A slip of masking tape over each jaw is a big help when the glue-up seems likely to be messy. Some people prefer to tape a piece of rubber or plastic in place over the tips, in order to prevent glue buildup. Such tip covers are reusable if cleaned and stored properly.

Band clamps

One of the more useful clamps for round, octagonal, or similar shapes, a band clamp can range from light through heavy duty. The bands are from 1" to 2" and wider, with heavy-duty mechanisms that can draw them very tight. Most bands are heavy nylon or canvas, and the better-quality clamps can apply as much as 2,800 PSI (pounds per square inch) of pressure. Shorter, light-duty bands are usually about 10' long, while heavier-duty types may be twice that, or even longer. They are ideal for round, bent laminations and stave work.

One-handed clamps

This clamp's design allows the user to slip it closed and clamp it down with one hand. This allows the other hand to hold the parts in place. The clamp comes in tiny versions for light-duty work, and spreader clamps are available for repair jobs such as removing and replacing chair rungs and splats. One-handed clamps are one of the most useful developments in the past few years. They make jig builders' jobs a great deal easier.

Spring clamps

These small, one-hand spring clamps are useful for many light clamping duties. They come with resin (plastic) or steel bodies.

Opposite page: The truest of wood shop mantras: "You can never have enough clamps."

Below left: Band clamp

Below right: One-handed bar clamps

ROUNDING OUT THE TOOLBOX

Since the advent of electric scroll, circular, jig, reciprocating, band, and table saws, few woodworkers use handsaws anymore. There are some specialized situations where they are still a better choice, such as cutting dovetails, or trimming protruding dowels. For these tasks, the popular choice is a Japanese backsaw, which has teeth that cut on the pull stroke, rather than the push, an arrangement that offers more control. For trimming dowels, a version is available with an offset handle that allows the blade to sit flat on the workpiece and cut flush.

Rasps and files, most often found in the shops of carvers and refinishers, are a smart addition to the general woodworking toolbox, too. In addition to standard bastards and flat files, a set of rifflers can be extremely useful, especially for detail work. These are curved, thin files that will fit into the tightest spaces, or touch up fine work.

The bit and brace, a staple of carpentry for more than three centuries, is now an antique hung on the walls of wood shops. It has been replaced by an advancing army of ever more powerful cordless drills (see chapter 5). There are few practical reasons to own a brace, though it does have romantic connotations.

A good 10- to 16-ounce claw hammer is essential in woodworking. Some models now come with an engineered handle designed to reduce vibration, which is wonderful where extended use is required, or for those with arthritis or similar afflictions. The weight should be suited to the worker's hand and arm strength, as fatigue is an issue.

People who are framing buildings generally prefer a heavier tool in the 21-ounce range, because framing nails are larger than the headless finish nails that are used in the wood shop. Plastic-handled chisels are perfectly suited to hammer blows, but wooden-handled ones without a steel shaft work better with a mallet instead of a hammer. The head of the mallet can be wood, resin, plastic, plastic weighted inside with lead or steel ball bearings (known as a dead-blow mallet), or even rawhide. A

barrel-shaped mallet is available for gentle carving with smaller, specialized chisels.

Along with a good hammer, every toolbox should have an assortment of nail sets designed to set 4d through 10d finish nails. These are small punches with hollow heads that can be centered on a headless finish nail and tapped with the hammer, to "set" the heads. Setting just means driving them below the surface, thereby creating a small dimple that will hold wood putty and so disguise the presence of the nail.

Screwdrivers have essentially gone the way of many other hand tools. Cordless drill/drivers are now equipped with magnetic holders that accept various screwdriver heads. Hand tools have taken a back seat to these in recent years. When the occasion arises where a cordless tool won't do the job (batteries sometimes fail, or perhaps an opening is too small for the tool's body), a hybrid is the best solution. This is a hand tool that accepts those hex-base bits that were originally designed for power tools. It generally comes with a pretty good selection of flat, square, and Phillips bits and sometimes even includes some more exotic offerings such as Allen or star bits. Many models are equipped with a rachet drive, which cuts down on the effort required to drive a screw. The key here is that one tool has replaced a whole family of individual screwdrivers.

Keeping all of these hand tools clean is a job for wire brushes, which seem to fill several other essential roles in the shop, too. It's a good idea to keep some steel brushes to clean hard surfaces like files, and a couple of brass brushes for more sensitive surfaces.

Rounding out the toolbox, a simple apron/tool-belt combination can be as useful as a second pair of hands, especially during assembly sequences when nails, hammers, nail sets, glue, sandpaper, screws, and drivers are constantly being called upon. A full apron is handy during finishing (especially if stain is involved), and a heavy canvas apron actually provides some protection from errant projectiles in the shop. Pockets in aprons are great places to store tape measures, pencils, and marking tools, but they are not an advisable repository for delicate items such as safety glasses.

The best place to store safety glasses is on your nose.

Opposite page, left: Japanese-style backsaw

Opposite page, right: A wooden mallet works best for wood-handled chisels.

Above: Hybrid screwdrivers

Below: Spring clamps

CHAPTER 5

Portable Power Tools

Portable Power Tools

The right tool for the right job.

Sometimes the right tool is a hand tool, and for that reason we can expect them to be with us forever. For many simple tasks, it's far easier and faster to use muscle power than electrical (or pneumatic) power. To tighten a single screw or trim the end of a single 2 x 4, the average woodworker is far more likely to reach for an ordinary screwdriver or handsaw, even with powered versions only a few steps away.

But when it comes to driving dozens or even hundreds of screws, or making several repetitive cuts in heavy stock, power tools take center stage to get the job done most efficiently. What's more, the learning curve is faster for power tools for many applications; it can take years to master the art of cutting dovetails by hand, for example, but with a router and the right fixture, even a new woodworker can make perfect dovetails with ease after only a few tries.

Power tools come in two categories: portable and stationary. There is sometimes a bit of overlap between the two, but for the sake of definition, the word "portable" as it is used here refers to generally handheld tools. In spite of the fact that many bench-based tools are marketed today as portable—thickness planers, for example—those will be covered in the next chapter on machinery.

The most important thing to keep in mind is that power tools are less forgiving than hand tools, so it is essential that power be disconnected (corded tools should be unplugged; batteries removed from cordless tools) when you are making any adjustment to the tool.

ROUTERS

Routers are widely regarded as the most versatile power tools in the shop. With correctly matched jigs and bits, routers can edge-joint and surface-joint rough stock; cut almost any type of joinery, including dadoes, rabbets, splines, miters, tongue-and-groove, mortises, and more; and excel at trimming chores. The router's real asset is shaping, with the possibilities limited only by the availability of bits of the desired profile—an availability that is, for all practical purposes, unlimited.

Routers come in three basic types, all sharing a straightforward design. Simply put, a router consists of a motor with handles attached on either side. A base plate allows the router to rest directly on a workpiece or to be mounted in an inverted position in a router table. A collet securely holds and extends a bit through the center hole of the base plate to make contact with the workpiece. Depth of cut is controlled by raising or lowering the motor housing.

Opposite page: Woodworker and author Bill Hylton uses a pneumatic brad nailer to quickly assemble cabinet components.

CHOOSING A ROUTER

As you sort through router candidates, assess the vital characteristics. Among the most important to consider:

- **MANAGEABILITY**
  Can you lift it easily and handle it with confidence? If it's too big or too heavy, or if the handles don't fit your hands, it will be difficult to use effectively.
- **ADJUSTABILITY**
  The best systems provide both coarse and fine adjustment capabilities, and you need to be able to lock the setting securely without wrenches.
- **COLLETS**
  Routers with both 1/2" and 1/4" collets can use the greatest variety of bits. Self-releasing collets make bit changing easier.
- **ELECTRONIC VARIABLE SPEED**
  Single-speed routers run at about 22,000 rpm, fine for smaller bits, but too fast for 2" or 3" diameter bits. Variable speed allows you to reduce speed to minimize burning in some hardwoods and increases safety for large-diameter bits like panel cutters. Variable units also help maintain constant speed under load.

- **SOFT START**
  Routers with soft start accelerate progressively to minimize the high-torque "kick" on startup.

With a fixed-base router, cutting depth is set before use and locked in. They are generally compact, with a low center of gravity making them a stable tool for most operations. Their handles are low enough to be gripped firmly and while still bracing the heels of your hands against the work. A variation on some fixed-base routers is a D-handle option with a large loop-style handle with a trigger switch, much like a circular saw. Fixed-base routers excel at work that does not require constant changes in cutting depth, such as dadoes, grooves, rabbets, and most edge profiles.

Plunge routers can do everything a fixed-base router can, but because their motors ride on spring-loaded posts rising from the router base, they allow for on-the-fly depth changes and for lowering—or plunging—the spinning bit into the workpiece in a controlled manner. A plunge router can begin and end a cut in the middle of a board, making it ideal for cutting stopped dadoes and for inside work with templates. The plunging action is essential for routing deep mortises.

"A tool is but the extension of a man's hand, and a machine is but a complex tool. And he that invents a machine augments the power of man and the well-being of mankind."

Henry Ward Beecher (1813–87)

Ideally, it's good if you can afford both types in the shop. However, most manufacturers produce combination kits that include both types of bases, and the motor housing can be swapped from the fixed base to the plunge base as needed.

Trim routers were originally designed for trimming laminate countertops. These little machines don't have handles and are used single-handed by gripping the motor housing. While full-size routers can take bits with shanks of ¼", ⅜", and ½", trim routers are limited to only ¼" shank bits. Their lower power also limits what they can handle, but they are ideal for light-duty jobs like hinge mortising, inlays, small-radius edge treatments, and rabbeting panels for glass. Although fixed- and plunge-base routers can be table mounted, trim routers aren't suited for table use.

Trimmers aside, routers are clustered in two general sizes characterized primarily by amperage and horsepower ratings. The largest number of brands and models of both fixed-base and plunge types are rated from 10 to 12 amps, and 1¾ to 2¼ horsepower. The second cluster includes 13–15 amp, 3 to 3½ hp machines, most of which are plunge models. Dedicated plunge routers tend to be heavier than comparable fixed-base machines, but in general the smaller machines weigh about 6–9 pounds, while the big ones can weigh as much as 14 pounds. For that reason, many routers of 3 hp and up are dedicated to router tables as opposed to handheld use.

JIGSAWS

Because they can use a variety of blade types, jigsaws—sometimes called saber saws—can cut just about everything: wood, drywall, conduit, cardboard, plastic, even metal and ceramic. They are light and easy to handle, and no handheld tool does better at cutting complicated curves, or creating cutouts in panels.

Jigsaws cut with a vertical reciprocating blade, which means simply that the direction of the blade alternates upward and downward to perform a complete cut. The teeth on the blade face upward and cut on the upstroke. (If you cut material with a finished side, like laminate flooring, the "good" side should be on the underside of the cut to avoid tear-out on the finished side.) Jigsaws work best on thin materials, as their cutting depth is limited to the exposed length of the blade, about 1½".

Cutting action on jigsaws is described as orbital, in that the blade moves in a slight circle as it goes up and down. On the upstroke the blade angles into the work to increase cutting power; on the downstroke it angles away from the work until at the bottom of the stroke.

The most common jigsaw design incorporates a handle mounted above the saw. Others forgo the handle

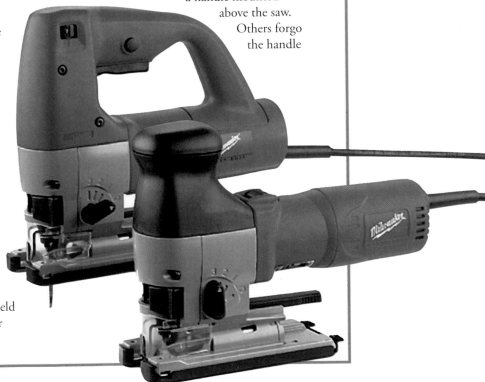

Left to right:
Laminate trimmer

Router bits are changed by loosening the collet with wrenches. Routers with a spindle lock, like the one shown here, require only one wrench.

Handle-grip jigsaw (top), barrel-grip jigsaw

entirely; for these, the saw is controlled by gripping the barrel-shaped motor housing. All models have an adjustable base plate or shoe, which allows bevel cuts by simply loosening the base, tilting it to the desired angle, and locking it in place. Corded saws are most common, but nearly every manufacturer has introduced at least one cordless model.

When buying, look for features such as variable speed control, tool-free bevel adjustment, quick-release blades, and dust control options.

CORDLESS DRILLS

Corded drills will likely be around forever, but when it comes to the woodshop, cordless drills have taken over. It's no wonder that manufacturers offer more drills than any other cordless tool—currently, about 150 cordless drill models. (Technically, these tools are called drill/drivers, as their variable-speed capability allows the low-speed, high-torque ranges needed for driving screws and other fasteners.)

All models handle the same tasks, but the variety of styles, power levels, and features can make choosing one (or two) for your shop difficult.

Start with power

Drills are rated by voltage and torque. Generally, drills with higher battery voltage and/or lower gearing have more torque. A 9.6-volt drill can successfully drive long screws, but it will drive them more slowly than a 14.4-volt or higher drill. Battery voltage also affects how long a drill runs between charges—the higher the voltage, the longer it lasts.

A battery's amp-hour (Ah) rating also affects run time; battery packs with a higher Ah number run longer. Unless used for installing a deck or sheathing a house, cordless drills in the 12- to 15.6-volt range are generally considered powerful enough for everyday use.

Size and weight

Bigger isn't always better. Higher-voltage drills tend to be bigger, heavier, and more expensive. Models with heavier construction (all-steel chucks, metal gears, etc.) aimed at more serious users are heavier than less expensive "light-duty" models. A typical do-it-yourself-level 12-volt drill might weigh only 3½ pounds, while a pro-oriented 18-volt model may be a hefty 6½ pounds.

For installation work and jobs around the house, consider a drill's overall size and body length. Longer drills are less likely to fit into cramped spaces under sinks or inside cabinets. Predictably, most lower-voltage drills tend to be shorter than higher-voltage models. Lower-voltage drills also tend to have more compact grips, an important factor for smaller hands.

Speed

A variable-speed trigger is a must for driving and removing screws, or for starting drill bits on sensitive or hard materials, like hardwood plywood or metal. Higher rpm is better for running small bits or driving screws quickly; lower rpm increases torque output when driving big bits and fasteners. Lower-priced 9.6- and 12-volt "economy" drills usually offer only a single-speed range, around 550–600 rpm, fast enough for occasional tasks around the house. Woodworkers and serious do-it-yourselfers, however, need the higher revs (typically between 1,000 and 1,600 rpm) that multispeed models offer. For greater speed-choosing versatility consider a three-geared model allowing high speeds up to 2,000 rpm.

Chuck and clutch

Cordless drill chuck capacity is usually ⅜" for drills up to 18 volts, and ½" for drills 18 volts and over. All-metal chucks are the toughest but tend to make these drills a bit nose-heavy. Plastic chucks are much lighter and are adequate for most users.

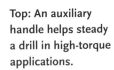

Top: An auxiliary handle helps steady a drill in high-torque applications.

Middle: Drill lengths vary. Shorter drills are easier to use in cramped quarters.

Bottom: Drill chucks come in a variety of styles, but all have a clutch ring set behind the chuck.

Left: Blades on reciprocating saws and jigsaws (shown) have an orbital action that maximizes cutting power.

An adjustable clutch sets the amount of torque the drill delivers to the bit, to prevent overdriving screws or screw breakage and head stripping. Most adjust by rotating a ring just behind the chuck. More clutch settings make it easier to fine-tune a drill's power output to suit a particular driving job.

Battery and charger type
Nickel-cadmium (NiCad) batteries, standard on most drills, have good power output, a long recharge life, and are perfectly adequate for most cordless

users. For best performance, choose a model with an advanced charger and follow good recharging practices, such as draining batteries fully before recharging and letting hot packs cool before and after charging.

Nickel-metal hydride (NiMH) batteries are more expensive but typically have higher ratings than same-size NiCad packs and offer longer run times.

Lithium-ion (Li), the newest battery technology, promises impressive performance, including excellent power output for battery weight, fairly constant power right up to when the battery is exhausted, and extremely long shelf life. However, Li batteries are more expensive and complex than other battery types, with built-in electronics and special chargers that carefully regulate the charge to each individual cell inside the pack.

Chargers for economy-grade drills often lack any charge-managing electronics and may require many hours to fully recharge a pack. Better-quality drills come with upgraded chargers that feature electronic circuitry that manages the charging cycle, maximizing battery performance and preventing heat damage, to increase a pack's longevity. Some deliver a full charge in an hour or even less. A few models employ a built-in fan to dissipate heat, while others are designed to charge two batteries at once.

Additional features

There is a long list of features to consider when buying a drill, including auxiliary handles (best on high-torque/high-voltage drills), belt hooks, built-in LED work lights, auxiliary bit holders, and more.

If your budget allows it, another buying strategy is to purchase two moderately priced cordless drills instead of a single more expensive one. Setting one up with a drill bit and the other with a driver bit can actually save a lot of time when making pilot holes and driving screws. Also, if one drill breaks down, you'll still have a drill on the job.

SCREWDRIVER BITS

If there is a specialized type of fastener out there, it's a safe bet that some manufacturer offers matching driver bits to fit it. Literally hundreds are available, and the number seems to grow daily. Common slotted and Phillips bits come in a large range of sizes, with either magnetized or lockable bases, plus extra-long versions for extending a drill/driver's reach into tight quarters. For woodworkers who drive more than common screws, driver bits are available in socket or nut-driver versions, hex, torque, square-drive, dodecagonal, Torx, Robertson, and many more. Specialized bits for "security-head" fasteners—screws and bolts often found in public spaces to prevent tampering and removal, such as spanner, fork, four-wing, star-drive, and others—won't be found at your local home center but can be ordered from a number of catalog and online sources.

Most cordless drill/drivers include at least a few representative bits to get the user started, but these are often limited to a pair of slotted and Phillips bits in two sizes. However, driver bits are relatively inexpensive, whether purchased individually or in sets, so it's advisable that a set with at least the most common bits be kept in the shop or inside a drill's

carrying case at all times. For common slotted and Phillips screws, get several and keep them everywhere in the shop: It's the rare woodworker who doesn't lose or wear out several of the most-used driver bits in the course of a year.

AIR TOOLS IN THE SHOP

Air-powered, or pneumatic, tools have been the choice of professional shops for years, but decreasing prices and a growing variety of tools have spurred interest in these tools among home woodworkers. To run tools on air, an air compressor is a must.

For carpentry and home repair, an ultraportable compressor easily carried from place to place may be your best bet. This type of unit has a 5–20 gallon tank and a motor rated from 1 to 3 hp. If most of your work is in a home workshop, consider a standard portable compressor. This has a larger tank and motor and is usually equipped with its own set of wheels.

Heavy use or high-demand pneumatic tools generally require a stationary compressor with a 50–60 gallon tank and a motor rated at 5–6 hp.

Air compressors generate moisture. Depending on the system size and ambient humidity, draining may be needed several times on a heavy-use day to prevent accumulation of water trapped in the compressor tank over time. If the compressor runs more than 5 or 10 times a day during the summer, the tank should be completely emptied at the end of each day.

Obviously, air tools require an air hose for their source of power and are limited in use by the length and weight of the hose. For occasional use, lightweight coiled hoses are handy but have a tendency to tangle easily when stretched. (They can also act as a long spring, tugging steadily at the tool while it is being used.) Standard air hoses can also be unwieldy. With an overhead or wall-mounted hose reel, however, the user can play out the exact amount of hose needed, while the reel helps support the weight of the hose.

AIR FASTENER SAFETY

Pneumatic nailers/staplers have special safety features and considerations. Merely squeezing a nailer's trigger does nothing; it won't fire a nail across the room. The spring-loaded safety is deactivated by placing the tool's nose on the workpiece and gently pressing. Most nailer/staplers can fire only a single fastener and must be lifted off the workpiece to reset for the next one to fire.

Errant nails are a significant hazard. Individual fasteners, especially in the higher gauges, are very limber. When fired into a workpiece, they follow the path of least resistance. Encountering gnarly grain or a knot, they can veer off course and burst through the surface in an unexpected spot. Particular attention must be paid to hand placement when using these tools.

Available air tools

Aside from spray-finishing applicators (see chapter 13), the most common air tool in woodworking is the pneumatic fastener, either a nailer or stapler. Models range from the smallest pin nailer to an industrially rated framing nailer. Each has its own purpose and limitations.

Pneumatic nailer/staplers come in a range of designs, but most are similar in size and weight, accommodate similar nail/staple sizes, and have tactile handgrips. The actual fasteners come bonded together in strips, and the tips are chiseled to help prevent splitting. Nailers and staplers load like desk staplers: Slide open the magazine, drop in a clip, and close it up. Almost all come with plastic pads on the business end, intended to eliminate scratching and to cushion the impact of recoil.

When choosing a pneumatic fastener, first determine your primary use. For small projects like jewelry boxes, an 18- or 19-gauge pin or brad nailer is best. These shoot headed or headless pins ranging in length from ⅜" to 2". For large projects like coffee tables and cabinets, you may want to consider a light finish nailer. This gun shoots 16-gauge finish nails or large brads, ranging from ¾" to 2½" in length.

If you are primarily building cabinets, a 15-gauge finish nailer is a good choice. Since the nail head is slightly larger, this has the added advantage of being able to pull workpieces together during impact. While a 16-gauge nailer works well for carcass work, a 15-gauge nailer is great for pulling window, door, and floor moldings tight to an uneven wall. For woodworkers who run the gamut of project size from jewelry boxes to full-sized cabinetry, the best bet might be a good 15-gauge nailer and a low-cost 18-gauge nailer.

Pneumatic staplers are sometimes interchangeable in applications with nailers but lend themselves well to thin materials such as cabinet backs, where nails have a tendency to pull through, or in material that experiences stress or movement, like flooring. Staplers

The fence of a biscuit joiner can be set at almost any angle, but 90° cuts, as shown here, are the most common.

are also a few pneumatic tools, such as impact hammers and grease guns, that have few applications in the wood shop.

Finally, in recent years a few manufacturers have come out with "cordless" pneumatic fastening tools. These use a variety of methods to provide air power, including small onboard compressors and even internal combustion. Extremely useful for on-site work where electrical power for a compressor is unavailable, or where excessive hose length is impractical, these tools are a good match for their hose-based counterparts nail-for-nail. Most of these tools are on the expensive side, however. All of them are quite heavy and don't lend themselves well to casual shop use.

are an especially good choice for attaching upholstery, ceiling tile, carpeting, and other soft materials. The choice in staplers is similar to that of nailers, with a variety of staple sizes available. A number of manufacturers have combination guns that shoot both nails and staples, but keep in mind that these combination nailer/staplers are usually limited to fasteners no longer than 1½".

Following nailers and staplers, one of the more popular pneumatic tools is the random orbit sander. In function, appearance, and applications, these sanders are comparable to their electrically powered cousins, discussed later in this chapter. As with sanders, many other common shop tools are available in air-powered versions, including drills, reciprocating saws, impact wrenches, grinders, and polishers. There

BISCUIT JOINERS

Biscuit joiners (sometimes called plate joiners) are among the newest tools to find a home in the wood shop and the only portable power tool dedicated to a specific type of joinery. The type of joint they create is a variation on an older form of joinery related to floating tenons and dowel joints, wherein an additional piece of wood is used to connect separate workpieces in combination with a glue joint. The distinction in the name is subtle: A jointer (see chapter 6) is a machine that creates an edge on a piece of stock to make it suitable for joining to similarly prepared workpieces, while a joiner is a machine

Below: Belt sander

Opposite page: Variable speed random orbit sander

that actually joins two pieces of stock together by creating the joint itself.

A biscuit joiner has a flat face that is placed against the edge of the workpiece to be joined. When the machine is powered up and pressed into the workpiece, the spring-loaded motor moves forward to extend a cutting wheel—similar to a tiny circular saw blade, but with only a few cutting teeth—into the wood to create a slot. Matching slots are created in the mating workpiece. With glue applied to the workpiece edges, thin wooden plates that look remarkably like small biscuits are glued into the slots to line up and strengthen the mating edges. Commonly used for edge-joining, biscuits can be especially helpful in strengthening end-grain joints of the type found in miters and face frames.

Biscuit joiners feature an adjustable, front-mounted fence system that makes it easier to align the joiner with the workpiece and keep it tightly against the surface when cutting. With the fence set and locked in the correct position, biscuit slots can be cut at nearly any desirable angle.

Biscuit joiners can be used to join boards to make larger panels for tabletops, to create and attach face frames to cabinets, and to attach shelves to cabinet sides. A variety of biscuit sizes are available, which can be matched to the size and thickness of the workpiece, and specialized two-piece locking biscuits have been developed that allow a tabletop to be taken apart and reassembled at will.

Biscuit joinery can also be performed with a router equipped with a slot-cutting bit.

SANDERS

Portable sanders play two main roles in the shop that neatly bracket the lifespan of the typical woodworking project. In the early stages, sanders help remove waste material to create complete workpieces like large panels. As a project nears completion in the later stages, sanders come to the forefront for surface finishing.

It isn't generally talked about, but there is also a third role sanders play: While there is no excuse for careless workmanship, portable sanders can often correct a world of honest mistakes or even downright sloppiness. Mismatched joints can be smoothed and corrected. Errant scratches and gouges can be minimized or even removed if they are not too severe. Minor tear-out in edge profiles can sometimes be made to disappear. Glitches in staining and finishing can be sanded back to a "clean slate" to allow finishing to be started over.

Portable sanders come in four main types, and although there can be some overlap in how they are used, each performs best for a specific function.

Belt sanders

The true workhorse of the group, belt sanders can hog a lot of material from stock in a short amount of time. The circular belt passes over a flat, rigid platen, helping to level workpieces far better than other portable sanders can. Belt sanders excel at flattening large panels glued-up from multiple boards, or shaping large curves.

Care should be taken when operating a belt sander. Unlike other portables that use an orbital pattern, the belt runs at high speed in a continuous straight line, so using both hands is a must—lose your grip and you'll find out why belt-sander drag racing has become a popular pastime. Also, belt sanders are very aggressive, especially when fitted with a coarse-grit belt. Let the weight of the sander do the work; adding extra weight by pushing the machine down into the workpiece can easily gouge the surface.

Belt sanders are easily the dirtiest machines among the four types and produce clouds of sanding dust. A dust collection bag, or better still a hose attachment connected to a shop vacuum or dust collection system, is a necessity.

Palm sanders

Inexpensive and available from nearly every manufacturer of woodworking equipment, palm sanders are a good choice for general finish work. They require no special type of sandpaper; full sheets of regular paper can simply be cut to size to fit the square sanding pad. Most palm sanders are sized to use fourths of a full sheet, but there are smaller palm sanders that use one-sixth of a full sheet. Paper is held onto the cushioned pad with a pair of clips, one on each side.

Although it may feel that palm sanders work by vibrating, they actually use a continuous orbital pattern; that is, the sanding pad moves the sandpaper in tiny circles against the work surface. These circular patterns repeat endlessly around a central point, so it's necessary to keep the

Below: The specialized pad on this contour sander allows it to reach into tiny crevices.

Opposite page: The highly portable circular saw is frequently used to resize full sheets of plywood and other large stock.

sander in motion at all times to prevent the creation of scratch patterns resembling tight swirls on the wood surface.

Although the dust produced isn't as great as with a belt sander, dust collection is still necessary. Most come with an attached dust bag, and adapters are available that allow connection to a vacuum source. Palm sanders draw dust through the pad, so holes must be punched in regular sandpaper to allow air to be drawn through.

Random orbit sanders
Similar to palm sanders in size, shape, and function, random orbit sanders add a unique refinement. While the pad makes an orbital motion, it also spins at the same time, making the scratch pattern totally random. Because of this spinning motion, the sanding pad is round and requires sandpaper disks sized specifically to the machine; 5" pads are the most common, but sanders with pads of 6" and larger are available. Most random orbit sanders use sandpaper with a hook-and-loop backing, allowing paper to be mounted or changed easily. However, a few models still use the old-style "peel and stick" pressure-sensitive adhesive (PSA) sandpaper disks. PSA disks can be used only once, as removing them usually destroys them.

Dust issues with these sanders are about the same as with palm sanders, but random orbit sanders are a bit better equipped to handle it. The pads of these sanders have a pattern of either five or eight evenly spaced holes that match holes already punched into the paper. All random orbit sanders come with dust bags or canisters, and hose adapters are available.

Random orbit sanders can be very aggressive, particularly when using coarse sandpaper, so care should be taken to monitor the amount of material being removed. Although the orbital action minimizes damage to the work when used properly, these sanders can still leave swirl marks if pushed down too hard into the wood instead of allowing the weight of the sander to do most of the work.

Contour sanders

Unlike the other three types of sanders, which are best suited for flat surfaces, contour sanders use a variety of sanding pads that can fit into just about any type of surface shape. Also called detail or profile sanders, these tools have removable pads available in a seemingly endless number of shapes and profiles that allow them to get inside tight curves, moldings, profiles, hollows, and even carved recesses. And while

most come in kits with a selection of pad profiles that can be used for common moldings and curves, some manufacturers include or make available as an option accessory kits that allow the user to create custom-shaped pads to fit any recessed area.

Since these sanders don't use traditional flat pads, dust collection ranges from difficult to impossible. Fortunately, they are used almost exclusively in tight profiles and so produce the least amount of dust of any type of sander.

CIRCULAR SAWS

To paraphrase an old adage, "If you can't take the wood to the table saw, take the table saw to the wood." Although no replacement for a good table saw, circular saws can perform many of the tasks done by their stationary cousins, plus some they can't. For accurate trimming of rough stock on-site—or reducing large stock too cumbersome to cut properly or safely on a table saw—few tools can do better. For cutting stock to rough length or reducing sheet goods to manageable size for cutting on a table saw, a circular saw can be used freehand. A straightedge can be clamped to the workpiece for cuts requiring more accuracy.

These tools are constructed like an upside-down table saw, with the angle of the cut determined by the relative angle of the blade to base plate. Unlike a table saw, where blade angle and depth are controlled by moving the blade, a circular saw's cut is adjusted by moving the base plate to the correct position.

Full-size corded circular saws typically use a 7 ¼" blade, but expect smaller blades on cordless versions. Manufacturers' specifications vary, but most 7¼" saws have a maximum cutting depth of about 2½" at 90°, and about 1⅝" at 45°—plenty to handle standard 2-by stock.

Circular saws come in two types: The most common types found in the home shop are called direct-drive or in-line saws, and have a side-mounted motor with the blade attached directly to the motor shaft. Generally lightweight and easily handled, direct-drive saws are a good choice for wood shops. "Worm drive" saws, meanwhile, have the motor mounted behind the blade and use gears to increase blade torque for heavy-duty tasks. These saws are usually more powerful and heavier than their direct-drive counterparts and are typically used for construction.

To use a circular saw, first set blade depth by positioning the unplugged saw on the edge of the workpiece. Pull back the blade guard and release the locking knob on the base plate, then slide the motor up or down until the blade projects about ¼" below the workpiece, and retighten the base plate. To start the cut, with both hands on the saw, rest the front edge of the base plate on the workpiece, being sure the blade isn't touching the stock. Start the saw and move it into the wood with the base plate flat against the workpiece, pushing steadily until you have cleared the other side (you know you are through when the waste drops off). If the motor bogs down during a cut, slow your forward movement.

Keep a circular saw's base plate clean at all times and frequently check the accuracy of the preset stops for bevel angles (most saws have positive stops at 45° and 90°). If the saw is dropped, examine the base plate carefully to ensure it hasn't cracked or bent, and recheck bevel stops.

RECIPROCATING SAWS

Strictly speaking, reciprocating saws are generally more useful taking things apart than building them. A real staple of the construction and remodeling trades, reciprocating saws—commonly referred to simply as "recip" saws—excel at creating cutouts for windows, doors, and sinks, or recesses for built-in constructs in walls. For that matter, they are often the tool of choice when it comes to dismantling walls and other framing.

A reciprocating saw functions mechanically like an in-line jigsaw; the blade moves in a direct line with the motor, usually with an orbital action that maximizes cutting power. However, their greater weight and larger blades can make them difficult to control for the fine cutout action for which jigsaws are known. Still, because their construction background means they usually have larger, more powerful motors than jigsaws, they can be useful for rough-cutting thick linear stock or raw lumber to length, or for hogging out large amounts of waste material. Also, their linear design allows for cutting in cramped or difficult-to-reach locations. Outside the shop, they can make short work of pruning chores for trees and heavy shrubbery.

As with most portable power tools, recip saws come in both corded and cordless versions.

ROTARY TOOLS

These handy little power tools can do just about anything—as long as it's small. Normally used single-handed, rotary tools consist of a barrel-shaped motor housing and a small collet (usually ⅛") that can take a variety of bits, cutters, and attachments. With the appropriate bit, rotary tools can be used for carving, cutting, engraving, polishing, drilling, grinding, sharpening, and more. With specialized attachments and bases, they can be converted into tiny handheld planers, routers, sanders, and cutout tools; there is even a pumpkin-carving attachment. Available in several sizes and power ranges from a number of manufacturers, rotary tools come in both corded and cordless versions.

HOT-MELT GLUE GUNS

While hot-melt glue is most often used in craft-related applications, it can have a number of woodworking applications. Because it sets very quickly, usually in just a few seconds, it works well to hold components in place until screwed or nailed.

Top: Rotary tools can accept a number of accessories. Here, a planer attachment is used to smooth a door edge.

Bottom: Reciprocating saws come in both corded and cordless versions.

For the same reason, hot-melt glue is usually more than adequate for mounting small moldings and detail appliqués. It should be kept in mind that hot-melt glue isn't as strong as traditional shop glues and should not be used as the sole means of adhering components that will be subjected to usage stress. Likewise, for carcass construction involving dovetails, mortise-and-tenon, rabbets, or other joinery techniques, it's better to stay with traditional glues.

As the name implies, these glue guns must be heated before use, so they are not particularly convenient for a single spot of glue. On the other hand, if a particular project calls for attaching dozens of small moldings or similar parts, they can earn their keep.

One of the shortcomings of hot-melt glue is that it works best only on porous or rough-textured materials. That same shortcoming becomes an asset, however, when there is a need to attach something solidly but temporarily. Jigs and fixtures made for one-time use can be quickly dismantled with little effort, and turners frequently use hot-melt glue to attach bowl blanks to waste blocks for faceplate mountings. Many woodworkers have discovered the quick trick of using hot-melt glue to attach a sample part to the front of plastic drawers used in parts bins. Because you can actually see the part, it works better than a handwritten label; and if you decide to use that drawer for different parts, it's easy to snap the old one off the smooth plastic on the drawer front and replace it with something else.

Machinery

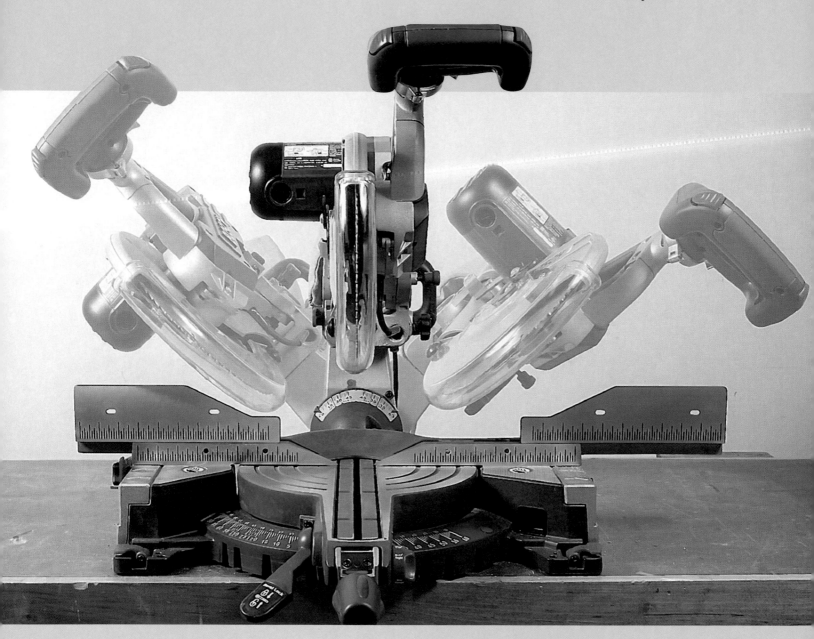

Machinery

Portable power tools handle myriad woodworking tasks, but their power, capacity, and flexibility are limited. The next step in powered woodworking is machinery generally intended to stay in one place as it is used.

On the smaller end of this category are benchtop machines, and although some are quite heavy, they can still be moved from place to place in the shop or taken easily to a job site. Stationary machines, on the other hand, are very large and heavy; once in place they are usually left where they are.

Today's benchtop machines are constructed from lightweight metals and advanced reinforced plastics, featuring sophisticated motor and drive technologies, well-designed ergonomics, and upgraded dust collection. Advanced models often boast features not found on even the most expensive stationary models. These compact machines carry price tags low enough to allow even the most space-challenged, budget-minded woodworker to buy a whole shop's worth of equipment for little more than the price of a single stationary machine.

Benchtop tools aren't for everyone. Many benchtop models employ universal-type motors, the kind used in portable power tools like routers. Universals have impressive performance for their size, but they are noisy and no match for the heavier induction motors found in stationary machines. Benchtop machines don't offer the depth or width of cut and rate of feed stationary models do, but limiting their capacity keeps them compact enough for a single adult to carry to a job site or store under a workbench.

In addition to space and price considerations, careful evaluation of the work you will do is the best guide when choosing machinery. Sometimes, the capacity of the tool is the issue: If you're planning on turning only small bowls, a big, floor-model lathe is clearly overkill. Likewise, if you plan to sell surfaced lumber planed from rough planks, you're better off investing in a durable stationary thickness planer that will handle the load.

TABLE SAWS

In most woodworking shops, a table saw is the central workhorse. That is not surprising when you consider that a table saw can rip wood, crosscut wood, size sheet goods, and shape workpieces.

The table saw is a tool with great potential, for both creativity and accidents. Safety on the table saw is primarily the responsibility of the user; learn how to set up and use it properly. Use guards and splitters when possible and select the right (and sharp) blade and insert plate for the job. Always unplug the saw when making adjustments or changing blades, and, of course, employ proper techniques.

Table saw blades tilt either to the left or the right. Tilt direction is a safety concern when beveling a narrow strip between a right-tilting blade and the fence. With a right-tilt saw, you can sometimes move the fence to the left of the blade, but there may be only 12" to 15" of capacity there. A left-tilt saw does give you more options for ripping bevels.

Saws come in four distinct varieties.

Benchtop saws

Benchtop table saws are lightweight, compact, and easy to transport and store. Most use the same miter slot-guided gauges and accessories other table saws do, and most models have built-in dust ports. However, arbors on most models are too short for a dado blade set; their direct-drive universal motors make for slow going when cutting thick, dense stock; and there's not enough rip capacity for cutting big sheets of plywood.

If you need a table saw for work at a job site, or for occasional craft work, woodwork, and do-it-yourself projects in a garage workshop, a benchtop saw's capacity and ease of transport and storage may be a good fit.

Opposite page: A dual-bevel compound miter saw tilts both left and right.

Contractor's saws

Halfway between benchtop machines and larger cabinet saws, contractor's saws were originally designed to be portable, practical, and sufficiently powerful for use at construction sites.

Most of today's contractor's saws are designed for woodworking, rather than home construction. Their well-engineered fences, polished cast-iron tops—many with significant extension tables—are all features more desired and practical in a wood shop than on a construction site. They are less expensive than a cabinet saw, but less substantial and powerful. A single-belt drive powered by a 110-volt motor can be expected to do only so much, as these motors generally produce less than 2 hp. Contractor's saw trunnions, the structural member inside the saw to which the motor is mounted, are less robust and attach to the underside of the table.

However, you will likely appreciate a contractor's saw's more powerful induction motor and larger table and rip capacity over a benchtop model. For general woodworking, it's a good choice as an all-around

ANATOMY OF A CABINET SAW

A basic cabinet saw is a study in calculated simplicity. Ample power, robust construction, and built-in accuracy are terms that describe the essential cabinet saw. Not every feature of every saw will be identical, especially when it comes to the European imports, but the internal workings of your saw are not as complicated as you might imagine.

power saw for carpentry, home improvement, and cabinet/furniture building.

Cabinet saws

The higher power in cabinet saws means they can cut through hardwoods at full capacity (about 3"), and some accept 12" or 14" blades for even more capacity. To take advantage of this power, you have to provide a 220-volt circuit.

Additionally, cabinet saw motor trunnions are attached to the cabinet and easier to tune, while the motor placement gives them better balance. They are also quieter.

Most cabinet saws have at least 3 hp, with tops about 27" deep and about 40" wide. European models have deeper tops, about 32" to 39" on most models.

Instead of a splitter, European models use a riving knife that comes right up to the back of the blade, matching the blade's contour. As the blade is raised or lowered, the riving knife stays in the same relationship to the blade. Finally, these saws have a completely enclosed base, aiding dust collection through a cabinet-mounted dust port.

Hybrid saws

The newest table saws are called hybrids and combine some of the best features of contractor's and cabinet models. Their power, capacity, size, weight, and cost usually fall about halfway between contractor's and cabinet saws. These models have enclosed bases and dust ports like cabinet saws, aiding dust collection.

EUROPEAN COMBINATION MACHINES

Combo machines merge a sliding table saw, shaper, jointer, planer, and slot mortiser into one unit, yet occupy about the same footprint as a decked-out table saw, about 5' or 6' square. These 220-volt machines hail from Europe, where shop space is in short supply and tool quality and safety standards are second to none.

Sizes vary, based primarily on the sliding table length and the jointer/planer capacity, but a unit with a 12" blade for the saw, a 12" jointer/planer, and a sliding table of about 6' is a good capacity for the average home wood shop. Prices vary from about $5,000 for a basic combo machine to $20,000 and up for an industrial model with frills.

The heart of the saw is the long, narrow aluminum table that slides back and forth next to the blade. Lengths range from 4' to 10'. By attaching a long crosscut fence to the slider, you get effortless and dead-accurate cutting at all miter angles. The sliding table can also be used with the shaper for supporting large work.

Opposite page: The typical contractor's saw has a cast iron top and an open base.

Below left: Dados are cut across the grain, using the miter gauge.

Below right: European combination machines meld several common shop tools into one.

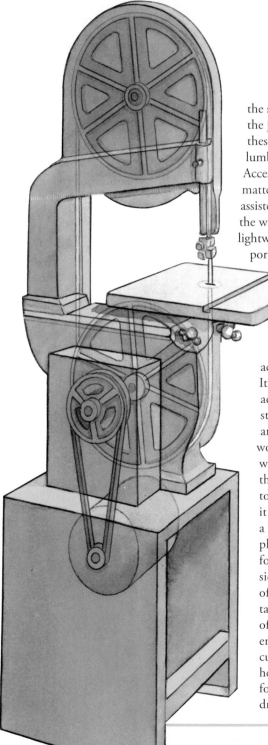

The planer shares the same cutter head as the jointer, and most of these machines will surface lumber up to about 9" thick. Accessing the planer is a matter of lifting the spring-assisted jointer tables out of the way and flipping up a lightweight planer hood/dust-port cover. The changeover takes less than a minute.

Combo machines have a horizontal mortiser that simplifies accurate mortising. It amounts to a fully adjustable table with stops for cutting depth and length, with the workpiece held down with a clamp. Once the table is adjusted to the correct height, it is maneuvered with a handle. The wood is plunged into the cutter for depth and moved sideways for the length of the mortise. The table mounts on the side of the machine at the end of the jointer/planer cutter head. The cutter head accepts a chuck for mortising and drilling bits.

MITER SAWS

Miter saws come in three types. A basic miter saw swings left and right to cut miters but will not tilt to do bevels. The smallest and most uncomplicated, it's arguably the most accurate because it has only two pivot points and only one adjustment that can be made: the miter angle. Most have a 10" blade, so capacity is limited to crosscutting a 2 x 6 or mitering a 2 x 4. Operation is uncomplicated. Lay the workpiece on the saw table, tight against the fence. Grasp the saw's handle, pull the trigger, and rock the saw head down in a chopping motion (hence the common nickname "chop saw").

A compound miter saw cuts miters, but its tilting saw head also cuts bevels. Tilt and swing the saw at the same time for compound miters of the type needed for crown molding. Operation is the same as the basic saw. Models are available with 10" and 12" blades; the larger blade typically crosscuts a 2 x 8 and miters a 2 x 6. Compound miter saws are larger, weigh more, and cost more. A subset of this type is the dual-bevel compound miter saw. It tilts to the right as well as the left.

The sliding compound miter saw—often known simply as a slider—is designed with about 9" of fore-and-aft movement of the blade. The cutting width capacity is increased by roughly 4", though thickness capacity isn't affected. To use the saw, position the work, then grasp the handle and pull the saw head toward you as far as you can. Switch it on, rock the blade down into the stock, and push it away from you, making the cut.

Sliders are made in three blade sizes: 8½", 10", and 12".

Some miter saws are equipped with a laser that shows precisely where the saw teeth will touch the work, so you can accurately align your board for a crosscut, miter, or bevel. Twin lasers, mounted in the blade housing, project beams that show exactly where (and how wide) the kerf will be. You can shift the independently adjustable beams to match whatever blade you use.

RADIAL ARM SAWS

Take the saw head from a miter saw, hang it from an overhead track on a bearing-mounted carriage, and put a table beneath it—in principle you've got a radial arm saw. Radial describes how the saw head can shift from left to right, swivel from side to side, slide front to back, and tilt to one side.

Radial arm saws can make any cut a table saw or miter saw can (including compound angles) and years ago were sometimes the only powered saw in a shop due to that versatility. However, with the advent of miter saws, especially sliders, and the fact that radial arms saws can be difficult to keep in adjustment, these saws have fallen out of popularity.

There is also a perceived safety issue, based on how the operator interacts with the saw. Ripping presents the same kickback dangers as a table saw does, but on a radial arm saw the

entire blade is exposed. In crosscutting operations, the saw is switched on and pulled through the workpiece on the table directly toward the operator. On older machines, the spinning blade could actually power the saw head toward the operator faster than anticipated, much like pulling a car toward you while the wheels are spinning. Further, radial arm saws were difficult to guard. Newer machines have addressed both dangers as a table saw does, but their use is mainly restricted these days to production shops and home centers.

Home shop models generally have a 10" blade, while production models can have blades up to 16".

BAND SAWS

Band saws are quiet to operate and can make both straight and curved cuts.

Take a welded band of metal, cut some teeth along one side, wrap it around two, three, or even four large wheels, and add a motor. Obviously, it's not that simple, but that is a pretty good description of a band saw. As the wheels are driven, the blade is thrust downward through a flat table, eliminating the kickback hazard associated with circular saws. Blade

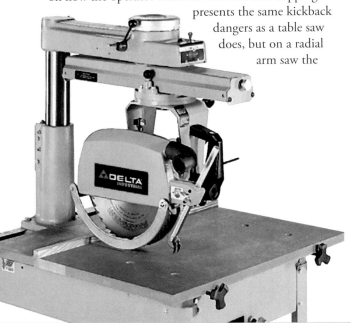

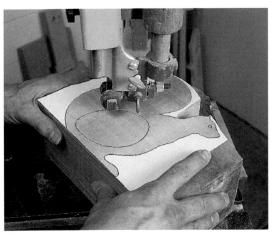

Opposite page: The basic inner workings of a typical band saw

This page left: Radial arm saw

This page right: Band saws excel at cutting intricate shapes.

tension is applied by adjusting the upper wheel on a two-wheel band saw or the rear wheel on a three- or four-wheel unit. Blade guides control the path of the blade to keep it from twisting as work is fed into it.

A band saw can be used for ripping and crosscutting, but it really shines when cutting irregular curves or resawing thick stock. When a band saw is used for intricate work, be sure to match the blade width to the curves you are cutting to reduce strain on the blade and increase accuracy. For cutting irregular curves, always keep the upper blade guide assembly close to the workpiece and never force the work, as this deflects the blade from its intended course.

Band saws excel at resawing, a method of vertical cutting that creates multiple workpieces from thicker stock. Generally, the widest blade available is selected for resawing purposes. Depending on the brand and size of band saw, this will be somewhere between ½" and 3". Wider blades follow a straight line better because they are more rigid and less likely to deflect. Resawing is controlled with either a standard fence or a pivot block jig usually no higher than the stock being cut. The chief difference between a standard fence and pivot block is that the latter allows you to pivot the back end of the work to keep the blade on the desired path, a technique that is not possible with a standard fence.

Band saws range from benchtop models to large stationary models, with capacity determined in two ways. First, the distance from the blade to the support beam is considered; this dimension determines the longest crosscut that may be made on the saw. Next, consider the distance from the table to the upper blade guide assembly at its highest setting. This vertical dimension determines the thickest piece of stock that can be cut.

For general cutting tasks, regular 14" band saws offer respectable capacity and power, but resawing is limited to 6" or 7" of cutting height at best. If your

saw's motor is less than 1 hp, it will also struggle to resaw wider material. A number of larger band saws are built specifically with resawing in mind. Most have high-performance blade guides, heavy-duty blade tensioners, reinforced saw frames, and higher horsepower.

These machines offer crosscut widths of 14" to 37" and cutting heights of about 9" to 24". Horsepower ranges from 1½ to 15, although machines for home use generally top out at 4½ hp.

Good things to look for include a footbrake, motor trip switches on both the upper and lower frame doors, and a kill switch next to the power switch.

JOINTERS

When it comes to flattening the face of a board and squaring an edge, a few minutes at the jointer can accomplish what would take an hour or more with a hand plane.

The core of a jointer is the cutter head, located between two long, parallel tables. The cutter head holds the knives that do the cutting. The outfeed table is set even with the apex of the knives' rotation, while the infeed table is set below the apex; this offset determines the amount of wood the knives will skim off. The length of the knives establishes the maximum width the jointer can surface.

Although 4" cutter-head benchtop models are available, the narrow width and short bed length make them suitable only for the smallest of projects. The typical home shop jointer is a

SNIPE HUNT

Snipe is a slight concave cut on the ends of boards, and it can happen with both planers and jointers.

In a planer, it's caused when just one of the two rollers on either side of the cutter head is pressing the wood against the planer bed. Without even roller pressure on both sides, the cutter head takes a slightly deeper bite when starting and ending a pass. Several manufacturers build anti-snipe locks into their planers to help anchor the cutter head and rollers.

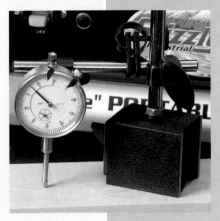

On a jointer, snipe occurs when the outfeed table is set improperly. If snipe appears on the front end of a board, the outfeed table is too high; if it's on the rear end of the board, the outfeed table is too low.

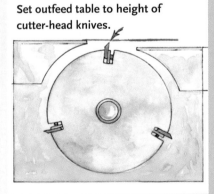

Set outfeed table to height of cutter-head knives.

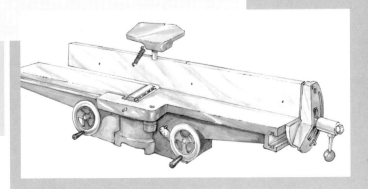

"Man is a tool-making animal."
Benjamin Franklin (1706–90)

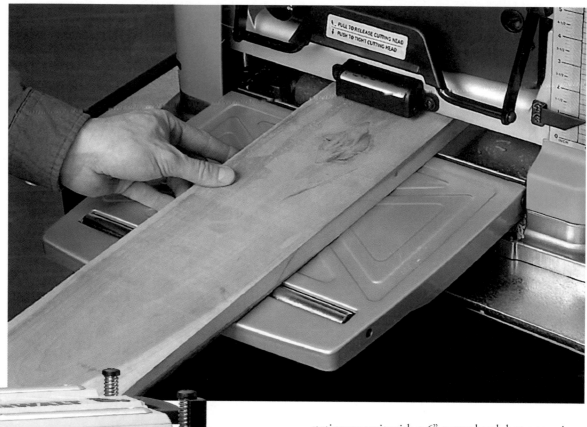

stationary unit with a 6" cutter head, but a growing number of 8" machines are demanding the attention of woodworkers.

Begin flattening a board by choosing the best surface for passing over the jointer and determining the proper feed direction. It's a good practice to joint the more concave side since it sits flat on the table, whereas a convex face will rock. To prevent tear-out, orient the wood so the edge grain runs down and back. Lay the board on the infeed table and push it slowly and steadily over the cutter head, using push sticks whenever possible. As soon as it's feasible, transfer your downward pressure from the infeed

"Man is a tool-using animal."

Thomas Carlyle (1795–1881)

table to the outfeed table. Flattening a board face usually requires several passes, especially since it's not advisable to remove more than ¹⁄₁₆" at a time.

Jointing an edge is basically the same action, but there are two more points to remember. First, make sure the fence is set square to the tables. Second, be sure to hold the jointed face of the work against the fence while keeping the edge firmly against the tables.

PLANERS

Similar to jointers in design and function, planers also employ a spinning cutter head mounted between an infeed and outfeed table. However, where a jointer's main task is to flatten or perform edge and face treatments on relatively narrow boards in preparation for joining, planers focus on surfacing and reducing the thickness of wider stock. A planer can be envisioned as an upside-down jointer, as the cutter head is above the work instead of below. The machine is enclosed and uses a pair of powered feed rollers flanking the cutter head to both hold the workpiece flat to the tables and advance it through the machine.

Planing is probably the only area of woodworking—especially as it applies to the home shop—dominated by smaller machines rather than larger ones. Although a professional cabinet or furniture shop clearly has a need for the higher power and larger capacity of a stationary planer 15" to 20" wide or larger, benchtop machines are usually more than sufficient for the home shop, and even a few professional ones. Their universal motors are considerably louder than their larger induction-motor cousins, but there is no shortage of 12" to 13" capacity benchtop planers loaded with features like dust hoods, sophisticated depth controls, cutter-head locks, and multiple speeds. Knife changing is generally easier with a benchtop machine, and most use double-edged blades that can be reversed once

before replacing. And, in spite of the fact that these are not truly portable machines, with a helping hand they can be moved far more easily than stationary machines for job site work.

Like jointers, planers produce a mountain of wood chips and are a mess to operate without some form of dust collection. Some newer machines have basic dust collection built-in, with internal impellers that help to clear chips from the machine and direct them to a fabric collection bag or trash can.

Before using a planer, it's important that the workpiece is flat on one side, which can be done on a jointer or with a hand plane. The flattening doesn't have to be pretty; it just needs to keep the workpiece from rocking on the planer tables so it moves smoothly through the machine, allowing the cutter head to plane the top face parallel to the bottom face.

To use a planer, first set the cutter head to the thickness of the workpiece at its highest point by slipping the workpiece into the machine and lowering the cutter head until the feed rollers make contact. Remove the board, turn on the machine, then slowly feed the workpiece into the machine. Stop pushing the workpiece when the feed roller takes the work on its own, but continue to support lengthy work. Support it again as it exits the other side. (A helper or a shop-made extension table can also handle this task.) Since only the bottom face is flat at this point, on the first pass or two the cutter head will likely not remove much wood—just the high spots. Once the work has cleared the machine, crank the cutter head lower and pass the board through again. Continue until the board surface is smoothed and the workpiece is at the desired thickness. If your machine has a cutter-head lock, be sure to engage it on the last few passes to minimize snipe.

Just about any planer will do a good job of surfacing and thicknessing, but here are several things to look for:

Top: Feeding stock into a planer

Bottom: Two-speed thickness planer

- **Multiple speeds.** Two-speed planers control the feed rate. At the higher setting, work can be planed faster, but knife marks may be visible on the surface of the work. The lower setting pulls the work into the machine more slowly, effectively increasing the number of cuts per inch, leaving a much cleaner surface requiring little sanding.
- **Internal dust collection.** Built-in fans help remove chips to a collection bag.
- **Cutter-head lock.** Secures cutter head and rollers to minimize snipe. Some machines have automatic locking built-in.
- **Three-knife cutter head.** Leaves a smoother, cleaner surface than a two-knife cutter head.
- **Double-sided blades.** Gives twice the life before knives need to be replaced.
- **Self-indexing knives.** Facilitates blade replacement.
- **Depth stop.** Allows machine to be set quickly to desired thickness.
- **Material removal gauge.** Shows exactly how deeply the machine is cutting on each pass.

Left to right:

A shaper can be used to cut extensive moldings.

Combination disk/belt sander

Edge belt sander

SHAPERS

A shaper is basically a router table on steroids, designed to handle large cutters and heavy stock. Like router bits, shaper cutters come in a wide range of shapes and sizes.

Anything a router table can do, a shaper can do bigger and, often, better. A shaper's beefy induction motor and stout spindle can handle heavy cuts in thick stock that would be difficult or impossible on a router table. A shaper's large-diameter cutters are also less likely than comparable router bits to burn stock or leave chatter marks, and its larger cutting arc makes cutters less apt to tear out woods with figured or interlocking grain. Factor in a shaper's reversible motor

and versatile fence and you have a machine that is worthy of consideration for any size wood shop.

The heart of any shaper is a motor-driven shaft, called a spindle, that protrudes vertically through a flat tabletop. One or more shaper cutters may be mounted on the spindle at one time, held securely with a locknut.

Shaper models are distinguished by the size of their spindles. Common spindle sizes include ½", ¾", and 1¼", while European machines typically have 30 mm spindles. Motor size is proportionate to spindle size—the larger the spindle, the higher the total horsepower.

SANDERS

Although larger benchtop and stationary sanders can do most of the things handheld sanders can, they can also do a few things they can't, including squaring stock and assembled projects like drawers or boxes, thickness-sand panels, and effortlessly smooth tight inside curves and cutouts.

Disk/belt sanders

With disk sizes ranging from 4" to
12", these machines have an attached
worktable that can be set from 45° to 90°
to accurately sand a specific angle. Stand-
alone disk sanders ranging from 12" to 24"
and larger are available, but a disk sander
of 12" or less is most often paired with
a belt sander, with
both sharing the
same motor.

    These belt
sanders do the same
tasks as portable units, but
instead of resting the sander on the
work, the workpiece is held against
the belt platen. Most disk/belt sanders
use a belt measuring either 4" x 36" or
6" x 48". Platens can be used horizontally,
or unlocked and adjusted to a
vertical position.

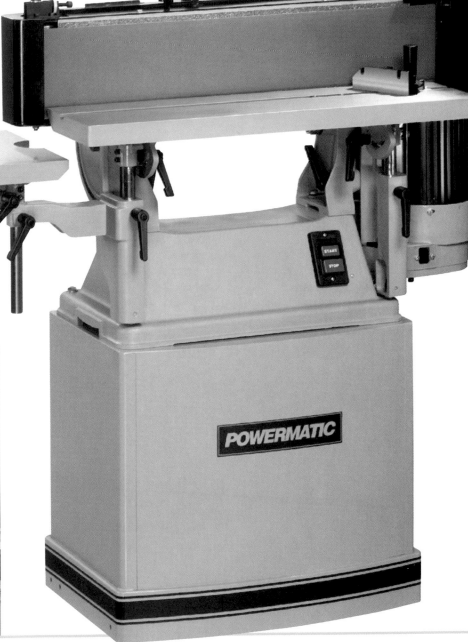

Clockwise from lower left:

Open-ended drum sander

Oscillating drum or spindle sander

Benchtop lathe

Opposite page: A panel saw can make quick work of large sheet goods.

Disk/belt sanders can kick up clouds of dust, but newer models come equipped with dust ports and shrouds that help minimize dust when attached to a vacuum system.

Edge belt sanders

These large machines take the horizontal belt platen and tilt it forward 90° to give a long vertical sanding surface ideal for edge sanding. For the home shop, most models use 6" x 48" to 6" x 108" belts, but larger production models are available. Most of these machines also feature an oscillating movement for the belt that shifts the belt a short distance side to side as it runs over the platen; this oscillating action minimizes sanding lines. Most of these sanders are stationary floor models, although a few smaller benchtop units are available.

Oscillating drum sanders

Used for detail work on inside edges and cutouts, these machines have a vertical sanding drum protruding at a 90° angle through a large cast iron or aluminum table. They come with a series of hard rubber drums in various sizes that can easily be changed to match the curves being sanded. Cylindrical sanding sleeves in a variety of grits slip over the drum. In use, the drum not only spins at high speed but also oscillates up and down to minimize sanding lines on workpiece edges.

Wide sanders

While not found in most home shops, extremely wide sanders designed specifically for panels are available. Using either a horizontal sanding drum or a very wide belt, these machines can handle flat panels from 12" wide up to full-size entry doors and tabletops. They resemble and operate like planers, except that, instead of overhead rollers, a moving platen beneath the workpiece pulls it into the machine. In addition to surface sanding, these machines are also used for thicknessing workpieces.

Home shop versions are generally from 12" to 18" in width and are open-sided. That is, one end is not enclosed, so wider workpieces can be fed through. In that manner a 20" workpiece, for example, can be fed through a 12" machine and sanded on one side, then flipped and fed into the machine again to sand the other side. A few benchtop units are available, but most are stationary machines. Larger models are usually closed on both sides to handle the higher weight of the machine above the sanding platen.

Wide sanders create more dust—especially fine airborne dust—than any other woodworking machine, so an adequate dust collection system is mandatory for their use.

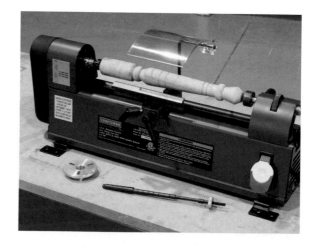

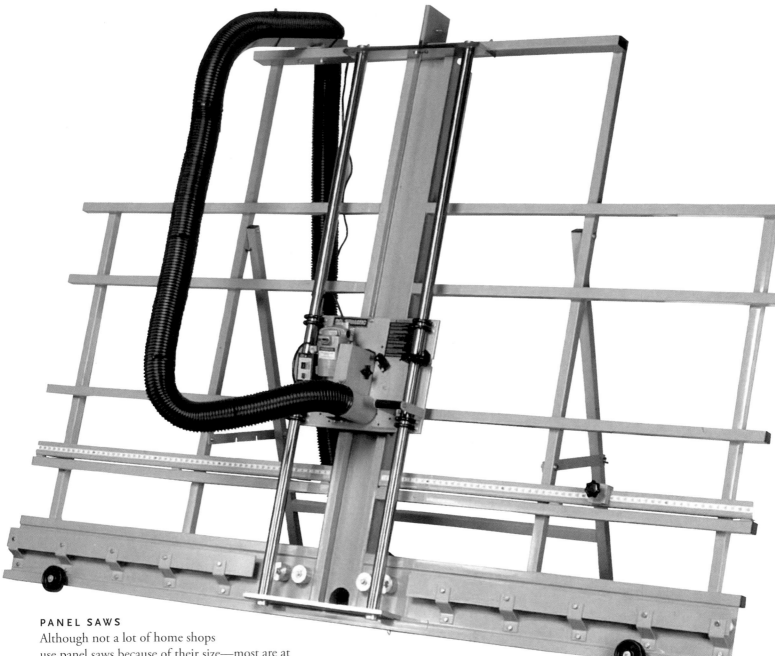

PANEL SAWS

Although not a lot of home shops use panel saws because of their size—most are at least 8' in length—they can be extremely useful in shops using a lot of 4' x 8' sheet goods. Panel saws use a moving carriage with a portable circular saw on a mounting plate that can slide the full length of the panel, as well as the full vertical width, and can reduce large panels to smaller workpieces very quickly and safely. (All home centers have these machines on the floor to reduce large sheets to more easily transportable pieces for customers.) Most panel saws have the ability to replace the circular saw with a router, for cutting full-length grooves, dadoes, and other joints in large panel stock.

LATHES

Few things can match the beauty of lathe-turned objects. Like a potter's wheel, a lathe can shape solid wood as fluidly as soft clay.

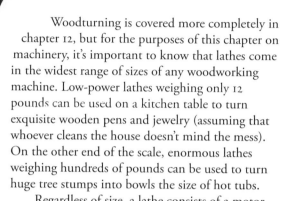

Woodturning is covered more completely in chapter 12, but for the purposes of this chapter on machinery, it's important to know that lathes come in the widest range of sizes of any woodworking machine. Low-power lathes weighing only 12 pounds can be used on a kitchen table to turn exquisite wooden pens and jewelry (assuming that whoever cleans the house doesn't mind the mess). On the other end of the scale, enormous lathes weighing hundreds of pounds can be used to turn huge tree stumps into bowls the size of hot tubs.

Regardless of size, a lathe consists of a motor, called a headstock, mounted to a metal bed. With a faceplate attached to the workpiece, flat or bowl shapes can be turned with chisels supported by a tool rest. Replacing the faceplate with a spur center, lathes can turn any type of spindle, from lampposts to table legs, and are limited only by their capacity. For spindles, workpieces are mounted between the headstock and a corresponding tailstock, allowing cylindrical work to spin freely.

MORTISERS

Mortisers are like drill presses, but they drill square holes. When lined up, a row of square holes creates a slot called a mortise, which will accept a tenon. Mortise-and-tenon joinery is among the strongest used in furniture making (see chapter 9).

Mortisers use an augerlike drill bit housed inside a square hollow chisel. When plunged into a workpiece, the drill bit clears the way while the sharp edges of the hollow chisel clean and square-up the sides of the hole.

The key advantage of a mortising machine over a mortise attachment on a drill press is the longer stroke of the machine, allowing for deeper one-step mortises. Mortisers come in both benchtop and stationary versions.

BENCH GRINDERS

A bench grinder is as suited to other shop tasks as it is to woodworking. The main use in the wood shop is for sharpening chisels, blades, and knives; attempting to tune a hand plane without one is a waste of time. A variety of wheels, or stones, is available in a wide range of grit sizes.

Bench grinders with the correct wheels can also be used to hone household cutlery, as well as lawnmower blades and other yard equipment.

DRILL PRESSES

The stationary version of the handheld drill, a drill press can bore holes at a perfect 90° or other preset angle. Available in both benchtop and floor-standing models, all drill presses have a tilting table that allows drilling any desired angle. Because the table can be set so precisely for angle and depth, a drill press is invaluable for dowel joinery (see chapter 9).

Beyond simply drilling, their chucks can accept almost anything intended to operate in a circular motion. Sanding drums can turn them into effective drum sanders. Hole saws can bore large-diameter holes. Using a mortising attachment, they can be converted to a hollow-chisel mortiser. With the right jig, enterprising woodworkers have even turned them into small vertical lathes.

For most shops, a 10" drill press (measured between the chuck and the support beam at the back of the machine) is sufficient. For regularly drilling wider stock, a larger machine is better.

Opposite page: Benchtop mortiser

Left: Bench grinder outfitted with a specialized chisel-sharpening jig

Bottom: 10" drill press

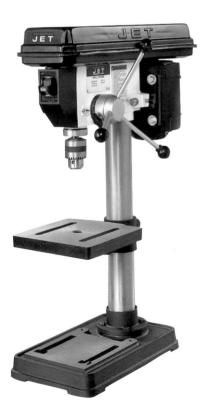

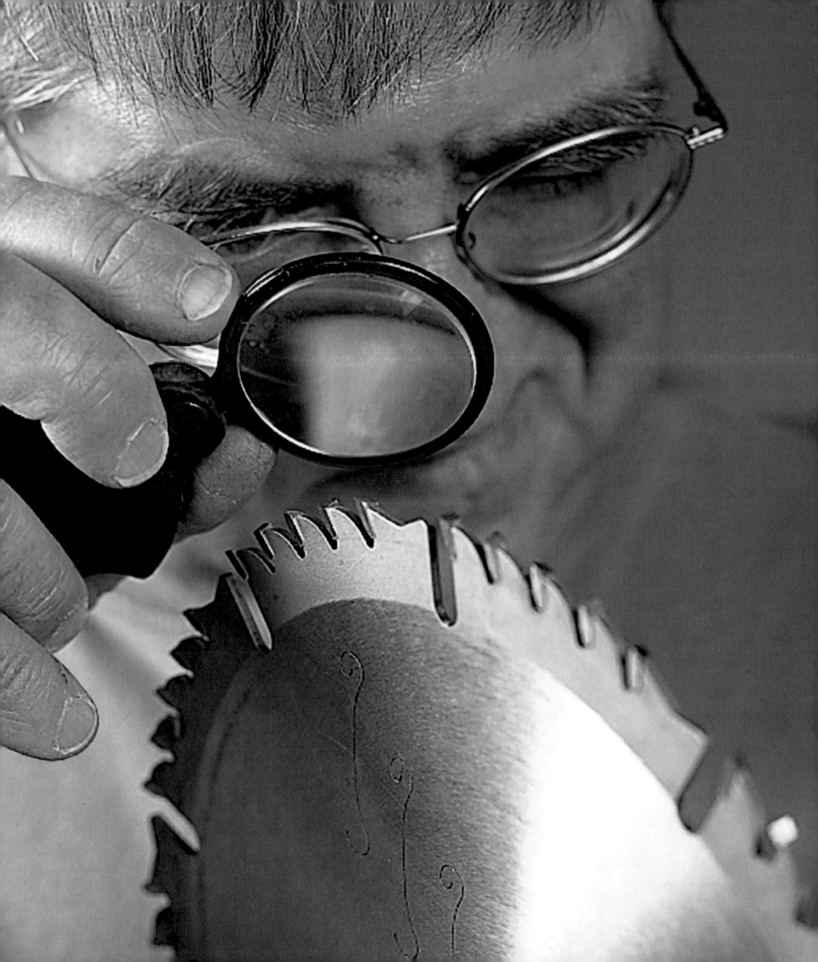

CHAPTER 7

Choosing Blades and Bits

Without sharp, precision-engineered blades and bits, powered woodworking is frustrating at best and impossible at worst. The good news is that the demand for more and better power tools has ushered in a host of improved blades and bits.

What may be challenging, especially if you are relatively new to woodworking, is how to assess your blade and bit needs. If you are limited by budget, is there one truly general-purpose blade for your saw? Should you buy one of each diameter straight bit for your router? Do you routinely need to drill metal as well as wood? If any (or all) of these questions apply, then you'll need to know which blades and bits are better suited than others for multiple material types. Product packaging won't always make a buying decision easier.

CHOOSING SAW BLADES

Saw blades vary considerably in terms of how the blade plates look, but the most important consideration is the composition, shape, and geometry of the teeth. The number and size of the teeth, and the size of the pockets in front of each tooth—called the gullets—all affect how the blade functions. Teeth may be square-edged or pointy, tipped forward or backward, and have the same or different shapes on a single blade. Regardless of appearances, every tooth on every blade is a tiny bit of tungsten-carbide, brazed or silver-soldered to the blade's steel disk. Steel-tooth saw blades are virtually a thing of the past, because carbide is much stronger and retains an edge far longer than steel.

The teeth are distributed evenly around the plate. Behind each tooth is the shoulder, a portion of metal that adds strength and support to the tooth and helps reduce kickback. In general, the more teeth a blade has, the smoother its cuts will be—but there are tradeoffs. When you have lots of teeth, more force is required to feed the workpiece through the cut, and cutting speed slows down. In addition, more teeth are in the kerf (the notch made by the cut) throughout the cut, generating more heat and dulling the blade more quickly.

Reducing the number of teeth on the blade reduces the force required to feed workpieces and increases the cutting speed. It also reduces the number of teeth in the kerf during the cut, thus yielding a cooler cut and extending the life of the blade. The tradeoff is that blades with fewer teeth generally cut less smoothly than blades with high tooth counts.

Tooth grinds

Beyond the numbers of teeth, there are correlations between their shape and orientation and cutting effort, speed, and quality. Three basic tooth shapes, which refer specifically to the cutting edge, are used in the following configurations.

• **Flat-top tooth:** The flat-top tooth (usually abbreviated FT) has a square cutting edge, like a chisel. A flat-top grind blade cuts like a chisel, plowing nicely with the grain, but splintering its way roughly across the grain. By itself, the flat-top tooth grind is used primarily on rip blades. Teamed with other grinds, the flat-top tooth is called a raker.

• **Alternate top bevel:** Teeth with an alternate top bevel grind (ATB) have cutting edges that angle from side to side. From tooth to tooth around the blade, the bevel angle alternates left and right. The bevel angle varies according to design intent, ranging from 5° to as much as 40°.

The pointed corner of the ATB tooth slices through wood fibers like a knife, creating a crisp edge to the kerf, while the beveled portion pares the waste. It seems to cut equally well with the grain and across it, which is why it is the most widely used grind on both general-purpose and cutoff blades. It even cuts chip-prone laminates cleanly. The steeper the bevel angle, the cleaner the cut. On the other hand, the steeper the angle, the less durable the edge will be out to the narrower pointed tip.

• **Triple chip:** The third basic shape is the triple chip. Here the corners of a flat-top tooth are chamfered at 45°. In the triple-chip grind, or TC, the characteristic tooth is alternated with a flat-top tooth (called a raker in this application). The triple-chip tooth cuts a narrow groove that the following raker tooth widens to the blade's final

kerf width. This grind is favored for various sheet goods, including melamine, because the chamfered teeth score the material to help minimize chipping and tear-out.

• **Alternate top bevel plus raker:** The most common example of teaming teeth with different grinds is the combination blade, which has what is called an ATB+R grind. This blade has groupings of five teeth: four ATB teeth and one raker. The ATB teeth score the stock, and the raker, with its extra-deep gullet, clears dust and chips.

The last bit of geometry in a saw tooth is

the hook. This is the angle between the front of the tooth and a line extended from the blade center to the cutting-edge tip. It can range from 20° or slightly more, down to negative numbers. A high hook angle provides an aggressive cut, but one that creates a lot of tear-out on the underside of the work. Low hook translates into a clean but sluggish cut. More feed pressure is required. In practice, rip blades have high hook angles, cutoff blades have low hook angles.

Overview of blade types

There are five common styles of blades you're likely to find when you shop. Each is designed for different cutting tasks or materials. It's important to be able to visually identify the differences between the various blade types so you can choose the correct blade for your saw or operation. Following is a brief description of each type of blade.

• **Rip blade:** Characterized by its big, uniform gullets, the rip blade typically has 24 flat-top teeth and 15° to 18° of hook. Variants include speed rippers with 18 to 20 teeth and 20° or more of hook, and glue-line rippers, with 30 teeth (sometimes with a triple-chip or ATB grind).

• **Cutoff blade:** Lots of teeth characterize the cutoff (or crosscut) blade. The quintessential cutoff blade has 60 to 80 ATB teeth and 10° of hook. The ATB grind slices cleanly across the grain, and high tooth counts ensure a smooth cut. Hook angles will vary from 0° to 5°.

• **Combination blade:** The "traditional" general-purpose blade will usually have 50 ATB+R teeth. For years, this has been the "jack-of-all-cuts" blade, capable of crisp crosscuts and acceptably fast rips. It cuts plywood and other sheet goods with a minimum of splintering. The versatility stems from its mixture of ATB and FT teeth on one body. The teeth are grouped in fives, with four in the ATB grind and one a flat-top raker. The raker is ground slightly lower than the ATB teeth. The ATB teeth are mounted in front of shallow gullets (referred to as the primary gullets), while the raker has a deep gullet in front of

Opposite page, top: Some saw blades are slotted to help reduce heat buildup.

Opposite page, bottom, clockwise from top right:

Cutoff or crosscut blade

All-purpose blade

Combination blade

Rip blade

This page, left to right: The top tooth has a positive hook; the lower one a negative hook.

Inspect blades frequently for missing teeth or other damage.

it. The deep gullets visually separate the groups of teeth. Often, the last shoulder in each group, the one opposite the raker, has an anti-kickback spur.

• **All-purpose blades:** These are the reigning favorite do-all saw blades. The prototype is the 40-tooth ATB blade, but some versions have only 30 teeth. A number of manufacturers offer ATB+R versions.

CARING FOR SAW BLADES

Pitch, gum, and resin buildup will cause a blade's plate to heat up, promoting further buildup and accelerating tooth dulling. Dirty blades with teeth that are fouled with baked-on debris need cleaning. Soak the blade in blade cleaner or ammonia for a few hours, then scrub it clean with a nylon or brass brush. To prevent rust, dry the blade (use a hair dryer) and apply a light coating of WD-40 or other metal protective spray.

Once the blade is clean and dry, look at the cutting tips with a magnifier. If the cutting edges shine in reflected light, they're rounded over and in need of resharpening. Most blades can be resharpened several times. Competent sharpening services can even replace a missing carbide tip. A local metalworking shop might be your best resource for blade sharpening referrals to facilities accustomed to reaching better tolerances and finer edges than many less-well-equipped shops. Another good option is to call the blade manufacturer; many offer factory sharpening services and are usually best equipped to service their own blades.

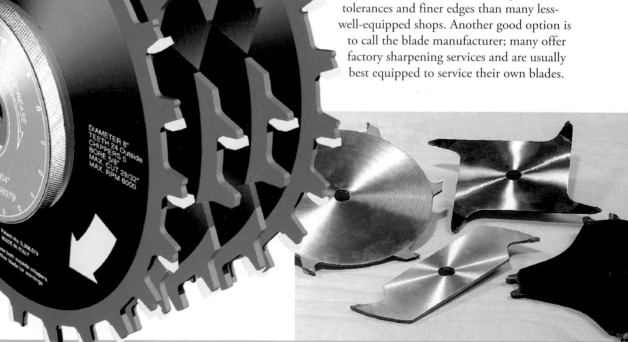

CHOOSING DADO BLADES

A dado blade, used to cut square-channeled grooves, is one of the most common accessories used on a saw. Dado blades can be adjusted infinitely for cuts greater than ¼" and up to ¹³⁄₁₆" wide. This popular accessory is used to make dadoes, rabbets, lap joints, and tongue-and-groove joints. Some woodworkers also use the dado head to cut box joints or finger joints and tenons (see chapter 9).

There are two types of dado blades, each with unique characteristics that make it appropriate for certain operations.

Stacked dado blades

The stacked dado blade is made up of two cutters and up to eight chippers. The cutters look like circular-saw blades and are usually 6" to 8" in diameter. While these cutters look like saw blades, they are intended for cutting dadoes and have a special tooth profile. Usually, all the teeth point in one direction, unlike other blades with teeth that point both right and left.

Chipper blades have from two to eight teeth on them and are designed to be "stacked" between the cutters. The teeth on chipper blades will vary in width from ¹⁄₁₆" to ¼", and you'll get a collection of various widths with the blade. By stacking chipper blades in different combinations, it's easy to create a dado of virtually any width. Thin shims can be placed between the chippers to enlarge the cut by fractions or even thousandths of an inch for cutting odd-width dadoes.

Wobble dadoes

The wobble dado resembles a single 6" to 8" standard saw blade with a fat hub. The hub, which is actually two separate pieces in a triangular shape, can be twisted on itself to tilt the blade so it cuts in a skewed, wobbling fashion. The hub will have increments stamped into it to help set width adjustment. As the blade turns and wobbles, it removes any wood in its path to form a dado. Up to ¹³⁄₁₆" can be cut by adjusting the amount of wobble in the blade.

A variation on the single-blade style is the V-wobble dado, which has two blades mounted on the hub instead of one. The blades open into a "V" shape to establish the cutting width. Wobble dadoes are generally less expensive than stacked dadoes, but the tradeoff is that they tend to cut more roughly and create uneven—rather than flat—bottoms in the cut. However, for quick work where a high degree of quality isn't at issue, a wobble dado may be a good investment.

Dado blade safety features

Dado blades are much heavier than standard saw blades and can remove a substantial amount of material in a single pass, depending on how wide and high you set them. If you use a dado blade on a radial arm saw, there's also a chance that it can climb up and out of the cut and cause the saw's motor carriage to lurch forward and at you. On a table saw, dado heads increase the chances for kickback, since dado and groove cuts can only be made with the splitter (and usually the guard) removed.

Opposite page, left: A stacked dado set with six chipper blades. **Inset:** Chippers can have from two to eight teeth.

This page: Regularly cleaning blades to remove residue helps them run cooler and stay sharp longer.

Set = Total width of the blade with the teeth bent. The more set a blade has, the wider the kerf.

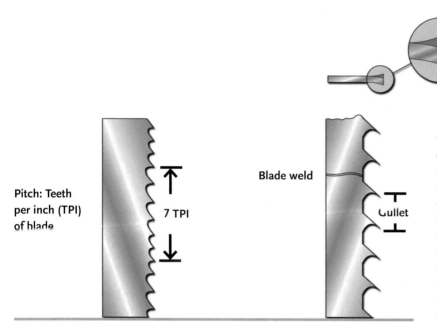

Kerf

Pitch: Teeth per inch (TPI) of blade

7 TPI

Blade weld

Gullet

Aside from adopting safe sawing practices, a way to increase your safety is to use a control-cut or chip-limiting dado blade. A control-cut dado blade is a stacked dado that has shoulders behind each tooth on the two cutters and chip limiters in front of the teeth on the chippers. The shoulders and chip limiters control the amount of wood each tooth can remove. It's also important to use the correct blade diameter for your saw size. Use a dado blade at least 2" smaller than the standard blade size for your saw. For instance, a 6" to 8" dado blade is the correct size for a 10" table saw. If you have a light-duty saw, choose the smaller of the two blade sizes, just to be safe.

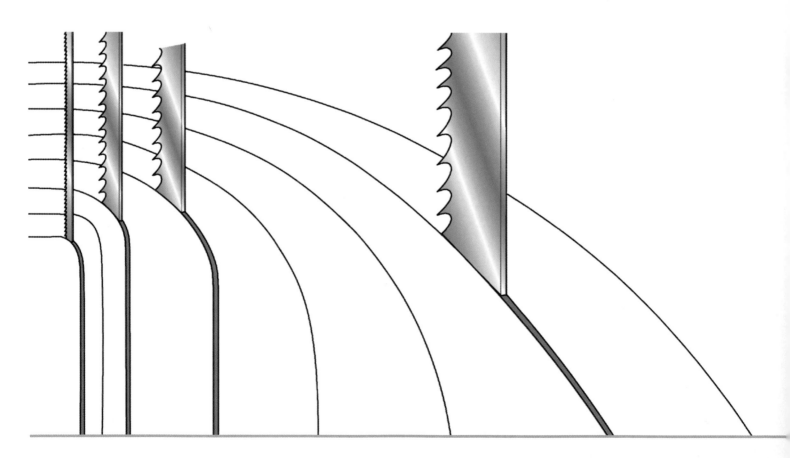

"If I had eight hours to chop down a tree, I'd spend six sharpening my ax."

Abraham Lincoln (1809–65)

CHOOSING BAND SAW BLADES

With the unique ability to make straight or curved cuts in wood of all thicknesses, the band saw offers more creative potential than any other saw, but exploiting its full potential requires picking and adjusting the best blade for a given task. Here are some important blade characteristics to keep in mind when matching the blade to the task.

Selecting the right blade, for the right reasons
Choosing the proper blade for a particular job prolongs blade life and tooth sharpness, while using a blade for the wrong application is the best way to abuse it. A number of key factors including width, pitch, and tooth style all impact performance.

• **Width and thickness:** Band-saw blades are usually classified according to width, which determines how tight a turn the blade can make. Blades vary in width from ⅟₁₆" to ₁", in typical sizes of ⅛", ¼", ⅜", ½", ⅝", and ¾". The narrower the blade, the tighter the turns it can make. The wider the blade, the more likely it is to resist deflection and cut in a straight path. A ¼" blade is the most frequently used blade for general-purpose work. Narrow blades are made from thinner-gauge metal than wide blades, and there are many blade

Opposite page, bottom: The thinner the blade one a band saw, the tighter the turn it can make.

Below, from left: Standard tooth, 0° rake; skip tooth, 0° rake; hook tooth

BLADE TOOTH STYLES

Band-saw blade teeth are ground in two basic shapes. The face of the tooth is either milled at 90° to the body of the blade, which is called a 0° rake, or it has a slight positive angle that makes it hook-shaped. A blade with a 0° rake cuts with a smooth, scraping action, but it produces more heat during cutting than a hook-toothed blade. A blade with hook teeth cuts more roughly and aggressively, but it can be used for a longer period before it develops excessive heat.

Woodworking blades can be broken down into three general groupings according to the configuration of their teeth:

• **Standard tooth:** Teeth are spaced closely together; 0° rake. Offers a smooth cut especially useful for cutting small details and for cutting across the grain of the wood, because it doesn't tear as it cuts. The best blade to use when smoothness is a consideration.

• **Skip tooth:** Teeth have a 0° rake, but every other tooth is removed, leaving large gullets between the teeth. Because a skip tooth blade is coarse, it cuts much faster, especially when the blade is used to cut with the grain. This blade is best suited for cutting long, gentle curves. Although it doesn't cut across the grain as well as a standard-tooth blade or rip as well as the hook-tooth blade, it is often the most widely used blade because it provides the best compromise.

• **Hook tooth:** The most aggressive blade, with a positive rake angle and the fewest number of teeth. It is particularly efficient at cutting thick stock with the grain. This makes it the best choice for ripping and resawing.

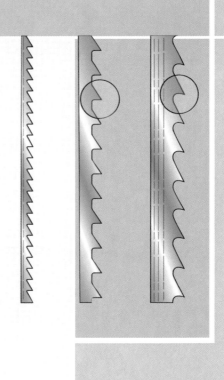

QUICK GUIDE TO BAND SAW BLADES

A collection of three to five different band saw blades should be sufficient to cover most sawing tasks, from fine scrollwork through demanding rip cuts and resawing. Here's a quick guide for what to buy.

• Tight scrollwork and fine cuts in hardwood: Choose a 3/32" blade with 24 teeth per inch (tpi) or a 1/8" blade with 14 tpi.

• General-purpose cutting: Choose a 1/4", 4-tpi skip- or hook-tooth or a 1/4", 6-tpi standard tooth. These two blades provide a wide range of cutting options, and either can be left on the saw as a general-purpose blade. The 6 tpi is better for a finer finish cut in harder woods, while the 4-tpi skip or hook tooth is better in thicker stock for quickly cutting out curved parts. In a pinch the 4 tpi can even be used for resawing.

• Straight cuts and resawing: Choose a 1/2", 3-to-5-tpi hook tooth. For your most demanding resawing jobs, set aside a sharp 1/2" blade just for resawing.

thicknesses. Focus on blade width more than thickness when you're selecting a blade.

One way to help choose the correct blade for your cutting application is to use the size of the details in your intended cut to determine the blade width. Choose as wide a blade as possible, yet one that will make the tightest curves with ease. In practice, you'll develop tricks to decide the best blade for the job. For instance, to test if a 3/16" blade would work for a particular curve, place a dime (roughly 5/8") over the pattern. The 3/16" blade can cut a curve bigger than the dime, but not smaller. A quarter is the size of the tightest cut that can be made with a 1/4" blade, and a pencil eraser is the size of the tightest turn that you can make with a 1/8" blade.

• **Pitch** (tooth size): Pitch is usually given in the number of teeth per inch of blade There's an easy logic to understand the cutting characteristics of blades with different pitch. A "coarse" blade has few teeth. A "fine" blade has many teeth. The coarser the blade, the faster, and rougher, the cut. A blade with more teeth will give a smoother cut, but one with too many teeth will create problems such as excessive heat and slow cutting.

It is important to match the pitch of the blade to the material being cut. At least three teeth should be in the material at any given time during the saw cut. Feedback from the cutting process will tell you if you're using a blade with a suitable pitch: When you've got the pitch right, your blade will cut quickly and smoothly.

SELECTING ROUTER BITS
Routers are arguably the most versatile woodworking tools, and myriad bit styles are part of the reason why. Despite the vast number of bits available, you don't

need one of each type to tackle most woodworking applications. A core group of a dozen or so bits may take care of the majority of your general needs. Here is a survey of essential bits by type.

Cutting joints

Straight bits are the first style to buy, because they are sufficient for making the majority of joinery cuts—dadoes, grooves, mortises, tenons, laps, half-laps, and even rabbets. But even within the category of straight bits, the choices can be confusing. A good way to begin accumulating straight bits is to start with the basics and add special-application bits as your skills and needs grow. Collect a core group of straight bits in ¼", ⅜", ½", and ¾" cutting diameters with cutting edges between ¾" and 1¼" long. They'll handle a wide range of jobs, from ⅛"-deep dadoes to 1"-deep mortises.

Almost every bit set includes a rabbeting bit and some bearings. Change the bearing size, and you change the width of the rabbet it cuts. The bearings enable a single bit to make cuts of perhaps half a dozen different widths. Rabbeting bits with interchangeable bearings are a better value than those with only one bearing.

Most basic sets also include a dovetail bit, which may seem unnecessary unless you have a dovetail jig. However, even without the jig, a dovetail bit allows you to cut numerous joints, including sliding dovetails. Once you buy a dovetail jig, it may come with the appropriate-geometry dovetail bits, or you can add those at that time.

Profiling edges

A decorative profile—basically a contoured relief—lends an air of character and style to a workpiece. The profile can be machined directly on the edge of a tabletop or door, or applied as an attached molding. The range of profiles available is unbelievable, and new options are being developed all the time. Typically, a profile cutter has a pilot bearing on the tip. The bearing rides along the work edge, ensuring that the cut can't veer into the middle of the stock. Some profile bits can also be used in the middle of a board. These groove-forming profile bits don't have a pilot bearing.

With interchangeable pilot bearings, a rabbeting bit can cut rabbets of varying widths, as shown on the wood samples.

Opposite, upper right: Profiling router bits

Begin assembling your collection of profiling bits with cutters that produce simple profiles such as roundovers, coves, and ogees. You'll probably find that you end up using small-radius roundovers (⅛" and ¼") more than larger ones (⅜" and ½"). Smaller bits break an edge without making it look bullnosed. When you want a bullnose look, a roundover bit can produce it in two passes.

Shaping parts

Template work is one of the router's most beneficial applications (see chapter 8). Here, you fix a template

LARGE-DIAMETER ROUTER BITS

If you have a shaper, you already have the perfect tool for milling raised panels, large decorative moldings, and unique profiles like handrails. But if you don't, the infrequent call for such work makes it hard to justify the cost of a new machine, especially one that takes up space in a small workshop.

Those considerations, and the needs of industrial users, have led router bit manufacturers to explore another option: large-diameter router bits that essentially do the same work as a shaper. These bits can be used safely only with 2½-hp or larger, table-mounted routers equipped with 1/2" collets. Here's a brief overview of the large-diameter bit options available to you as well as some important safety considerations for using them.

The most common use for large bits in the home shop is to raise panels. Panel-raising bits come in two styles: Vertical bits enable you to raise a panel on edge or end by feeding it against the fence. The horizontal style requires that the panel lay flat on the router table as it's pushed along the fence. While you can buy individual raised-panel profile cutters, manufacturers also offer door-building sets that include a pair of stile-and-rail cutters.

Also popular are large-profile roundover and bullnose cutters. While they have innumerable applications, these are especially popular among craftsmen who build with children in mind, using them to shape table edges, handrails, and other child-safe features. Other options include lock-miter, multiprofile, and finger-jointing bits.

Large panel-raising or profiling bits are not designed for use in handheld router applications. They must be installed in an adequately powered, table-mounted tool equipped with a fence. Use the fence to guide your work even when the bit is equipped with a bearing. The bits are intended to remove a small amount of waste on each of several passes, so a fence is an integral part of the system.

to a blank, then guide the router around it, cutting the workpiece to a specific shape. You can make countless duplicates of the template. But you need the right bit, either a flush trimmer or a pattern bit.

A flush-trimming bit is basically a straight bit with a pilot bearing on the tip, below the cutter. The bearing's diameter matches the bit's cutting diameter. The bearing rides along the template's edge, and any material projecting beyond the edge is removed. A pattern bit, on the other hand, has a pilot bearing mounted on the shank above the cutter. Each bit style influences where the template is fixed to the workpiece, either above or below but always so it contacts the bit's bearing.

With template routing, it's easy to exceed both your router's capability and your own experience. Start out with a ½"-diameter flush trimmer with 1"-long cutters. Down the road, you can add a larger, longer bit. For a pattern bit, simply get a bearing and stop collar for whatever ¾" straight bit you already own.

Router bit sets

Unless you know exactly what you need, a wise way to start or upgrade your collection of router bits is by investing in a packaged set. Every vendor offers sets, and invariably one is a "starter" set. These multibit assortments include joinery and profiling bits, all in a handy box. The specific selection may vary, but it usually includes three or four straight bits, a rabbeting bit, three or four edge-profile bits, a V-groover, a dovetail bit, and a flush-trimming bit. This provides the means to sample the primary categories of router operations. The economy is that the set's price is lower than the aggregate cost of the individual bits.

Shopping for bits

If you buy bits from the local home center or lumberyard, prepare to find a limited selection. A better avenue is to order through mail-order catalogs or Internet suppliers. While shopping by mail prevents you from examining the bit before you buy it, the fact is that critical characteristics aren't visible to the naked eye anyway. The only way to truly assess bit quality is in actual use.

There are, however, a few visual clues to quality you can look for. Look for bits with thick carbide, smooth and even brazing where the carbide meets the bit body, and the smoothness (and sharpness) of the cutting edge. Also, buy profiling bits engineered with anti-kickback, chip-limiting features whenever possible. This will greatly reduce the chances of overloading the bit and causing it to grab your workpieces unexpectedly. Also, if your router is equipped with both ¼" and ½" collets, buy the larger shank size. Half-inch shank bits don't cost substantially more than ¼" shank bits and offer greater resistance to deflection and vibration.

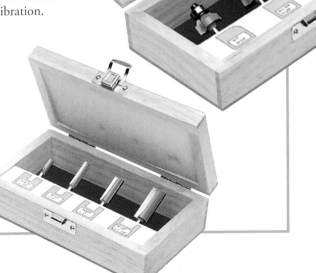

Opposite, top: The pilot bearing on this flush-trimming bit follows a template to create an exact match in the workpiece below.

This page: Router bit sets may include several of the same type bits in various sizes, as shown, or a collection of different bits.

Opposite page: Twist bits come in three point styles (from top)— standard point, stepped point, brad point.

Right: Twist bits are often packaged in large sets.

CHOOSING DRILL BITS

Whether you're using a drill press or handheld drill, there's a good chance it has a twist drill bit in it right now. Twist drill bits are, by far, the most common accessory used by do-it-yourselfers and woodworkers for all manner of drilling tasks—mounting hinges, putting up shelves, hanging light fixtures, assembling cabinets, just to name a few.

Versatile twist bits will quickly bore clean, precise holes in a wide range of materials. Twist bits are also affordable and come in a wide range of diameters, from hair-thick to 1" in diameter and larger.

Hardware stores and woodworking and machinist's supply catalogs now feature so many different kinds of twist drill sets that buying bits can be confusing.

Bit sizes and sets

When it comes to drill bits, one size definitely doesn't fit all. For everyday shop drilling tasks, you'll definitely want to purchase a basic set of fractional-sized twist drills. Sets come in several different size ranges. A big 30-piece set will prepare you for the majority of wood-shop drilling tasks. Fractional-sized twist drills are also available up to 1½" or more in diameter, but these are expensive and primarily designed for metalworking. Better-quality sets come in handy metal index boxes that keep all the bits organized and prevent them from getting lost or knocking about.

Fractional drills may be the most commonly used kinds of bits, but they are far from the only type available. For installing European hardware, or to tap holes in metal or plastic for metric-sized bolts, it's essential to have a set of metric-sized drill bits (1 mm to 10 mm or 13 mm) on hand.

Bit materials and coatings

As with router bits or saw blades, cost is often a good indicator of drill-bit quality. The cheapest bits, made from lower grades of carbon steel, won't stay sharp as long and won't perform as well as bits made of better-quality metals, such as high-speed or cobalt steel. Another way that manufacturers improve the performance of twist drill bits is to treat them with oxides or coat them with ferrous oxide, black oxide, or titanium nitride.

Twist drill bits manufactured from high-speed steel (usually marked "HSS") are a good choice for general shop drilling tasks. High-speed steel bits stay sharp up to 10 times longer than carbon steel bits. Better yet, HSS can withstand the high temperatures created when drilling thick metal. Uncoated HSS bits are a bit more expensive than carbon steel bits, but they are definitely worth the price difference if you use your drills for more than just wood and plastic.

Heat-resistant cobalt steel, a second option for bit composition, can last many times longer than regular high-speed steel bits, especially in demanding applications where heat buildup is a problem. Cobalt bits are a dull gold color because of a special heat-

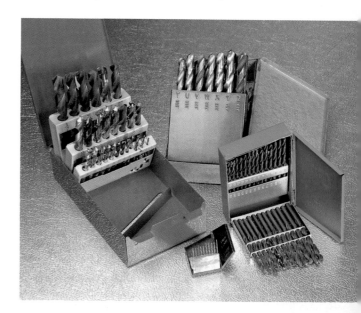

treating process that hardens them. Unlike coated bits, cobalt drill bits can be sharpened without reducing their performance.

Bits coated with titanium nitride ("TiN" for short) have a distinctive rich gold color, which is said to dissipate heat and help bits last up to seven times longer than uncoated HSS bits. The TiN coating increases the hardness of the surface of bits even further and adds self-lubricating properties. This makes TiN bits terrific for drilling both ferrous and nonferrous metals, as well as nonmetallic abrasive materials like concrete-based sheet goods.

Point styles

A basic twist drill works by using a pair of cutting edges (called lips) to shave a thin layer of material off the bottom of the hole as the bit spins. The design of these lips, as well as the shape of the entire point, significantly affects the way a twist drill performs. Commonly available twist bits feature several different point styles, some made for general use, others for handling a limited range of materials and applications.

• **Standard and split-point:** The degree of a drill point's angularity determines how easy or difficult the bit is to start, as well as how aggressively the bit bites into the material being drilled. Standard bits with a 118° point (sometimes called "mechanic's bits") or steeper 135° points are good for general-purpose drilling jobs and offer satisfactory results in a wide variety of materials. These bits also center very well in existing holes, allowing you to enlarge them easily.

• **Stepped-point:** Stepped-point bits have a tip that looks like a short twist drill that is about half the diameter of the bit's shank. This point not only prevents the bit from skating around when starting a hole but also makes it easier to center the bit on a pencil mark or center-punched dimple. A stepped point also helps keep the bit from veering off-center when drilling thick materials and causes less tear-out on the underside of the stock when drilling completely through the material. The complex tip geometry of stepped-point bits means that sharpening isn't an option; once the point is damaged or dull, the bit must be replaced. They are not suited for enlarging existing holes.

• **Brad-point:** If quickly drilling perfect holes in wood, without tear-out, is your goal, it's hard to beat the clean drilling performance of brad-point bits. A brad point's sharp middle tip allows the bit to be positioned with great accuracy and eliminates skating as the hole is started. The bit's raised side spurs score the wood around the circumference of the hole, providing a very smooth cut and reducing chipping on the top surface of the work, as well as reducing splintering where the bit exits the underside.

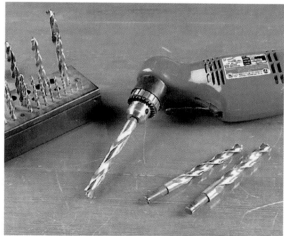

On the downside, these bits are strictly for drilling wood, soft plastics, and solid-surface materials. Like stepped-point bits, brad points aren't a good choice for enlarging existing holes, as they won't center properly. Brad point bits can be resharpened only with a needle file or fine stone, a difficult procedure to execute properly.

Special twist drills

General-purpose twist drills come in a variety of sets, but there are occasions when these bits won't do the trick and it's time to reach for a specialized type of twist bit.

• **Self-centering bits:** For perfectly aligned hinges, latches, and other hardware, nothing beats drilling screw holes with a self-centering bit. Also known by the brand name "Vix bits," self-centering drill bits surround a standard twist drill bit with a retracting, spring-loaded sleeve. The sleeve's tapered end fits snugly into the chamfered mounting screw holes found on most hardware, to guide the bit as the hole is drilled. The bits come in several sizes, each made to work with one or two standard or metric screw sizes.

• **Tapered drills:** Made primarily for drilling pilot holes for traditional tapered cabinet woodscrews, tapered drills have shanks that go from thick to slender and come to a fairly sharp point. The holes these bits create give the threads of tapered wood screws good "bite" along their entire length. This not only produces strong connections, but also decreases the chances of screws stripping out or snapping.

Tapered drills are sized to match different-size screws. A typical set for all the typical cabinet screws you are apt to use in a small shop would include #6, #8, #10, and #12 tapered bits. Most sets include removable countersinks that slide onto the shank of each tapered bit, as well as stop collars that allow you to set the exact depth of the countersunk hole.

• **Stepped bits:** A stepped drill bit is like two bits in one, with a smaller-diameter drill at the tip attached to a larger-diameter shank. With a stepped bit, you can drill two holes at once: a smaller pilot hole for a screw, and a larger hole for recessing the screw's head below the surface of the work. Stepped drills are also perfect bits for drilling pocket-holes for joining face frames with screws using a special jig (see chapter 9).

Opposite page, left: Self-centering bits are ideal for drilling pilot holes for hinges and other hardware.

Right: Regardless of actual bit size, shanks are always sized to fit drill chucks, as shown.

This page, left: Stepped bits drill a hole that is narrow at the bottom and wide at the top to allow screw heads to be countersunk slightly below the surface.

Right: Tapered bits match the profile of screws commonly used in cabinetry.

CHAPTER 8

Techniques for Making Project Parts

Techniques for Making Project Parts

There are many steps to transforming an unsurfaced board into a precisely made project part. The first stage involves flattening, squaring, and reducing your stock to correct thickness, followed by gluing boards together to make larger panels. From this point, a variety of machining steps like sawing, routing, and shaping brings components to their final proportions. This chapter will teach you how to use a jointer, planer, table saw, band saw, and router safely and effectively, how to make a core group of basic cuts, and how to turn your router into an effective part-duplicating machine. Once the workpieces are milled to shape and size, you will be ready to proceed to joinery (chapter 9) to bring everything together for final assembly.

SQUARING-UP STOCK

Cupped, bowed, or twisted stock can wreak havoc on the best-laid plans and make assembling a project difficult. Trouble is, lumber has a natural propensity to warp due to internal stresses that are often present and its ability to absorb and release moisture unevenly. That's why a careful job of preliminary jointing and planing can true up lumber so that it's flat and square, which lays a solid foundation for the rest of your project construction. Here is what you need to know to prepare your lumber properly.

Select and acclimate lumber

It's important to select and buy good-quality lumber, and you're off to a great start when you choose a reputable supplier. Select straight boards, pleasing in color, grain pattern, and condition. After you bring the lumber home, let it adjust to your shop for at least one to two weeks so it can stabilize in its new environment. This may result in a bit more warping, but that's what you can remove in the next steps if you purchase lumber thicker than what you finally need.

Cut to rough size

The first step is to cut boards about 1" longer and ½" wider than their final measurements. Be sure to allow for tenons, if necessary, in the final board length. Use a circular or miter saw to crosscut to rough length. The ideal tool for rip-cutting rough lumber to initial width is a band saw, but a table saw will also work, as long as one edge of the board is flat. For more on rip-cutting with a table saw, see page 146.

Joint one face flat

A jointer is the tool most woodworkers use for flattening cupped or bowed lumber, but you can also use a long-soled handplane for this task. Your jointer must be in tune to deliver good results, with the fence set at 90° to the table and both tables properly aligned.

To joint a board face, place one edge against the jointer fence. Take thin passes and cut with the grain to reduce tear-out. Use push pads or push sticks to feed narrow boards over the cutters in order to keep your hands out of harm's way. Never take off more than ¹⁄₁₆" per pass. Use a push block, and keep all guards in place. If the board is bowed, orient the concave face down. Don't push down too hard or the entire board will be cut instead of just the high spots.

Plane the other face flat

After flattening one face, plane the opposite face by running it through a thickness planer. Plane with the grain as much as possible to avoid tear-out, and take thin passes—again, no more than ¹⁄₁₆" at a time. Feed boards with irregular grain as slowly as possible and using even lighter passes. Don't bring your stock to finished thickness in one day; leave the boards about ⅛" too thick, then let the wood adjust to the change overnight. Instead, proceed to straighten one edge.

Above: Three common board defects (from top to bottom): nonparallel faces, cupped, and end checks.

Opposite: Gail O'Rourke of Hometown Woodworking in Plymouth, Massachusetts, uses a router to make a component for a workbench.

FOUR STEPS TO SQUARE STOCK

1. On a radial arm or miter saw, rough cut your stock 1" longer than its final measurement. Then turn to a band saw to get the width within 1/2" of its final size.

2. Use a jointer to remove cups or twists, flattening one face of the board. Joint the concave face but don't push down too hard or you'll shave the middle instead of just the edges.

3. With the flat (jointed) face down, run the board through a planer to create a parallel surface on the opposite (top) face.

4. Use a jointer or a straightline jig on the tablesaw to clean up one band-sawn edge of your stock. Then rip the second edge parallel to the first on the table saw.

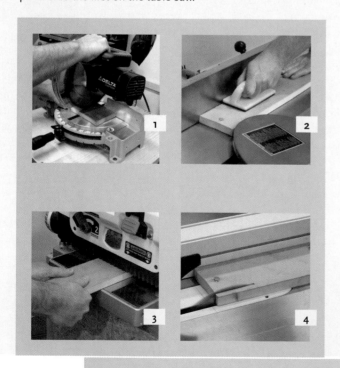

Joint a reference edge

Joint the first edge flat, this time with one board face against the jointer fence. Since you have already flattened both faces, either one can be run against the fence. Be sure to joint with the grain to avoid chipping; if the jointer tears out the wood, flip it so the other face is against the jointer fence and try again. That will usually remedy a tear-out problem.

Cut to final dimensions

The last two steps that complete the squaring process are to rip your board to final width on a table saw, with the reference edge against the rip fence, then crosscut it to final length. Congratulations! You have now completed the first and perhaps most important step in woodworking: creating flat, smooth, and square reference surfaces on your wood.

EDGE-GLUING AND MAKING PANELS

Gluing the edges of narrower boards together to create larger panels is a necessity for many projects. Simply gluing the pieces together is only part of the technique of making attractive panels that will stand the test of time. How you arrange the boards, flatten and clamp the edges, and even how you apply the glue all contribute to your success.

Planning a panel is the first step of the process, before you even reach for the glue bottle. Look over your wood and decide how many boards to use in the panel and which ones are the best matched. Try to choose an odd number of identically dimensioned boards. This creates a uniform appearance and avoids a center glue line (defeating the eye's propensity to divide objects in half). Arrange interesting areas of the boards in a balanced, random pattern. Don't cluster knots or swirly grain at one end or in the middle where they will be distracting. Try to disguise transitions from board to board by placing similar grain patterns together.

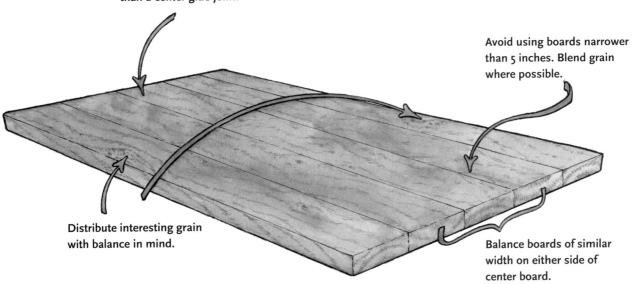

A center board looks better than a center glue joint.

Avoid using boards narrower than 5 inches. Blend grain where possible.

Distribute interesting grain with balance in mind.

Balance boards of similar width on either side of center board.

Next, orient the boards for stability. Some woodworkers flip the boards so the end-grain arcs alternate from "smile" to "frown" on the theory that the minor cupping of each board will go in opposite directions, preserving the general flatness of the panel. Other woodworkers assemble all the boards with their end grain the same, resulting in a panel that cups uniformly in one direction. They counter this cup by fastening a batten to the center of the panel. Let appearance and the project's structural design guide you here.

For a long-lasting glue bond, board edges should meet square and true even before clamping pressure is applied. If your jointed edges are slightly out of square, alternate which face bears against the fence when edge-jointing each board. This method produces complementary surfaces that meet in a good joint, even if the edges aren't perfect. Boards that touch along their entire length or touch at their ends with a slight concavity at the center are best. Remember, you only increase the stress on a glue joint if you have to force the boards together with clamps.

Aliphatic resin glue—usually called "yellow" or "shop glue"—plastic resin, or white glue are all good choices for edge gluing. Gluing a panel together requires preparation and a certain degree of

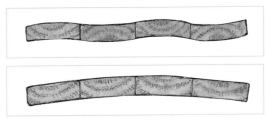

speed, so first clamp the parts without glue to make sure you have the clamps set to the right lengths and that the boards pull together as they ought to. Sometimes, clamping a wide surface encourages it to bow, which in turn opens the joints on one face. To avoid this situation, place adjacent clamps on alternate sides of the panel. Support the boards on a few straight sticks to hold them above the clamp bars.

Don't rush the process by trying to glue too much at once. Too many "wet" glue joints will result in the parts sliding out of place when you tighten the clamps—a frustrating problem. When you're making a wide panel from many narrow boards, glue it up in subgroups. Wait for these to dry and then glue them together to form the final panel.

Spread glue thinly and evenly on both edges of every joint. Too much glue just makes things messier and more slippery. Tighten the clamps a little at a

Left: Alternating the "smiles" and "frowns" of growth rings in edge-joined boards evens out panel cupping; edge joining boards with the growth rings in the same direction can result in a cupped board (cupping exaggerated for clarity).

can get a clear view of the cut, but avoid standing directly in line with the blade. Have both the splitter and guard installed for this operation.

Start by sawing a test piece and checking it with a try square. Adjust the miter gauge as necessary. It's possible to hand-hold the workpiece against the miter gauge fence, but the cut will be more accurate if the piece is clamped in place. Begin the cut slowly so the saw eases into the wood, then speed up to a constant rate. Whether the workpiece is clamped or not, hold it against the fence with both hands. Stand to one side so your wrist and elbow are not in line with the saw cut.

As soon as the workpiece clears the front of the blade, it will be cut into two pieces. If you are holding the workpiece, slide it away from the blade along the miter gauge fence and then return the miter gauge and workpiece to the start position. If you clamped the workpiece to the fence, simply pull the gauge back.

Shaping cuts

Making shaping cuts on a table saw involves any operation that does not separate the wood into two pieces. Common shaping operations include making grooves, rabbets, dadoes, and moldings, raising panels, and cutting joints. Shaping is done using a regular saw blade, a dado blade, or a molding head.

Most shaping operations can be done in several ways. For example, you can make a rabbet with two passes over the saw blade or with one pass over a dado blade. Deciding which way to proceed involves the blades available, the amount of wood to be removed, the number of passes required to remove the wood, and the number of pieces you intend to machine.

The saw blade, dado blade, or molding head should be guarded for all shaping operations, but if the splitter interferes with the cut it must be removed. Combination guard-and-splitter units standard on many benchtop and contractor's saws cannot be used for shaping cuts.

For most shaping cuts, you'll need to set the blade low so the teeth are fully buried in the wood. Because the cutting resistance is low, you may be tempted to feed the work too fast at the expense of accuracy, but feed at the same rate as for regular sawing. Since tight contact between workpiece and fence is critical, you're liable to put considerable pressure against the fence. If your fence deflects under side pressure, clamp the free end to the saw table. Stand on the left side of the saw table. This gives you a good view of the line of contact between the workpiece and fence and allows you to press the workpiece tight as you advance it.

Sawing grooves

The simplest groove is one pass over the saw blade, making a groove the same width as the blade (3/32" or 1/8"). To make wider grooves using a standard blade, make the two outer cuts first, then make multiple cuts to remove the waste from the middle. Wider grooves are quicker to cut with a dado blade.

Sawing rabbets

A rabbet is a rectangular cutout along an outside edge made for decoration, to make a joint, hold glass, or retain a panel. Using a standard blade, square rabbets can be sawn with two passes on a single setup. With a dado blade, rabbets can often be cut in a single pass.

Left to right: Cutting a groove in the edge of a workpiece

Cutting a rabbet on the table saw

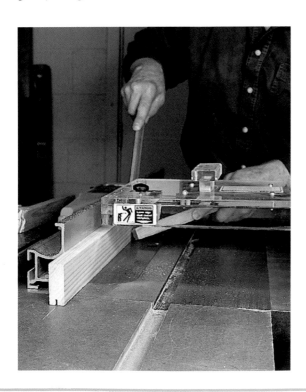

**Above:
A tapering jig**

Right: To cut raised panels on the table saw, first score the front face on all four sides.

Complete the raised panel by cutting a bevel on all four sides that just meets the scored lines on the face.

Opposite page, left: Using a tapering jig to cut furniture legs on the table saw

Right: Resawing on a band saw

Sawing dadoes

A dado is a groove made across the grain in the interior of the workpiece. Dadoes are often made to partially enclose another piece of wood, such as the end of a shelf. In wide workpieces you can saw dadoes by guiding the end of the workpiece against the fence. For narrow pieces, feed the workpiece with a miter gauge as for crosscutting.

RAISING PANELS ON A TABLE SAW

Creating the broad bevels on a raised panel involves two cutting operations. First you make four shallow cuts to form the shoulder lines that surround the panel's rectilinear center area, then you cut the panel on-edge with the blade raised high and at an angle to meet these shoulder cuts.

Begin by raising your blade just less than ⅛" above the table, and use this setup to score the front face of each door four times to create the panel's shoulders. Set the rip fence appropriately to make each of these cuts, according to your panel's dimensions. For a typical ¾"-thick panel, the fence would be at 1⅝".

Place the panel on edge, then set the blade at about 12° and raise it until the teeth meet the shoulder kerfs. Set the fence ¼" from the inside edge of the blade and cut across the grain first, then with it. The first round of cuts will likely produce some burning and blade swirls. Now nudge the fence ⅟₃₂" closer to the blade and repeat these four bevel cuts to clean them up.

MAKING TAPER CUTS

A taper cut is essentially a rip cut made at an angle to the edge of a workpiece. Tapering is a common practice for cutting table legs. It's an easy technique, especially with a tapering jig on a table saw or band saw. With the shop-made jig shown at top left, two straight pieces of wood are hinged together at one end, and a lid support near the other end lets you change and lock the angle. A small block of wood screwed to the side of one arm acts as a stop. If you don't want to build a tapering jig from scratch, you can buy aluminum versions that work essentially the same way.

To use the jig, make the gap between the arms at the stop block equal the amount you want removed from the bottom of the legs. Align the saw blade

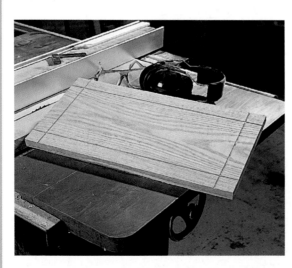

with the top of the taper layout line, slide the rip fence against the tapering jig, and lock it down. When cutting tapers, the cut always starts near the top of the leg and works down. Use a push stick to keep the workpiece pressed tightly against the tapering jig. Slide the jig past the blade to complete the cut.

RESAWING

Slicing a board in two through its thickness is one of those nifty ways to create a pleasing, symmetrical match, get more mileage out of your thick lumber, or create perfectly color-matched workpieces. It also allows you to match wood grain and color perfectly on parts that should match. Resawing isn't complicated; it's similar to ripping, but the board is cut to thickness instead of to width.

   Grain matching adds a lot to the appearance of your finished projects. By splitting the thickness of a board and then flipping the pieces open like a book, you will get a grain match called a book

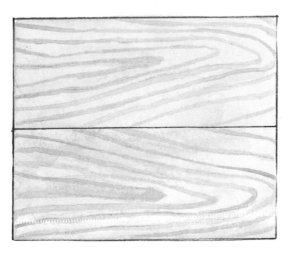

Resawn workpieces can be joined three ways to create panels.

From top: Book-matched panel

Slip-matched panel

Swing-matched panel

match. It's a sure sign of intentional, good design if used prudently. If you slide the pieces apart instead of flipping them open, and then set them next to each other, you'll get a slip match. And if you flip one piece end to end and set it next to the other piece, you'll get a swing match. Each type of grain match pattern can be useful, depending on the look you want.

Resawing is a good way to get a color match for things like face frames and tabletop edging. It's hard to color-match wood that comes from different boards, even though they are the same species. But if you resaw thicker boards, you will at least double the amount of color match you can get from a single board.

As with most shop techniques, the pros have developed several different approaches to resawing. Most use a band saw, while some prefer their table saw; both methods have their limitations. Resawing on a band saw is confined to boards that will fit under the blade guide, and proper blade tension is critical to maintain a flat cut. Resawing on a table saw is limited to boards twice as wide as the cutting height of the blade. You have to make two cuts instead of one band saw cut, and settle for a wider kerf. Or, if you have both a table saw and band saw, you can make the first pair of cuts on the table saw to create most of the kerf, then finish up on the band saw to slice the board in two.

If you use your band saw for resawing, you'll find it easier to resaw when you use a ½" wide, 3 tooth per inch (tpi) hook-tooth blade. This type of blade makes a rough but straight cut quickly. Fewer teeth per inch allows the blade to remove sawdust more effectively. Wider blades track better and cut straighter—exactly what you want when resawing. If your machine will accept a ¾" or 1" blade, you will have the ideal width for resawing. Start with the presumption that you will have to thickness-plane—

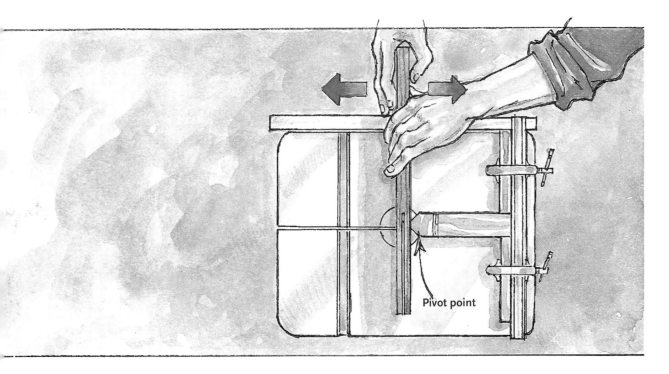

Pivot point

When resawing, keep the stock vertical and held firmly against the pivot point of the fence. As you feed the workpiece, adjust it left or right at the back end to keep the blade tracking in a straight line.

or at the very least sand—any wood you resaw. Plan on losing about ¼" of thickness for each resaw cut and the necessary cleanup planing involved.

Making a resaw cut

Wide boards that are thinner than ¾" are hard to keep upright when you resaw. To combat this, start with flat, square-edged stock and use a pivot fence clamped to the band saw table as shown here. By having a single point to register the cut (placed adjacent to the cutting edge of the saw blade), you will be able to swing your stock left or right to correct for blade drift. You might be able to get away with using a standard fence once in a while, but if you are trying to slice off a ¼" piece of expensive hardwood and your blade drifts toward the fence, you are powerless to correct it.

Feed the wood through the blade slowly and evenly, keeping a close watch on how the blade progresses through the cut. Make left and right adjustments as soon as the blade wanders off course. Keep the wood pressed against the edge of the pivot fence at all times.

Another thing to be aware of is that band saw blades tend to wear unevenly on the sides of the teeth. Using an unevenly worn blade will cause the saw cut to wander off center. You know this is happening if you find yourself feeding the board across the saw at an angle in order to follow your cut line. If the wandering is excessive, it's time for a new blade.

Don't be surprised if you resaw a straight board and the resulting pieces are warped. Resawing can release internal stresses in the wood. Most of the time warping will be minimal, and generally it can be remedied when you plane to remove the saw marks. Plan for a bit of warping and you won't be disappointed.

CUTTING CURVES

A band saw is ideally suited for cutting curves. Its blades are thin and generally narrow, which helps minimize friction during tight curve cuts. The wheels provide tension on the blade both from above and below the saw table, so the blade will cut uniformly if it's tensioned correctly. There aren't many guidelines you will need to follow for cutting curves successfully, but a few helpful pointers should be kept in mind.

First, choose the correct blade for the curve you need to cut. As a rule of thumb, the tighter the curve cut, the narrower the blade you'll need to use. For more on choosing a blade, see chapter 7.

Wider blades only increase the friction during cutting and bind the saw kerf. It should go without saying, but make sure your blade is clean and sharp for best results.

Second, try to make the full curve cut in one smooth pass rather than cutting partway and backing the blade out of the cut. Withdrawing the blade,

especially when the saw is running, can pull it out of the blade guides and even off the flywheels if you aren't careful. If a cut is particularly complex and will require several passes to execute, cut the shortest portions first to minimize the amount of backing out you need to do. Then make the longest portion of the cut last to complete the curve.

Finally, use a series of short relief cuts when necessary to help the blade navigate particularly tight areas of a curve. Create the relief cuts by making several short cuts in from the closest waste edge of the board to divide the tight area of the curve into segments. As you make the actual curve cut, the relief sections will cut free and provide the blade a less restrictive turning radius.

ROUTER BASICS

As one of the most versatile machines in the shop, a router can do a lot. With only a few important techniques, it can do it better.

For most cutting operations, feed against the bit's rotation. One of the most confusing aspects of using routers is figuring out the correct feed direction. The answer lies in an old shop rule that says you should always cut against the direction of the bit's rotation. If you think about that for a minute, you'll realize that a portable router—with its bit facing down—should always be moved counterclockwise around the outside of a workpiece and clockwise on an inside cut. You'll know you've got the feed direction correct if you feel the bit pushing back at you as you feed the tool along. If it pulls rather than pushes, you're going the wrong way.

Avoid tear-out. As a bit travels around the corner of a board, how do you stop the wood from chipping out? The best way to avoid this is to rout across the end grain first, then finish up with the grain. The long-grain passes will remove any tear-out that occurs at the corners of the end-grain cuts.

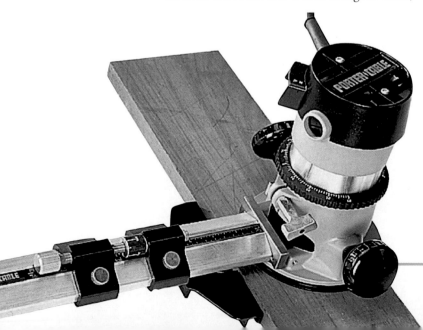

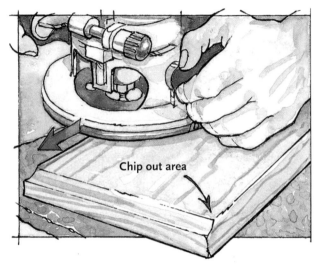

Chip out area

Rout narrow parts on wide stock. Machining narrow stock with a router can be both difficult and dangerous. The pros figured out a long time ago that it's safer and easier to rout small or narrow parts while they're still part of a wider board, then trim off the routed piece on another machine. If you have no option but to rout a small or narrow workpiece, use push sticks or push pads to keep your fingers as far away from the bit as possible.

Don't bottom-out the bit. When installing router bits, push the shank fully into the collet,

then pull it back out about ⅛". Many bits have a funnel-shaped flange below the cutter; if this gets caught in the collet, the bit won't tighten down securely and could work loose during cutting. Also, any shock the bit experiences, such as hitting an extra-hard knot or being dropped on the bench, is not transferred directly to the router's shaft and bearings.

Make every cut a controlled cut. If you are hand-holding the router, keep both hands on the handles at all times and use a piloted bit to guide the cut. In situations where the bit has no pilot bearing, use an edge guide, a clamped straightedge, or another reference surface to guide the edge of the router base along the cut. It's difficult to make an accurate cut, especially if the bit is set for a deep pass, by guiding the router freehand.

Finally, when changing bits, always unplug the router. Make sure the switch is turned off before plugging the tool back in. Routers don't have magnetic switches like many larger stationary machines do, so "On" is always on. Hold the tool with two hands so you're prepared for that quick jerk as the motor powers up. Above all, when you switch the router off, hold on to it until the bit stops spinning to keep the cutter out of harm's way.

Opposite page: An edge guide helps control a router to make perfectly straight cuts.

Left: To remove tear-out on corners, rout across the grain first and with the grain second.

Below: Always rout in the opposite direction of the bit's rotation—counterclockwise on the outside edges, clockwise on interior edges.

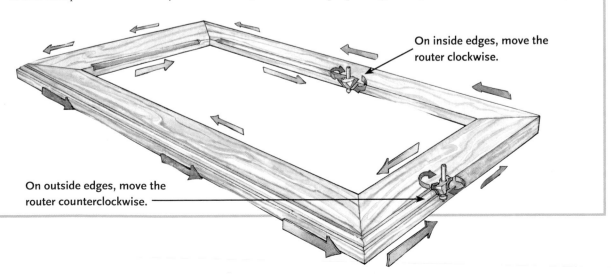

On inside edges, move the router clockwise.

On outside edges, move the router counterclockwise.

Template routing
A router's versatility extends far beyond simply softening and shaping the edges of parts. You'll learn in the next chapter that it's an excellent joint-cutting tool, but it's also adept at duplicating parts and forming flat, smooth edges. By using a flush-trim or pattern bit (see page 135) guided against a shop-made template, you can trim an oversize workpiece so it matches the shape of the template perfectly.

Template routing is particularly useful if you have several identical parts to make or when the shape of the workpiece is curved and intricate. If you guide a piloted straight bit along a straightedge, your router transforms into a makeshift jointer. You can also use a modified template-routing technique for creating inlays.

The secret to successful template routing is to do a careful job of making the initial template. The router bit's pilot bearing will follow the edges of the template exactly, so any discrepancies in the template will transfer to the workpiece. Make your templates from any stiff, void-free material: MDF, Baltic Birch plywood, plastic, or scrap wood will all work. Templates should be at least ¼" thick, so there is plenty of material for the pilot bearing to ride against. Sand the edges of the template thoroughly.

You'll want to mount the template on your workpiece so it stays in place securely during routing but is easy to remove later. Double-sided carpet tape is an ideal choice for mounting templates, but a few beads of hot-melt glue or several short brads will also do the trick if you don't mind nail holes in your workpiece.

Template routing is easiest and safest to do on a router table. You can mount the template above the workpiece, in which case you will need a piloted flush-trim bit with a bearing mounted on the tip. Set the bit height so the bearing touches the template only, and feed the workpiece counterclockwise against the bit. Another option is to arrange the template below the workpiece. Use a pattern bit with a shank-mounted bearing instead for this setup.

If your template involves shaping the interior of a workpiece, the feed direction reverses from shaping the outside edge. Feed the workpiece clockwise so the bit's rotation is always opposite the direction you are feeding the workpiece.

Regardless of how you set up the cut, don't overload the router by cutting more material than necessary. Before attaching the template, cut the workpiece about 1/16" larger than the template using a band saw. The less material the router bit has to remove, the better. You'll get smoother, cleaner cuts and prolong your bit sharpness.

Inlay routing

A variation on template routing, inlay routing allows you to excavate an area with your router, then fill it with a piece that matches the excavation. To do this, you will need an inlay kit, which consists of a guide collar that mounts to the router base, a removable bushing that fits over the guide collar sleeve, and a 1/8" diameter straight bit. To rout the female

workpiece that will accept the inlay, stick your template with a cutout shape of the inlay to the workpiece with double-sided tape. Install the guide bushing in the router and slip the collar over the guide bushing. The collar essentially creates an oversize guide bushing and follows the template to create a slightly undersize recess for the inlay. You can use the inlay bit to remove all the waste in the recessed area or, if there is a lot of material to remove, substitute a larger-diameter straight bit.

To cut a matching inlay piece, use the same template but now remove the collar from the bushing. By removing it you effectively move the router bit 1/8" closer to the template, which compensates for the thickness of the router bit. Attach the template to your inlay workpiece, which should have a thickness that matches or is slightly thicker than the depth of the recess you have routed. Make one or more passes carefully around the template cutout area to create an inlay the exact size of your recess. If you have done a careful job of routing both the recess and the inlay piece, the parts should fit together like a hand in a glove.

Opposite page, top: Routing an inlay on a paneled door with the template fixed in place

Opposite page, bottom: A complete setup for routing inlays

Below: Creating inlays is a two-step process. Using a template, rout the female workpiece with a bushing covering the collar (top). To create the matching inlay piece, use the same template guide, but remove the bushing from the collar.

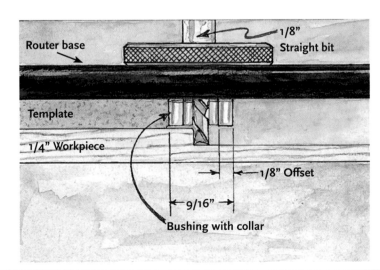

Router base

1/8" Straight bit

Template

1/4" Workpiece

1/8" Offset

9/16"

Bushing with collar

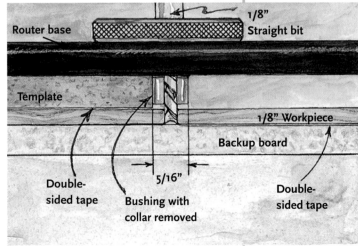

Router base

1/8" Straight bit

Template

1/8" Workpiece

Backup board

Double-sided tape

5/16"

Bushing with collar removed

Double-sided tape

CHAPTER 9

Joining Wood

**Top: A classic
dovetail joint**

**Bottom: To close
a dovetail joint,
tap gently with a
hammer or mallet.**

HAND-CUT
DOVETAILS

Hand-cut dovetail joints are a fine
woodworking signature and can be used
to form boxes, drawers, or cases that hold drawers or
doors. There are a number of variations on dovetail
joints, but learning to make the through dovetail lays
the base for making others.

    While exact shapes and angles can vary, a through
dovetail consists of two matching parts, each made on
the ends of mating workpieces. The tails, as the name
implies, are triangular cutouts shaped like a bird's tail.
The mating workpiece has pins, which slip into the tails.

    With dovetail joints, strength and durability are
built in. Appearance thus becomes the major concern
of dovetail joinery.

    Joint appearance comes from the slope or
angle of the tails and pins, and the layout or size
relationship between tails and pins. The best angle for
dovetails is 83° (1:8) in hardwood; in softwood
it's 80.5° (1:6).

Hand-cut dovetails are
straightforward but take practice to master.
The best practice wood is mahogany, which
saws cleanly down the grain and chisels cleanly
across the grain. Poplar is an acceptable second
choice, but it doesn't always chisel crisply across
the grain.

The cutting process
Start by cutting the tail and pin pieces and complete
the joint by removing waste, flattening the tail and
pin sockets, and dry assembly.

    Because the tails will guide later cuts, make them
first. Square the end of the wood. Set the marking
gauge to 1/32" less than the thickness of the wood.
Knife a line around the end of the piece and set it
upright in a vise. Square a series of sharp lines across
the end grain about 3/8" apart, then mark tail slope
lines from the end grain lines with the sliding bevel,
extending the lines well below the gauge line. With
the saw at an angle to saw the tail, these longer lines

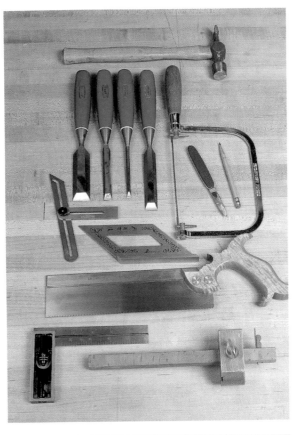

Clockwise, from top left:
A complete tool kit for making hand-cut dovetails

To start a dovetail, follow the squared line and angle the saw by sighting down the elongated guide line. Use light pressure and keep the saw teeth horizontal.

With the saw still horizontal, cut the slopes of the tails to the shoulder line on both sides.

Remove the waste with a coping saw.

A mitered corner sets off an elegant through joint layout.

Left: This table apron is typical of frame-and-panel construction.

Right: Cope-and-stick joinery is commonly used for doors and windows. Note how the intricate shapes match each other perfectly.

Mortises can be made in a number of ways. Waste can first be removed with a drill, followed by squaring the sides with a chisel and mallet. Mortises can also be made with a dedicated mortiser using a square, hollow chisel (see chapter 6). Finally, they can be cut with a dedicated slot mortiser—a machine that bores elongated holes in a workpiece held flat on the work surface—or with a router using a straight bit. These last methods produce mortises with rounded corners. These can be squared with a chisel, or the edges of the corresponding tenon be can rounded to match.

Tenons can be cut with a handsaw, but most often they are made on a table saw with either a regular blade (requiring a combination of cuts), or with a dado blade. They can also be made with a straight bit in a router table.

Sizing issues
The configuration of mortises and tenons can vary depending on how and where the joint is made.

Generally, stopped mortises are cut about halfway into the stile. In narrow stock, it is best to go a bit more than halfway for greater strength.

If a mortise is placed too near to the end of a workpiece in a corner joint, the piece may split if stressed. Therefore, make the tenon shoulder nearest the end of the workpiece one-quarter the total width of the tenon.

When joining two pieces of wood of the same thickness, divide the thickness roughly in half to create a balanced joint. For example, if the wood is ¾" thick, make the tenon ⅜" thick and each mortise cheek (the sides that meet the tenon faces) ³⁄₁₆" thick. Since each piece has an equal amount of tissue, each is equally able to resist stress and the joint is balanced.

FRAME-AND-PANEL CONSTRUCTION
A variation on mortise-and-tenon joinery, frame-and-panel construction also features a slot into which a tenon fits. Tongue-and-groove joints are another such variation.

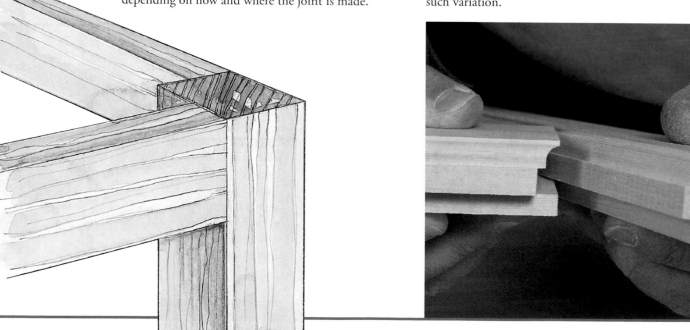

The classic frame-and-panel is a two-dimensional frame with a solid panel trapped in a groove. This construction remains the only method for making a stable frame from unstable solid wood, as in a paneled door.

Three-dimensional frames are a bit different, and are used to make table bases, chairs, and the skeletons of large cases. Three members connect, for example, a table leg and two rails or aprons. In most uses the vertical leg is more or less square in section, while the incoming rails are flat.

COPE-AND-STICK JOINERY

Commonly found on panel doors and windows, cope-and-stick joinery is among the most popular way to join stiles and rails. The router table or shaper is the tool of choice for this method and normally uses a matched set of profile bits or cutters.

One bit forms the "stick"—a decorative profile edge—on door and window stiles. Most of these bits also produce a groove for a panel or a rabbet for glass at the same time. The second bit then creates

a complementary image of the profile to "cope" the ends of the rails. The cope itself fits against the contours of the profile perfectly, to form yet another variation on mortise-and-tenon joinery.

Setting the router bits to the correct height is critical. Just a bit too high or low and the joint will not go together correctly. Use scrap material and trial and error to get the settings correct. Once the setting is perfect, it's a good idea to create a setup block for future use. After making all your stick cuts, before moving on to the coping bit, cut one more sticking cut along the edge of a short piece of scrap hardwood that matches the stock used for your workpiece. After making your coping cuts, make a coping cut on the end of your piece of scrap. You now have a guide block that can be used to accurately set your router bits the next time.

To make a simple frame with such a set, cut two stiles and two rails to size. Cope the rail ends first so that any tear-out created on the end grain will be corrected by the sticking cut. Back up the cut with a scrap block to minimize tear-out. Rout the sticking cuts after all the copes have been cut.

If accurately made, the cope nests neatly against the sticked edge. Be sure to do a test fit of all parts and check for square before gluing. When you are satisfied that everything is ready, disassemble and apply glue to the rail ends. Assemble the parts, then clamp them.

DOWEL JOINERY

Doweling has been a standard technique in the furniture trades since accurate boring tools became available. Dowels offer speed, ease of installation, and versatility in some projects. Doweling jigs and dowel centers have made dowel joints easier for all woodworkers.

Dowels can align edge-to-edge joints in wide panels. Here, dowels cross the grain of the lumber

Setting up the router for cope-and-stick joinery can be tedious. Once your setup is perfect, making a setup block out of an extra piece of material the same size as your workpieces will allow you to reset the router the next time you make these joints. Using the setup block as a guide, the correct router height and fence distance can be set quickly and accurately.

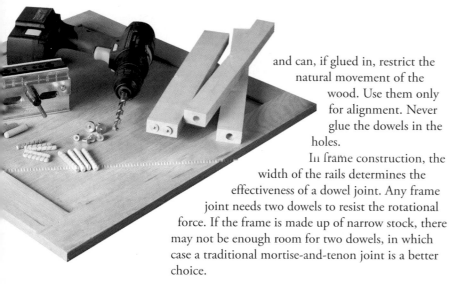

and can, if glued in, restrict the natural movement of the wood. Use them only for alignment. Never glue the dowels in the holes.

In frame construction, the width of the rails determines the effectiveness of a dowel joint. Any frame joint needs two dowels to resist the rotational force. If the frame is made up of narrow stock, there may not be enough room for two dowels, in which case a traditional mortise-and-tenon joint is a better choice.

Dowel joinery, a tried and true method with many applications, requires only a few tools.

Dowel joint mechanics

The spacing, size, and number of dowels in a joint are critical to its final strength. Dowels set too close to an edge or to each other can split the wood. Allow a minimum space of one dowel diameter between the edge or end of a board and the first dowel hole. This rule of thumb also applies to spacing between dowels. Fit as many dowels as you can within these guidelines for greatest strength. The size of the dowels used in a joint determines how much stress the joint can take in two ways: Larger-diameter dowels have both more gluing area and greater strength. In edge-to-edge joints, ¼"-diameter dowels are fine because they don't bear the load. In frame and miter joints made of ¾"-thick stock, ⅜" dowels provide the most strength and gluing area.

The fit of a dowel in a hole is critical. Glue needs a lot of wood-to-wood contact, so a loose-fitting dowel risks failure. Holes that are too small increase pressure on the wood as the dowel is driven in, making a split more likely.

The best joinery dowels are ready-made pins that are cut to length and feature spiral or straight flutes along their sides. Flutes allow air and glue trapped in the hole to escape as a dowel is driven in. This relieves the pressure that builds up in the holes. Fluting also helps keep glue on the hole walls and dowel pins for better adhesion—unfluted dowels scrape the glue off the walls and force it to the bottom of the hole.

To make sure joint members make full contact, countersink the dowel holes slightly. This provides a reservoir for excess glue that might otherwise interfere with the fit. As with mortises, drill all your dowel holes about ¹⁄₁₆" deeper than needed to leave room for excess glue (and to avoid problems with overlength dowels).

Apply glue to both the dowels and the holes. Use a smaller dowel or toothpick to spread glue on the walls of the holes; use a small brush to coat the dowels.

BISCUIT JOINERY

Although dowel joinery has much stronger shear strength, biscuits are faster and easier to use and have the ability to join very narrow workpieces.

Biscuit joiners (see chapter 5), also known as plate joiners, create joints similar to those with floating tenons. The biscuits or plates are flat, football-shaped, and 0.148" thick, regardless of width. The joiner's cutter cuts a slot 0.156" thick, to provide a loose fit. The plates absorb water from the glue and rapidly swell to a snug fit.

Accuracy is easier with biscuits than with dowels, as the slot cut to accept the biscuit allows adjustment along the length of the biscuit, while a dowel pegs you to a point and keeps you there. If you have drilled your dowel holes a fraction of an inch off, your project is a fraction of an inch off. With biscuits you can move things around until the mate is perfect.

To use a biscuit joiner, align the cutter opening at the front of the machine to cut in the center of the workpiece, then mark the wood where you want the slots. Place the fence on that mark, then start the joiner and push it forward to slot the wood. It is quick, easy, accurate.

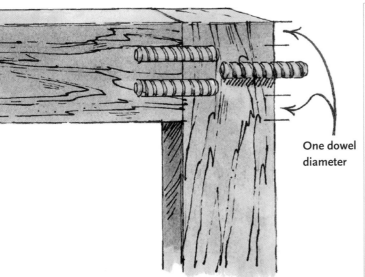

One dowel
diameter

Slight
countersinks

Top left: Allow a minimum space of one dowel diameter between the edge or end of a workpiece and the first dowel hole. This rule of thumb also applies to spacing between dowels.

Top right: To guarantee that the joint members make full contact along the seam, countersink the dowel holes slightly. This prevents wood raised during the drilling process from jamming between the boards, and also provides a reservoir for excess glue that might otherwise interfere with the fit of the joint.

Bottom: Biscuit joints, a variation on floating tenons, can strengthen traditionally weak joints like the miters in a picture frame.

A basic setup for pocket screw joinery. The toggle clamp holds a vertical workpiece steady, while the holes on top guide the drill bit at an angle into the wood. The stepped bits drill a pilot hole and recess hole for the screw head in a single step.

POCKET SCREW JOINERY

Pocket screw joinery—sometimes called pocket hole joinery—will not often be the first choice for fine furniture joints, but it has a place in any shop that produces cabinets, bookcases, tables, and similar projects.

Pocket screws are made specifically to secure butt joints so the screws are invisible (specialized plugs are available to close the visible holes). Self-tapping pocket screws don't split the wood, as drilling makes both a pilot hole and a counterbore. Both holes are made in a single step with a specially manufactured drill bit that combines a pilot bit and a ⅜" counterbore.

Several manufacturers have developed jigs to speed up the pocket hole process, locking the workpiece in place and setting the holes at the correct angle.

Top-notch pocket hole jigs use an industrial quality cast aluminum block set into a lightweight but very strong base that clamps the workpiece in place while you drill one to three holes. The aluminum block is replaceable and interchangeable and may be

used alone, there is a dust collection port, and the tool is quick to set up and very easy to use. Smaller and lighter-duty jigs offer nonproduction pocket hole drilling at low cost that is plenty fast enough for small-shop production.

These jigs are not just for face frames. They have many uses, from edge-banding shelves, to making convex and concave curves, to securing and bracing legs, and making picture frames.

WOODWORKING GLUE

No matter what type of joinery you might use, the one constant will be glue.

Most glues may be applied with a brush, stick, or roller. Check joint surfaces before application and clean off all dust, oil, old glue, loosened and torn grain, and chips. Do any machining that has to be done as close as possible to the time of gluing and assembly. For best results, always do a test assembly before gluing to check that all parts fit correctly.

For general uses, aliphatic resin (yellow glue) and polyvinyl acetate (white glue) are best. Commonly referred to simply as "shop glue," these adhesives allow some measure of reversibility and have worked for many decades in situations where moisture is not an ever-present problem. Cleanup can be handled with a damp cloth.

One step up in usability in wood glue is a heat- and water-resistant polyaliphatic resin glue that is sufficiently water-resistant to be used anywhere but below waterlines. It is similar in joint appearance to other yellow glues but sets more rapidly.

Polyurethane glue

Polyurethane glues are slightly more difficult to use than yellow or white glues, because they have a tendency to foam up, and because water cleanup doesn't work. Gluing surfaces also need to be moistened when wood is dry.

Polyurethanes are nearly totally waterproof, very strong, and become easier to use with practice, but they can be hard to store because any air entry hardens the glue.

Epoxy adhesives

Epoxies are outstanding in areas where the glue itself must be used as a support for a project part, such as gap filling. They readily attach metal parts to wood, and for oily woods such as teak, epoxies work better than anything else.

Most epoxies are two-part adhesives, in that a liquid hardener must be mixed with a liquid resin to create the glue. Cure is by chemical reaction. Heat is produced during the reaction.

Epoxies are toxic, limiting their uses in some shops, and can be extremely messy to use, so thin plastic gloves are recommended. Clean up quickly with acetone. Make sure all mixing containers and sticks are disposable.

Hide glue

The test of time proves the value of hide glue. Archaeologists have found 8,000-year-old artifacts held together with animal protein glue, and the earliest how-to record on hide glue appeared 4,000 years ago. It has been favored by furniture and violin makers throughout history. Hide glue is strong, versatile, reversible, convenient, and has many qualities that make it ideal for woodworking.

Hide glue is made from the hides, or skins, of animals, along with other connective tissue, like tendons (not hooves). It is a renewable resource that is nonhazardous, nontoxic, and biodegradable.

Hide glue makes an incredibly strong, rigid, shear-resistant bond that doesn't creep or move over time. It bonds wood, fabric, paper, leather, pearl, tortoiseshell, and even metal. Dried glue can be colored with dye stain. It is gap-filling, making strong bonds on joints, and works under all finishes. You can scrape, chisel, or sand off dried squeeze-out or scrub it off with a toothbrush and warm water.

Hide glue is indefinitely reversible with heat, hot water, or steam. Hide glue is not water-resistant, so don't use it for exterior projects or kitchen cutting boards.

Hot hide glue is typically sold in dry, granular form. Add water, let it sit until it turns into a gel, then heat it to create a syrupy liquid. It must be kept at 140°F during use, creating the need for some sort of glue pot. Liquid hide glue is the same material with urea added so that it remains liquid at room temperature and does not need to be heated.

Cure time depends on temperature and humidity.

Mix hot hide glue by adding a cup of glue granules to a cup of water. Let it sit for 30 minutes or longer. It swells and gels. Heat to 140° and it is a syrupy liquid. Add more water if it is too thick or more glue granules if it is too thin. At the end of the day, refrigerate leftover glue to prevent mold growth. It can be reheated and reused for about a week.

An electric glue pot for mixing hide glue

Veneering Basics

It may seem odd at first that carving, a woodworking discipline that involves heavy use of hand chisels as the primary tool, would be paired in the same chapter with scrolling, an area of woodworking that almost exclusively uses a power saw.

Yet while the methods and tools differ, carving and scrolling share many traits. Both generally require less shop space to enjoy, and only a limited number of tools are needed. They can produce projects that are complete in their own right, or can be used to adorn other types of woodworking such as furniture, clocks, and mantelpieces. And while the finished projects may be quite large, whether the wood is being carved or sawn, only a small portion of it is being worked at any given time. For that reason, carving and scrolling proceed at a slower pace than other forms of woodworking, and each can be a very intimate experience for the woodworker.

There is a further connection between the two, called intarsia. Like carving, intarsia generally requires that wood be carefully shaped and combined to form a sculpted image. That image can be a portrait, a landscape, or even an abstract design. However, most practitioners of intarsia rely on power tools—scroll saws, band saws, spindle and disk sanders.

CARVING

Carving is one of the oldest forms of artistic expression, with countless surviving examples in materials like bone and antler that predate historical records. Every culture on earth seems to have engaged in the practice at one point in its history.

An argument could be made that any type of woodworking could be accomplished today without power tools, as it was before the 19th century. And although carving—especially large sculptures—can indeed be done with powered equipment, it is the one area of woodworking today that remains mostly unpowered by choice of its practitioners. Power tools simply are not required, nor is a sprawling shop. Whether you live on an Iowa farm or in a New York City apartment, you can become a woodcarver with a few simple tools, the right wood, and a bit of practice.

All forms of carving involve using a chisel or knife to shape wood by removing waste, but there are distinct types of carving.

Relief carving transforms a flat piece of wood into a recognizable image or scene by removing waste to create a raised image. "Low relief" carvings generally stand no more than ½" over the background, and although features are distinct, the overall carving is quite flat. The image on a coin is a good example. "High relief" carvings can extend any distance above the background and can even have portions of the work that seem to hover outside the rest of the image. The work of Grinling Gibbons, a 17th- and early 18th-century master carver, often featured whole flowers, birds, and other objects carved in their entirety above the background.

A subset of relief carving is the woodcut, where the surface is left flat and the image is created by removing waste below the surface. In woodblock printing, ink was spread onto the flat surface of a woodcut, creating a printed image when the block was pressed onto paper. A variation on this theme is sign carving, where letters and words are carved, with or without an image. Today, woodcuts are sometimes done with a highly automated process using a laser.

Chip carving, as its name implies, is done by removing wood in very small pieces. As with relief carving, the design or image is created by cutting away waste below the surface. Chip carving is usually done as a continuous series of identical cuts, often triangular in shape, and arranged to form a larger

Page 188:
This carousel horse carved by John Garton of Petersburg, W.Va., is a beautiful example of carving in the round.

Opposite:
Sign carver and woodworking writer Simon Watts at work

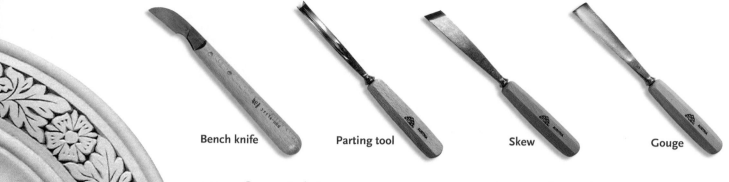

Bench knife   **Parting tool**   **Skew**   **Gouge**

pattern. Geometric designs are common in this type of carving, and it is frequently used to adorn furniture and other woodworking endeavors.

Carving in the round, or sculpting, is the method used to create fully three-dimensional works. Most large carvings are of this type. Wood sculptures can be abstract designs or true-to-life carvings. A growing subset of carving in the round is wildlife carving, with fish and birds among the most popular projects. Some can be incredibly lifelike.

Caricature carving is a whimsical offshoot of both relief and sculptural carving and usually depicts humorous characters or situations. Caricatures can be any size, but small hold-in-one-hand projects are among the most popular. Because caricatures are usually made from a single block of wood using only a knife, many caricaturists consider themselves whittlers.

CARVING TOOLS
A complete set of carving tools could easily include many score of individual chisels and knives, but there are really only four fundamental tool types; all others are variations on these four.

The most basic carving tool isn't a chisel, but a knife. Usually called a bench knife, it generally has a blade of 3" or less and is sharpened on only one edge. The tip commonly curves down to a point at the sharp side of the blade. Knives are very good at cutting fine details and are often the only tool used for chip carving and caricatures.

A straight chisel is just that—a chisel with a flat, straight edge that excels at flattening large areas and rounding off outside corners. A straight chisel with a cutting edge set at an angle is called a skew.

Gouges are the workhorses of carving. The curved cutting edge can hog out a lot of material quickly, so it is no surprise that gouges are often the initial tool used for rough work in carving (and in woodturning, as you will learn in the next chapter). Gouges come in a huge variety of curves, from broad, almost flat profiles, to very deep, tight curves sometimes called veiners for the type of cuts they make. Gouges probably have the largest number of variations of carving tools. They come in numerous sizes, and many—with names like spoon gouges and fishtails—are bent or oddly shaped for specialty cuts and accessing hard-to-reach areas of carvings.

Parting tools, sometimes called V-tools or V-gouges, have a sharp point at the bottom of the V shape that can be used for very fine detail cuts. They come with V's in several angles, but 45°, 60°, and 90° are the most common.

Straight-chisel sizes are expressed as simply the width of the cutting edge, while curved-chisel sizes combine the shape—expressed as a sweep number—with the width of the cutting edge. A #3 sweep indicates a shallow curve, for example, and a #8 a steeper curve.

Unfortunately, shopping for chisels can be complicated by the fact that there are two measuring standards. The most widely used standard is the Sheffield, or English, system, which uses a sweep number with width expressed in inches. Chisels

may also use the Swiss system, which uses a sweep number with width measured in millimeters. Like the width measurements, the sweep numbers of the two systems do not quite match.

In addition to the differences in blades, carving chisels come in

Above: A double-beaded-rim plate by Wayne Barton of Park Ridge, Ill., illustrates chip carving at its finest.

Right: This caricature carving—entitled simply "Jake"—was done by Wayne Shinlever of Knoxville, Tennessee.

different overall sizes and handle styles. Chisels for detail work may be very short, with handles shaped to fit a cupped palm. Larger chisels can have handles designed for a full-handed grip, and many may be worked with mallets.

WOOD CHOICES

When choosing woods for carving, there are several issues to consider, like resistance to tearing, splitting, crushing under pressure, warping, and checking. The wood should cut easily, yield crisp details, and accept finishes well. A few species that are naturals for carving include basswood, jelutong, sugar pine, and balsa—all of which are soft, light-colored, fine-grained woods that hold details well. These woods are easy to work, making them good choices for beginners, yet deliver results that please even the experts.

The basswood family, also known as linden and lime, is an overwhelming favorite of carvers. Many have described basswood as "cutting like butter," and while that may be an overstatement, it is certainly one of the easier woods to carve. Basswood also cuts in any direction with minimal splitting or tearing, and its subtle grain pattern never dominates the final workpiece.

MORE POWER

Although most carvers prefer hand tools, that is not to say that power aficionados are left out in the cold. Power carving is a growing subset of the form.

Rotary tools with an array of carving bits are common for detail work and smaller workpieces, while handheld grinders with specialized cutting wheels are often used for medium-size carvings. For the largest of workpieces, many carvers have even mastered the chainsaw to produce their work.

Jelutong, sugar pine, and balsa share characteristics similar to basswood, with a few notable exceptions. Native to Malaysia and Indonesia, jelutong is fast becoming a carving favorite. Its only drawbacks are that it can quickly dull carving tools, and it can be an allergen for some. Sugar pine is easy to carve but is more prone to splitting than basswood and has visible resin canals. Beginners often like to try their hand at carving with balsa, possibly the easiest of all woods to work. However, its soft, spongy texture dents easily and requires razor-sharp blades to produce clean cuts.

Butternut and alder are among other favorites, but for those starting out in carving, just about any softwood scraps are fine for acquiring the feel of the tools.

Carving chisels are sized according to the kind of work they do. The standard chisels on the left can be used by hand or with a mallet. The detail chisels on the right are sized to fit the palm of the carver's hand.

Right: The scroll
saw can turn out
very delicate work,
like the bookmark
shown here.

Bottom right: A
variable-speed scroll
saw. Note how the
controls and most
adjustment knobs
are easily accessible
from the front of the
machine.

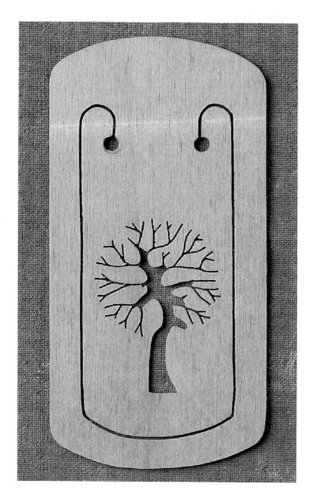

A scroll saw can be used as a shop's utility tool to cut out any number of small parts and components, inlay pieces, veneer, and appliqués. Its only limit is size: Most scroll saws have a thickness capacity of 2" or less, while throat capacity is usually 16"–20" between the blade and rear support.

When used to cut small parts, like those for intarsia, the scroll saw can make a complete cut in a single pass. However, its real talent is being able to make intricate cuts in the interior of a workpiece, as illustrated in the bookmark shown here. These cuts are made by first drilling small holes at key points in the desired pattern. One end of the blade is removed from its mounting and threaded through the hole, then remounted to make the cut. At the end of the cut, one end of the blade is again loosened to remove the workpiece. As many cuts as needed can be made in the same way to complete a pattern.

SCROLL SAWS

When it comes to tools for intricate cutting, the scroll saw is undeniably the master. As with carving, cuts are made slowly on small areas, with all subsequent cuts joining to create a larger whole. The cuts made by a scroll saw are often referred to as fretwork and were once done by hand using a fret saw—a U-shaped handsaw with a thin blade stretched taut between the two sides.

"I saw the angel in the marble and carved until I set him free."

Michelangelo (1475–1564)

Scroll saw tips and tricks

A pattern can be drawn onto a workpiece, or paper patterns can be attached to the wood with spray adhesive. Before putting a pattern onto the wood, sand the workpiece smooth to reduce sanding when finished.

Experienced scrollers have learned the trick of covering the pattern with clear packing tape. This tape acts as lubrication for the blade as it cuts, increasing blade life and reducing burning when cutting tight corners or with burn-prone wood like cherry.

When cutting fine details, always be aware of grain orientation. Long, slender pieces cut against the grain are unstable and break off easily; make these cuts with the grain when possible.

The best way to get reliably square cuts is to always be sure your table is at 90° to the saw blade, but the choice of blades is also a factor. Several kinds of blades can be used, including metal-cutting blades and spiral blades that can cut in any direction. Tooth count varies widely, but blades with higher tooth counts generally yield smoother, more accurate cuts. Skip-tooth blades that include a reverse tooth configuration at the bottom of the blade are best— the tooth pattern cuts in both directions, minimizing tear-out on the underside of the workpiece. Spending a little extra on precision ground blades is always advisable. When loading a fresh blade in the saw, tighten it as usual but add an extra half-turn to the tension knob to keep your cuts crisp.

Change blades often. One way to detect a dull blade is when you have to start pushing harder on the wood to get the same cut. The blade also tends to wander toward the softer grain, making it difficult to follow a pattern. In some cases, the blade will burn the wood in tight turns. If it seems your blades are wearing out too quickly, check the tension of the blade.

Scroll saws come in a huge range of models, from small single-speed benchtop units that sell for less than $65, to heavy floor models going for several hundred dollars. Here are some things to look for when shopping for a scroll saw:

- **Quick-release blade clamps.** In use, especially when the blade has to be threaded for interior cuts, scroll saws require the blade to be loosened frequently. Most current machines have quick releases, but some inexpensive units and many older machines may still require a hex wrench or proprietary tool to change blades.

- **Front-mounted controls.** Power switches, blade tension levers, and table tilt levers should be easy to reach and operate from the front of the machine.

- **Blade type.** Depending on model, a scroll saw will use either plain-end or pin-end blades; better machines can use both. Plain-end blades are flat and held in place by being pinched in the blade holder; pin-end blades are the most versatile and simply hook into place, making them very easy to change and adjust quickly.

- **Variable speed.** Sometimes blades cut better at different speeds, and it isn't always the highest one, so you will want to adjust blade speed to match the wood species and thickness of your workpieces. Saws can have a single speed, a number of preset blade speeds, or a variable range.

- **Dust blower.** Because most scroll sawing involves following the thin lines of a pattern, keeping the surface of the workpiece free of dust is mandatory. All but the most inexpensive models have a built-in blower that keeps dust away from the blade.

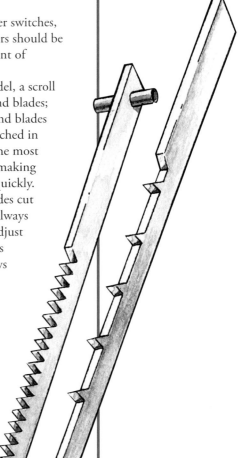

Scroll saw blades: On the left is a pin-end blade, on the right a plain-end blade.

INTARSIA

Intarsia is a three-dimensional mosaic or sculpture in wood. The process involves cutting and shaping individual pieces of a pattern, then gluing them together. Using different species of woods and varying their thickness, color, and grain can produce dramatic effects of depth and perspective.

There are no limits to the subject matter for intarsia: Wildlife, landscapes, religious icons, even corporate logos are popular. As with carving, there are no set rules to follow. A successful intarsia piece pleases the eye, balances form and composition, and satisfies its creator.

Tools for intarsia include a scroll saw, a sharp knife, some files and chisels, and a selection of sandpaper. A drum or spindle sander can be a real time-saver.

Intarsia patterns are commercially available, but your own drawings and photographs can also be used. A simple pattern—no more than 10 or 12 pieces—is best for getting a feel for the technique.

When selecting wood for your project, always use dry wood, and set aside the natural instinct to choose clear, straight grain; knots, color variations, and other faults like wild grain patterns can lend the finished piece dramatic highlights. Any wood can be used, but hardwoods tend to be more predictable for color selection. Wood with natural figuring can be used to enhance an image; tiger maple, for example, makes great fur on a dog or wolf.

The process

Start with two identical patterns, with all the parts numbered on each. Lay one pattern on a flat surface to be used as the assembly area and cover it with waxed

paper to prevent parts sticking to the pattern as they are glued together. Cut out each piece of the second pattern and either trace its shape onto the wood surface or use spray adhesive to secure these cutouts to the various pieces of raw wood.

To ensure a good fit, cut each piece just outside the pattern line, then sand to the line later. Blade speed and size are factors, but the critical element in successful cutting is feed rate. Go slowly; pushing too fast flexes the blade and results in cuts that are not square. Cut each piece out one at a time and compare it to the full pattern on the assembly sheet.

Sanding is the most efficient way to achieve the final shape and detail of each piece. The edge of a disk sander and the contoured face of a spindle or drum sander work well for initial shaping, while refinements can be done by hand or with a rotary tool equipped with a sanding head. All the edges in intarsia must be contoured to some extent. Keep in mind that the varying thicknesses of the wood will help here, but larger pieces may need extra contouring. Check the fit frequently against finished pieces already on the assembly pattern. Once each piece is sanded to shape, finish sand up to 220 grit.

Any woodworking glue except polyurethane can be used to join the pieces. (Polyurethane's tendency to foam up will turn your intarsia project into a mess.) If your project is made primarily of very thin pieces, spot glue them together at various points to hold everything in place until the entire assembly can be glued permanently to a backer board. Projects using thicker pieces can be securely glued together without a backer.

When the glue has dried, the project can be finished with varnish, spray lacquer, or shellac, given several coats of a penetrating oil, waxed, or just left natural, depending on the look you want.

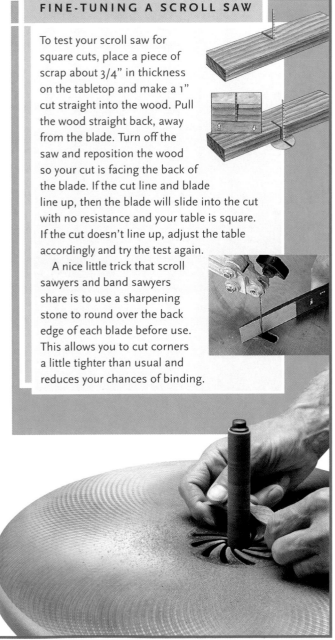

FINE-TUNING A SCROLL SAW

To test your scroll saw for square cuts, place a piece of scrap about 3/4" in thickness on the tabletop and make a 1" cut straight into the wood. Pull the wood straight back, away from the blade. Turn off the saw and reposition the wood so your cut is facing the back of the blade. If the cut line and blade line up, then the blade will slide into the cut with no resistance and your table is square. If the cut doesn't line up, adjust the table accordingly and try the test again.

A nice little trick that scroll sawyers and band sawyers share is to use a sharpening stone to round over the back edge of each blade before use. This allows you to cut corners a little tighter than usual and reduces your chances of binding.

Opposite, far left: These intarsia flowers use different wood species to bring the colors to life.

Opposite, bottom left: Transferring the pattern to a workpiece before cutting

Opposite, bottom right: Cutting out a pattern piece on the scroll saw

Bottom right: Using a benchtop spindle sander to shape a pattern piece of an intarsia project

Woodturning

Woodturning

Woodturning is both enjoyable and uniquely satisfying for creative woodworkers.

The lathe is the only stationary power tool that lets you be the cutter; shaping and removal are literally in your hands. Results are immediate, and the process of shaping the wood to the desired effect depends on your own skills and abilities. As you become adept, the chisels become extensions of your hands: You simply reach out and shape the wood by putting the edge in the proper place.

A lathe has no spinning blades, bits, knives, rollers, or gears waiting to damage unwary digits, but you must respect the laws of physics and kinetic energy, and you must protect your lungs and face from dust and debris, so proper safety gear is essential.

The best way to learn the lathe is to take a lesson or two from an experienced turner. Fortunately, that may be easier than you think. Woodturning is one of two areas of woodworking that has spawned the greatest number of clubs across the country. (The other is carving.) One large national organization—the National Association of Woodturners—has more than 250 local chapters.

Further, there are many types of projects that help develop skill. Small boxes and vessels, jewelry items, and writing implements all can be made quickly and easily on the lathe and are good projects for beginners.

In addition to being beginner-friendly, turning is the perfect pursuit for woodworkers with limited shop time. A great aspect of lathe work is that you can shape, sand, and apply finish right on the machine for most projects. Even many complex forms seldom take more than a few hours to produce. A bowl or a box can be turned from beginning to end in a single session.

The lathe is a versatile tool. With the right machine, you can turn a bowl with a diameter over 7' (yes, that's feet)—or a delicate wine goblet a mere ¼" tall. You can turn between centers, on a faceplate, or using chucking systems. You can turn outboard, offset, and on multiple axes. Natural-edge work is possible, and green woodturning is fast and fun. Furniture makers justify the lathe's presence in their shops by using it to expand design horizons: Legs, pedestals, rungs, balusters, newels, finials, and more.

All you need to get started is a lathe, a basic set of turning chisels, and some wood. Almost any wood can be turned—shop scrap and even your firewood pile can yield some prize workpieces.

LATHES

Lathes come in a variety of sizes and configurations, and although they can be constructed of different materials and in slightly different styles, they are all essentially the same simple machine.

With rare exceptions, a lathe consists of a motorized unit called a headstock, mounted on the left side of a metal bed or "ways." At the opposite end of the bed is the unmotorized tailstock, which can be slid back and forth along the ways to adjust for workpiece size. Each lathe has a means of mounting a workpiece, called a blank, so that a tool-rest attached to the ways can be slid to support tools to cut the workpiece. All of this can be designed to rest as a unit atop a workbench, or can be attached to a leg set.

Let's take a look at the individual parts and how they function.

Opposite page: Several marvelous examples of the types of woodturnings that can be done on the lathe (from left): a small plate, hollow vessel, flute, matched bowl and platter set, wooden hairpins, child's rattle, natural-edge bowl, bottle stoppers, goblet

The two major categories of lathe work are bowl turning (upper left), and spindle turning (bottom).

The major
components of
a typical lathe
(from left):
Headstock, tool-
rest, tailstock.
All three
components
attach to
the lathe's
bed ways.

Headstock

The power center of the lathe, the headstock can have the motor mounted behind it in a fashion similar to a contractor's saw, or below it.

Speed can be controlled in one of three ways. For lathes with manual speed control, the motor cover must be opened and a belt adjusted on a pulley system by hand to change speed. Some versions use a front-mounted lever that adjusts an internal system to control the belt through a series of preset speeds. Both belt-type systems generally have a set number of speeds, usually five to seven. Units with electronic variable speed can adjust motor speed directly through an infinite range from the motor's lowest to highest speed.

At the front of the headstock is a spindle that spins the blank. The spindle is threaded on the outside and hollow on the inside to provide a means of mounting blanks.

The outside threads can accept a screw-on faceplate—a threaded metal flange that attaches to workpieces that are general flat, such as bowls and plates, with screws or mounting blocks.

Blanks can also be mounted to the spindle with a chuck system. Like a faceplate, the chuck screws onto the threaded spindle, but instead of using screws to hold the blank in place, a chuck uses a system of jaws, similar to a drill.

The hollow spindle also accepts a Morse taper, a slender metal post that slips snugly into the spindle. A Morse taper is generally found on a spur center, a sharp, star-shaped apparatus that drives the workpiece. Spur centers are almost always used for turning long, narrow workpieces (also referred to as spindles). Morse tapers can be also be used to mount a chuck and other accessories.

Bed ways

A lathe's ways are composed of two lengthwise components. The most common style bed is a single piece of cast iron, with the ways consisting of a flat slotted platform; but a few lathes have a bed made of two parallel pipes. In both types, the headstock is mounted rigidly on the left. The tool-rest and tailstock have adjustable mountings designed to be loosened and slid along the length of the ways for positioning.

Tool-rest

The tool-rest is what gives the lathe its ability to cut wood. Placed and locked into position close to the workpiece, it rigidly supports a chisel as the wood's

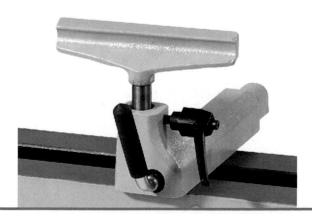

surface spins into the cutting edge, sometimes at great speed. The tool-rest should always be used as close to the workpiece as possible, to minimize the distance a chisel hangs over its edge, giving adequate support. (A chisel extended too far from the tool-rest can flex and vibrate, giving poorer cuts and compromising control.)

The tool-rest should always be adjusted with the lathe turned off. Once the tool-rest is in place, turn the blank by hand before attempting to cut the wood under power, to ensure that it does not contact the tool-rest at any point in its rotation. The tool-rest height should be set at a point where the cutting edge of the chisel is at approximately the center of the workpiece, so let the shape and thickness of the chisel determine the height setting.

In use, a chisel is held against the tool-rest, with the cutting edge pivoted up and away from the spinning blank. Using the rest as a fulcrum, slowly angle the cutting edge into the wood. Until the blank is perfectly round, the chisel will contact the spinning wood only intermittently. As more waste is removed, the chisel moves in closer and the cutting action becomes smoother. To keep the chisel fully supported at all times, be sure to adjust the tool-rest closer to the workpiece as the piece's diameter decreases. Always adjust the tool-rest with the lathe turned off.

Tailstock

Opposite the headstock is the tailstock, which is moved back and forth along the ways to accommodate a long workpiece and hold it in place. Large movements are made by loosening the tailstock and sliding it; when it is locked in place, minor adjustments can be made by turning the handwheel at the back of the tailstock to move the spindle an inch or two in either direction. While the headstock uses a spur center that grips and spins the workpiece under power, the spindle in the unpowered tailstock uses a live center, a freely spinning pivot point that allows the workpiece to spin with a minimum of friction. The live center is also based on a Morse taper and can be removed so other accessories can be inserted into the tailstock.

The tailstock is used most often for "turning between centers," but it can also be moved up close to the headstock to give additional support to large faceplate-based turnings like bowls while they are being turned into rough shape. When the interior of the bowl is being cut, the tailstock can be moved out of the way.

Lathe capacity

Length and width are the two determining dimensions for lathe capacity.

Length is expressed simply as the distance between the tips of the centers mounted in the headstock and tailstock. This is the maximum length of a workpiece that can be turned on the lathe and can generally not be exceeded. However, a few manufacturers offer bed extensions for their lathes that can greatly increase a machine's length capacity.

Width is expressed as twice the distance between the headstock's center of rotation and the surface of the bed ways. This capacity is often expressed as the *swing* of the lathe. For example, if the distance between the headstock center of rotation and the bed is 6", the lathe is said to have a swing of 12". This is the widest blank that can be mounted on the lathe. Keep in mind that because the tool-rest mounting base must often be placed beneath a blank as it is being turned, the maximum width may be smaller for some projects.

Many full-size lathes have the ability to loosen the headstock and swivel it away from the bed. With the headstock so adjusted, and using a tool-rest with a floor stand, much larger faceplate turnings can be made. This is known as outboard turning.

Mounting a blank

For faceplate turning, you will use a generally flat, square workpiece, or blank; the faceplate is attached securely to the center of the blank. The faceplate and blank are then screwed onto the spindle as a single unit.

With woodturnings where the point of attachment will later be cut away or otherwise discarded as part of the turning process, the faceplate can be screwed directly to the blank. For example, the outer convex portion of a bowl can be turned and sanded. The faceplate can then be unscrewed, and the workpiece reversed and mounted back on the lathe using a chuck to hold the base of the bowl, allowing the interior of the bowl to be hollowed out. As that is done, the screw holes are cut away with the rest of the waste.

A bowl can also be turned in a single orientation by using a faceplate with a

mounting block. Screw the faceplate to a round wooden block thick enough to accommodate the mounting screws. The mounting block, in turn, is attached to the bottom of the bowl blank with glue or double-stick tape. In this fashion, the turner has access to both the outside and interior of the bowl without having to turn it around.

With either faceplate method, the blank should be trimmed on the band saw to a round shape before starting to turn.

For turning between centers, first find the exact center on each end of the workpiece. Because workpieces are generally square in cross-section, this can usually be accomplished simply by drawing lines between the opposing corners. Use a handsaw to score these lines on the headstock end of the blank about 1/8" deep to create X-shaped grooves. Fit the spur center into these grooves on the headstock end and hold the workpiece in place as you move the tailstock up to the center of the other end and lock in place. With the workpiece thus lightly suspended between centers, turn the handwheel on the tailstock until the piece is held firmly in place, and lock the handwheel down.

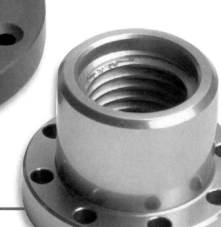

For all types of turning, keep in mind that no matter how carefully you have cut the workpiece and mounted it, it will never be completely on-center at first. That means it will not be entirely balanced as it begins to turn. For this reason, once the blank is securely mounted on the lathe, your first task is simply rough turning the work.

Always begin every turning with the lathe at its slowest setting, and use a roughing gouge to bring the blank into round before increasing speed. As you start to turn, your chisel will hit only the high spots, which can feel as if the chisel is being repeatedly hit with a hammer. At the same time, you may feel the lathe itself vibrating a bit because the turning is unbalanced; this will be more pronounced with larger workpieces. Go extremely slowly, removing waste from the high spots a little at a time. As waste is gradually removed, so is the imbalance. Increase lathe speed only after turning begins to go more smoothly and vibration disappears.

LOOKING AT LATHES

In spite of the fact that enterprising woodworkers have made fixtures that allow them to do rudimentary turning using a drill press, you really can't efficiently turn without a lathe. Fortunately, there are a number of low-cost lathes a beginner can reasonably consider.

For small-scale woodturning—like pens, bottle stoppers, and jewelry—small benchtop units are perfect. Most lathes in this class offer three or fewer speeds. Weighing less than 15 pounds, these lathes can be used just about anywhere. Going on vacation? You can tuck your lathe into a suitcase. Usually called pen lathes, these machines sell for less than $200.

For larger work, the category called mini lathes can handle workpieces up to 10"–12" in diameter and 14"–16" in length (most offer bed extensions that can increase length capacity to about 36"). Mini lathes can be used on a benchtop, but most manufacturers offer leg-stand options. Most units offer five or six speed settings, and some have a variable speed control. These machines weigh between 60 and 80 pounds and sell for about $250–$350.

For full-size work, like large bowls and bedposts, a full-size lathe is a must. These lathes can be incredibly heavy out of the box, usually several hundred pounds, but many offer ways to fill them with additional ballast to increase machine stability for the largest of turnings. Almost all lathes in this class offer motors with several speed ranges or have variable speed controls; some have motors that pivot to the side to allow even larger capacity for bowl turning. The machine shown here features a 12" disk sander built into the back side of the headstock. Full-size lathes can sell for as little as $400, on up to several thousand dollars.

Bottom left:
A variety of turning tools in several sizes makes working at the lathe an efficient, enjoyable experience.

Bottom right:
Bench grinder for sharpening

Inset: Detail of bowl gouge

TURNING TOOLS

Bowl gouge, spindle gouge, detail gouge, roughing gouge—with new tools rapidly appearing in catalogs and on store shelves, it's easy to get confused.

Today's turning tools are of higher quality and better design than their carbon-steel predecessors. Most are made from high-speed steel, which holds an edge longer than ordinary carbon steel. While HSS tools are a bit more expensive and sharpening takes a little longer, they are well worth the investment.

There is a lot of overlap among chisels and the types of turning they can do, but most can be broken down into two main categories: bowl turning and spindle turning.

Tools for bowl turning
A roughing gouge is essential for both bowl and spindle turning. These chisels are large and heavy, with a short bevel, and are used for taking square stock down to round. Their heft and size make this process quicker, easier, and safer than using smaller gouges. Start with a ¾" size.

Once the bowl has been roughed to shape, bowl gouges take over. A ⅜" bowl gouge is appropriate for small bowls, while ½" or larger is best for bigger bowls. For miniature turning, use a set of miniature gouges, smaller than ⅜".

Larger gouges provide more stability than smaller gouges. If you turn a large bowl with a 3/8" gouge, it will take longer and the tool will flex as it hangs off the tool rest, decreasing your ability to achieve a good cut. Be careful when shopping and be sure to buy bowl gouges, not spindle gouges. Although similar, bowl gouges have a deeper flute than spindle gouges, making them easier to control when turning a bowl, especially on the inside.

Additionally, a ¾" or 1" round-nose scraper can be used to clean up curves on the inside of a bowl. Make sure your scraper is significantly thick; thin scrapers flex too much, resulting in poor cuts.

Hollowing tools are small-ended scrapers designed specifically for making hollow vessels.

Coring tools make it possible to produce several bowls from one turning blank

Tools for turning spindles

For spindle turning, you'll need a roughing gouge, a spindle gouge or two, a skew, and a parting tool.

Spindle gouges have shallower flutes than bowl gouges, giving the tool more stability when the bevel is ground back. Generally, the bevel of a spindle gouge is ground at a steeper angle than for a bowl gouge. Start your chisel collection with a ½" spindle gouge, but as with bowl turning, size your chisels according to the size of your workpiece. If you are making bedposts, use a ⅝" or larger spindle gouge.

Skew chisels come as square-edged, oval profile, round, or flat with rounded top and/or bottom. Oval skews are not as successfully mastered as flat-stock skews with a rounded top and bottom. Round skews are a relatively new item. For your initial skew purchase, start with a ½" or ¾" size in flat stock with a rounded or rolled top and bottom.

Parting tools are used for establishing the diameter of different sections of a turning and for removing completed turnings from waste sections. They can also be used to cut small flat areas.

Tools can be purchased with or without handles. Handles can be long, short, or standard length. If you are just learning to turn, start with standard-length handles.

SHARPENING BASICS

When you turn using sharp chisels, shavings curl off cleanly and pile up like wooden snow. But the edge is the critical factor; the cut you get is only as good as the cutting edge you apply to the workpiece. Dull chisels grab and catch and make the fun into hard work. If it's not sharp, don't use it.

Grinders

A good-quality grinder is essential for woodturning. Slower-rpm machines run "cooler"—that is, they do not heat the metal edge of the chisels as quickly as high-speed machines. Excessive heat can ruin cutting edges and make the metal brittle. Use soft, white aluminum-oxide wheels (60 and 100 grit), which work quickly and with lower heat. Ceramic type wheels run even cooler.

After a lot of use, grinding wheels can load with debris, much like blocked sandpaper. Take the time to dress your wheels with a diamond dresser as needed to clean them.

Sharpening jigs

There are a number of good grinding jigs designed to make specific angles and bevel styles, such as skews and gouges, much easier to sharpen. These jigs are great for beginners and pros alike to minimize excess grinding, giving your tools a longer life and allowing you to duplicate the more difficult bevel angles easily. They are a worthwhile investment, and many come with a dressing attachment as well.

Hones

Learn to hone your edges as you work with a stone or diamond lap. Use a hone to dress your tools as soon as they start to dull, and avoid the grinder as much as possible. A thin slip stone also works well to take the wire edge (a raised burr created during sharpening) off the inside of a gouge after grinding.

Gouge sharpening

Gouges do most of the work, so they require frequent sharpening and honing. With a jig holding the angle you want (or freehand on the rest), bring the bevel of the tool to the wheel as if you were actually turning wood. Start grinding at the center of the flute, with the bevel of the chisel running on the wheel at the

TURNING TIP: COLOR EDGES FOR SHARPENING

One way to develop a razor edge on turning tools is to first use a permanent felt-tipped pen to coat the entire cutting edge.

This way, you can see how you are progressing while you grind and hone the edge. It's an old machinist's trick that really works.

desired angle. With light contact, roll and swing the gouge from center to shoulder with an even motion, keeping the bevel in even contact. Repeat the process from center to shoulder on the other side of the gouge, and alternate as necessary until you achieve the angle and edge you require. Remove the wire edge with a slip stone or leather buffing wheel, and get back to turning.

There are almost as many ideas about proper gouge angles as there are turners, and types of grinds for gouges are numerous. A basic spindle gouge will have about a 30°–35° grind and an oval tip that protrudes roughly as far as the width of the gouge's flute. A finishing gouge's angle will be more acute, with a longer point to allow almost skewlike work to be done. A roughing gouge is usually ground almost straight across at a bevel angle of 45° to give the edge a lot of support in heavy cuts. It doesn't have much bevel area and doesn't leave a perfect surface behind, but it removes waste quickly. For bowl gouges most turners use a "fingernail" type grind, with the bevel ranging from about 60° at the tip to 45°–50° or less at the shoulder. This allows smooth cutting with bevel contact on both the wall and bottom of a bowl's interior and will work for exterior cuts as well.

Skew sharpening

Skews fall into two grind profiles: straight and convex. The straight variety is easier to sharpen—for hollow-ground skews, simply run each bevel of the skew on the outside diameter of the wheel, maintaining a combined angle of about 40°–50°, or 20°–25° on each bevel, depending on the type of gouge. The angle of the edge to the shank (toe to heel) is usually about 70°. Then take a few passes on each face across a large stone to remove the wire edge and create a flat microbevel at the cutting edge. You can do this quite a few times before having to regrind.

Convex skews are more difficult to grind. You can grind them freehand, but it requires swinging the skew handle horizontally in a clean arc while maintaining an even bevel angle at the same time. For convex skews, using a jig is the best method.

Scraper sharpening

With the advent of HSS scrapers, the best course for sharpening is to burnish up an edge as you would a cabinet scraper. Grind the scraper bevel at about 40°, and then hone the top surface flat to remove the wire edge with a stone or hone. This leaves a fine sharp edge on the tool, but it's pointing in the wrong direction. To change the edge angle upward, simply pass the edge across a piece of hardened steel, like a drill shank, at 90° to the edge. One pass only. This will roll the edge up to an angle that will cut quite well, and the solid steel of this edge will last a long time.

TURNING GREEN WOOD

While most woodworkers avoid using green wood, woodturners can grab a block almost right off the stump and start making shavings. Green wood isn't actually green in color but rather not yet seasoned by either kiln drying or air drying. It can range in wetness from dripping wet (cut in springtime) to only slightly wet (cut in late fall or winter).

Freshly cut (green) wood with a high moisture content is, by nature, unstable and prone to warping and cracking as it dries. The movement is caused by the cells of the wood shrinking and changing shape as the moisture leaves. Outer layers dry faster than the inner ones, creating stresses in the wood that causes checking. Left to itself, drying is a slow process, with thicker air-dried material often requiring years of seasoning. However, air-dried wood is preferred by experienced turners over kiln-dried wood. It cuts

Opposite page, left: This sharpening jig allows a gouge to be rotated easily against a grinder wheel for a perfectly uniform bevel.

Opposite, right: Sharpening a skew chisel

Below left: Burnishing the edge of a scraper after sharpening

Below right: Turning green wood produces mounds of long, thin shavings.

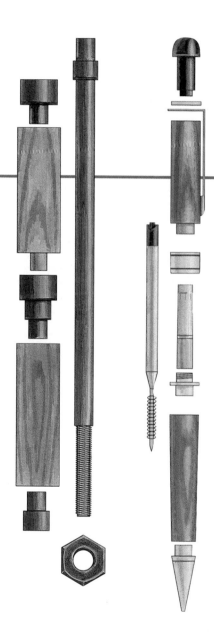

onto the rod and are surrounded by bushings the same size as the finished pen's diameter.

Pen hardware comes in kits that include all parts and usually retail for just a few dollars through turning-supply sources. The hardware kit you buy should include two brass tubes—one for the main body and one for the top or cap— and other various pen parts. Check the package to find the recommended size bit to use for drilling the wood blanks. The kit may also include bushings sized to match the pen.

The wood will cost from nothing (scrap bin) to a couple of dollars. Pens may just be the ultimate scrap-wood projects. With such small blanks, you can really be selective in the material

you choose. Pens can also be turned from a variety of plastic materials.

Preparing turning blanks

To get started, machine the pen blanks into ⅝"-square strips if they don't come this way already. Crosscut a group of blanks to the exact length of the brass tubes. For some pen kits the tubes are the same length, for others one will be longer than the other. In any event, keep the sets together (use a matching number on each set) and be sure your blanks are crosscut perfectly square. This results in a pen with tight joints between the turned material and the fittings.

Use a drill press to bore holes through all the blanks, lifting the bit out of the stock frequently to remove waste as you drill.

Roughen the surface of the brass tubes from the pen kits with steel wool or fine sandpaper. Apply cyanoacrylate glue to the inside of one end of the blanks and quickly push the brass tube into this end until flush with the opposite end. This glue dries very quickly, so apply glue to only one blank at a time

during the process. Once all the body and cap blanks have brass tubes inserted, remove any excess glue.

Turning and assembly
Slip the bushings and blanks onto the mandrel, finger-tighten the nut, and mount the mandrel on the lathe.

Turn the blanks round with a spindle gouge almost to the bushings, then sand through the grits until the blanks are flush with the bushings. Apply finish when the blanks are polished smooth.

Before you start fitting the two halves of your pens together, take time to align the grain. Pens look most attractive if the grain lines up when the pen isn't being used—for twist pens the grain should be aligned when the writing tip is withdrawn inside the pen; capped pens look best if the grain is aligned when capped.

Use a clamp to apply moderate force to press-fit the pen parts and blanks together. The fit will be snug—once together, it's just about impossible to separate.

Once you get the hang of the process, you should be able to mount, turn, sand, finish, and assemble a pen in about half an hour.

LATHE SANDING

Sanding is a necessary step in most woodturning projects, especially bowl turning, but it's a bit different from sanding other projects. Sanding scratches created on spinning wood are usually cross-grain and are far more visible. For that reason, it is wise to sand wood on the lathe much finer, often going to 600 grit or higher, depending on the wood. Harder woods require finer sanding.

The rule of thumb is that if you can see scratches, go finer—anything you see will be amplified when applying finish later.

Sanding on the lathe is potentially dangerous. Always remove the tool-rest before sanding, to prevent catching fingers between the wood and the tool-rest. If you use any type of rag for wetting the wood, use a small piece.

Opposite page, left: Exploded view of a mandrel used for pen turning

Opposite, center: Exploded view of a typical pen

Opposite, top: Pens can be turned from a variety of materials, both wood and plastic. Note how a clamp is used to gently push the pen components together.

Above left: Using a jig to drill pen blanks before turning

Above right: When turning a pen, remove waste almost down to the bushings. Use sandpaper to bring the pen the rest of the way to the same diameter as the bushings.

Sanding on the lathe produces large amounts of dust, and the rotation throws it right in your face. Be sure to protect your lungs with a mask, and use your shop air cleaner if you have one.

There are two categories of sanding: power sanding and hand sanding. With hand sanding, the turner holds the sandpaper against the spinning workpiece by hand. Power sanding involves the use of sanding disks mounted on a powered or unpowered device, which in turn is held against the spinning work.

Additionally, there are significant differences between sanding bowls and sanding spindle work.

Bowl sanding

Hand sanding is best for small bowls and other tight, concave areas.

Fold a small piece of sandpaper in thirds. The piece is kept small to allow it to conform to the bowl's curves. Folding it keeps the paper from slipping, because smooth back will not be positioned against

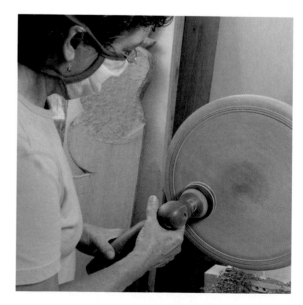

smooth back. And finally, this approach also keeps your paper from rubbing and wearing out, because abrasive doesn't touch abrasive.

You will most likely need to start with 80- or 100-grit paper for hand sanding a bowl. After completely removing all tool marks, proceed to the next finer grit. A good rule of thumb for grit progression is 80, 100, 150, 220, 320. As with sanding furniture and other projects, don't skip grits.

When finished, take the bowl off the lathe and hold it up to a bright light to highlight any remaining sanding scratches on the end grain. These can be minimized by sanding to a finer grit. Put the bowl back on the lathe and sand to 1,200 grit or even finer.

Power sanding

Power sanding is a much quicker process but can be used only on bowls large enough to accommodate the disks. Power sanding can be accomplished using an angle drill with a sanding disk holder attached or by using a handheld rotating sanding device. For power

sanding, you can usually start with 120-grit abrasive. It takes only a minute or two to sand an entire bowl or platter with each grit.

Progress through each grit to finer and finer. As you do, the swirl marks diminish. After sanding, you can buff to get rid of remaining sanding swirls.

When you are power sanding, take care not to oversand. Run your lathe slowly. This truly is a fast process; if you are spending more than a few minutes, you are oversanding.

Sanding spindles

Spindle sanding is easier than bowl sanding. Spindle sanding should be minimal if you are cutting the wood properly to begin with. The tops and bottoms of areas like beads and coves should be the only areas that might need a bit of touchup, and then only with 150 or higher grit to start with. Oversanding spindle turnings causes the elements to be less crisp and to run together. You can sand spindles at a relatively high speed, but it's also all right to slow down your lathe.

As a final step for both bowls and spindles, use this old turners' trick of burnishing to get a polished sheen on unfinished hardwood: After sanding, grab a handful of your shavings and press them against the spinning surface under a bit of pressure. Since the turned material is just as hard as the shavings, they polish one another rather than scratching. Burnishing works best on spindles. Be careful with this process, as the heat it generates can burn an unprotected hand. A leather glove is a good idea.

If you intend to paint the surface of a turned spindle, then sanding with 150 grit is recommended, but don't sand above 220 grit. Paint adheres better to a lightly sanded surface than to a burnished surface.

Opposite, top: Hand sanding on the lathe

Opposite, bottom left: Sandpaper should be folded in thirds into a small piece that gives better control in use, and longer life for the paper.

Opposite, bottom right: Using a power sander

Left: Burnishing a spindle with wood shavings

FINISHING ON THE LATHE

As with sanding, a few extra safety precautions should be noted when finishing on the lathe.

When applying any finish under power on the lathe, remember that centrifugal force will sling off any excess. Protect your face and especially your eyes from potential spray. Take care when using rags or pads while finishing under power. Use small pieces, and keep all corners and ends tucked in to prevent possible wrap-up. Be sure you can release any material that might wrap in the turning, and never wrap the rag around your hand. Steer clear of irregular or natural edges, as they will grab the rag.

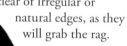

Sealing your work

The process of turning produces both end grain and flat grain on the final surface. And as the two will absorb finishes at remarkably different rates, it's a good idea to use a sealer coat, especially on exposed open end grain. This is particularly true if you are trying to achieve a uniform stain color or build up to a glossy surface. One of the best sealers is shellac, thinned with denatured alcohol and mixed with a small amount of linseed oil. Furniture finishers will recognize this formula as French polish—described later—and indeed it can be used as a finish all by itself if you build successive coats.

Wax

Wax is easy to apply and remove and requires little or no drying time. Solid sticks of wax are available in different colors and degrees of hardness, from soft beeswax to hard carnauba. Harder wax-sticks buff to a high shine.

Press the wax onto the spinning wood until friction melts it onto the surface. Follow by pressing with a clean rag to spread the wax evenly and remove any excess, buffing it in the process. The same process works with paste wax, but because most paste waxes contain solvents, you may have to

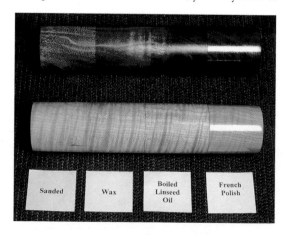

| Sanded | Wax | Boiled Linseed Oil | French Polish |

let the wax dry for 10 minutes or so before you start in on the buffing.

Remember that waxes are a soft finish that will have to be periodically renewed.

Oils

While wax leaves wood looking clean and natural, oil adds depth and a small amount of color. Both drying oils like linseed and tung oil and nondrying oils like mineral oil are good choices. Drying oils cure either atop or in among the wood fibers, but nondrying oils stay wet indefinitely.

The easiest way to apply any oil is to flood it on, let it soak in for 10 minutes or so, then wipe off the excess. Some turners like to sand oil into the wood, creating a slurry of swarf and oil that helps fill tiny pores.

Oil is often used in combination with wax, resulting in a finish that applies with the ease of wax but offers the enhanced definition of oil.

Film finishes

Anything that cures to a film falls into this category, including shellac, lacquer, polyurethane, and water-based coatings. Most of these coatings require more drying time than wax or polish and build up thicker than oils. They are a good choice when you need more protection or want a thicker finish, in any sheen from satin to high gloss.

Once film finish is dry and cured, you can rub it either to satin or gloss just as you would any furniture finish. Use 0000 steel wool and paste wax to bring a film finish to satin, or automotive rubbing compounds to buff lacquer, polyurethane, shellac, or French polish to high gloss.

French polish

Applied with a cloth pad to the spinning wood, shellac-based French polish lets you apply a built-up gloss film in just minutes. Technically, even pure shellac is considered French polish, but without additives it takes some skill to apply it. Put it on too wet and it will form ridges, called curdling. Press too hard and you will burn it right back off the wood.

Start by shutting off the lathe and sealing the sanded wood with thin, dewaxed shellac. Flood it on liberally, and wipe off anything that does not absorb immediately. After 15 minutes, it should be dry enough to sand with 600-grit or finer paper. Turn the lathe on slow speed, charge a cotton or linen cloth pad with a modest amount of French polish, and gently wipe on a thin coat of finish, coating the whole surface evenly. In a minute or two it will be dry enough to pad on another thin coat, and you may continue to build up coats until the surface looks the way you want it. If you get impatient and mess it up by going too fast, let it dry, sand it smooth, and continue with more thin coats.

Friction polish

One of the most common terms you hear among turners is "friction polish." Like "French polish," the term is used to mean both a material and a method of application. Almost anything you rub onto turning wood that creates friction, and subsequently heat that cures it, can justly be called friction polish. Thus wax sticks are friction polishes, just as is any shellac-based French polish.

What confuses the issue is that several companies sell mixtures specifically called "friction polish." Most are amalgams of common coatings laced with something that provides lubrication, so as to create an easier-to-apply film finish. How durable or glossy the finish is depends on what is mixed with what, and such friction polishes can run the gamut from something barely more than wax, to nothing less than shellac or lacquer.

Opposite, left: Finishing expert Michael Dresdner shows a variety of finishes suitable for lathe work.

Opposite, right: How finishing on the lathe changes the appearance of the wood's surface (from left)—plain sanding, wax, linseed oil, French polish

Jigs and Fixtures

CHAPTER 14

Hardware

STICKLEY HARDWARE

Gustav Stickley, one of the most influential furniture makers of the 20th century, still inspires countless woodworkers. For Stickley, construction and decoration were inseparable. Thus, he was particular about his hardware.

He respected the ancient crafts and filled his factory with metalsmiths trained in Old World traditions. Stickley's workshops made and offered hardware in a variety of metals—iron, copper, brass and pewter—as well as, sometimes, in wood.

Round or pyramid-shaped wooden pulls were less expensive for his customers and were used more frequently in nonpublic areas of the house such as the kitchen or bathroom. Showier rooms generally had hand-hammered copper or iron hardware for pulls and hinges. Strap hinges were a predominant style, while the pulls tended to be of the ring or bail variety.

The iron was in the Old World armor-bright finish, while the copper and brass went through a firing method that produced a texture, but they were left unlacquered. Just as Stickley believed in letting age darken the wood in his pieces, he also regarded age and exposure as the only agents "required to produce beauty and variety of tone" in hardware.

For today's woodworker completing a Mission or

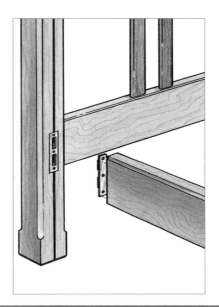

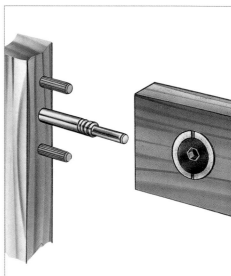

"Drive a nail home and clinch it so faithfully that you can wake up in the night and think of your work with satisfaction— a work at which you would not be ashamed to invoke the muse."

Henry David Thoreau (1817–62)

Arts and Crafts–style project, the hardware is the final touch—both functional and decorative.

BED HARDWARE

Beds are very popular woodworking projects, but some woodworkers resist using specialized knock-down bed frame hardware, concerned that these fasteners do not belong in a handcrafted bed. Nothing could be further from the truth. When you think of all the stresses and weight a bed must endure, and how hard a fully assembled bed is to move, quality hardware to join the bed rails to the head and foot is essential.

Fortunately, there is a wide and varied selection of bed hardware, from sophisticated Murphy bed and futon-style articulating systems to simple screw-on connectors. Bed hardware, essentially a form of specialized knock-down fittings, makes an otherwise difficult joinery task simple. In fact, the characteristics that make these fasteners practical in their traditional use—strength, durability, ease of installation—are exactly why they should be considered.

Use the connector hardware that best suits the bed you wish to build. Bunk beds, for instance, create a different set of challenges from a four-poster. Recessed bolt/cam fittings work extremely well when very strong joints are required. They call for a special bolt wrench and a fair bit of installation work but are well worth the effort. The more familiar steel bed-rail fasteners, whether surface-mounted or mortised into place, are all most bed designs need.

Mattress size will affect some other bed hardware components. A twin bed spans a smaller distance than a king-size mattress and therefore would not need a center leg support. Center-rail fasteners are an excellent way to snap your cross supports firmly in place. There are decorative bolt covers, bunk bed safety rail catches, ladder hooks, and numerous other offerings that will add to your bed building projects.

If your bed project is more utilitarian, don't overlook steel bed rails. They make for a quick-to-build but long-lasting bed.

TAPE

You buy it in a hardware store, but strictly speaking, tape is not hardware. However, since you can use it to assemble or fasten things, it is worth including here.

When it is time to apply paint or some other finish to a project, masking tape protects areas where you do not want the finish to go. For most woodworking applications, the blue painter's tape is often preferred because it holds securely and is easily removed without leaving behind any residue.

Duct tape is handy to have in your workshop because it is good for repairing and sealing all kinds of items besides ducts. Wrap some duct tape around the handles of tools like hammers to give yourself a more comfortable grip. You can even use it for emergency clamping, but be sure to put something between it and your workpiece, because, unlike masking tape, duct tape can leave residue. Reinforced clear packing tape can handle many of the same tasks as duct tape.

Veneer tape is a special perforated paper tape made to keep the edges of book-matched veneers together while being pressed. Its adhesive shrinks slightly as it dries, keeping the veneer pieces tight to one another. It also peels off easily with a damp sponging.

This product is not to be confused with edge-banding tape, which actually is veneer, primarily used to dress the visible edges of plywood. Edge-banding tape comes in rolls and is generally self-adhesive, either peel-and-stick or with a heat-activated glue that is applied with a household iron.

Opposite page, counterclockwise from top: Gustav Stickley, 1858–1942

Hardware manufactured at the Stickley factory is still available today from Rockler.com.

Stickley often used wooden rather than metal knobs.

Bed rail hanger

Bed bolt with cam lock

CHAPTER 15

Sanding and Finishing

A carefully made woodworking project deserves a top-quality finish to add the crowning touch. However, it can be easy to rush this last important step in the fervor of completing the job. Unfortunately, rushing a finish usually leads to disappointing results. If you temper your enthusiasm, sand carefully, and choose an appropriate stain and finish for your project, you'll never regret the time and effort spent achieving a spectacular finish. This chapter will help you navigate the waters of finishing—from proper sanding techniques through a final rubbing out—so every finish will leave your mark of fine craftsmanship.

PREPARING WOOD SURFACES FOR FINISH

Sanding can be a dirty, laborious, and sometimes frustrating process. Most woodworkers dislike it. Yet, ironically, both sanding too little and sanding too much can lead to inferior finishes. Woodworkers often blame the choice of finish or their application technique for less than perfect finishes, when in fact they are fighting with poorly prepared surfaces. You can't eliminate sanding from the finishing process, but an overview of how to do it efficiently and what tools and techniques to use can lead to a beautifully prepared surface in the quickest time with the least amount of effort.

Sanding goals

Sanding has four objectives. You need to know what each is, along with the fastest way to achieve them.

Step one is to remove tool and machining marks from the wood. If you just finished using the planer, jointer, saw, hand plane, or chisel, there are most likely some marks. Perhaps the surface is uneven or not quite flat, or curves are too bumpy. Use a coarse (80- or 100-grit) aluminum oxide paper, sanding

diagonally, to flatten or contour the surface. As soon as the tool marks are gone and the surface is smooth and flat, move on to step two.

Step two also has only one purpose: to remove the coarse scratches left by step one. Switch to 120- or 150-grit aluminum oxide paper to remove the sanding scratches. If you are sanding by hand, change directions so you are sanding diagonally at 90 degrees to the last sanding. When the scratches disappear, move on to the next step.

Step three is similar to step two. Use 180-grit aluminum oxide paper to remove the scratches left by the last sanding.

Step four—final sanding—is simply to straighten out the 180-grit scratches instead of removing them. The quickest way to do that is to use the same grit paper, only this time switch to garnet paper and sand with the grain. In most cases, 180-grit garnet will leave the surface smooth enough to finish; but some very hard woods, like boxwood or ebony, may require finer sanding steps. If you can still see obvious and offensive scratches in these woods, continue sanding to 220 or even 320 grit.

Abrasives and backing options

The four main categories of abrasives are briefly described in the sidebar on the following page. These days, flint paper is almost obsolete. Garnet is the preferred choice for hand sanding, while aluminum oxide is recommended for power sanding. Silicon carbide generally comes into play after the first coat of finish is applied and can be used wet (with water, naphtha, or rubbing oils) or coated with zinc stearate, a load-inhibiting talc that prevents the paper from clogging up and burnishing the surface.

Sandpaper is backed with paper, cloth, fiber, or polyester film. Here, too, there are choices to be made. The letter after the grit number on the back of the sheet designates the weight of the backing. Paper is available in "A" (too light for power sanding but

Opposite: The key to a good finish is properly preparing the wood surface.

TYPES OF SANDING GRITS

Flint: A natural abrasive made from silicon dioxide quartz. Inexpensive, and deservedly so. It dulls rapidly and is considered practically worthless in the woodworker's shop.

Garnet: Another natural abrasive and ideal for hardwoods, garnet is made from a semiprecious stone with a reddish-brown color. Garnet grits fracture when rubbed, exposing new cutting edges, which extend their life. The right choice for hand sanding, it's also preferred for end-grain sanding.

Aluminum oxide: A synthetic abrasive made of crystallized bauxite with other materials added for toughness. Aluminum oxide is by far the most common sandpaper in use today, particularly with machine sanding. This grit's cutting surfaces round off with use, which can cause a surface to burnish and lead to uneven staining. Hand sanding with garnet will cut through the burnish easily.

Silicon carbide: The hardest synthetic abrasive in common use, silicon carbide does not burnish wood because its cutting edges do not generate enough heat to cause a glaze. Though harder, it is not as tough and durable as aluminum oxide. Most commonly used to rub out a finished piece.

1.

2.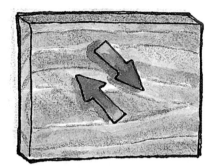

3.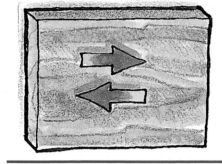

4.

good for sanding moldings and carvings), "C" and "D" (intermediate, cabinet-grade papers), and "E" (the heaviest paper, used for drum sanding).

Coated abrasives differ in the amount of grit applied to the backing sheet. An open-coat sheet of abrasive has 40 to 70 percent as much abrasive as a closed-coat sheet, which has its full surface covered. The open coat allows for easier chip removal and is generally suitable for rough work. Closed coats cut more, last longer, and give a smoother finish but tend to clog up faster and burnish the surface. Most aluminum oxide paper is open coat, while silicon carbide is closed coat.

Sanding process in a nutshell

All sanding is done in steps, starting with a coarse grit and proceeding to finer-grit papers. When moving from one grit to the next, never skip more than one grit, otherwise you will leave coarser scratches behind. Always sand with the grain, taking long strokes on

the stock and overlaying your strokes slightly. Keep a positive but light touch, checking constantly that you are not rounding over a corner that is meant to be sharp. When hand sanding, use blocks whenever possible to cut down high spots and span low spots to produce a more uniform surface.

Machine sanding

Belt and orbital sanders are mixed blessings. Because they are motorized they can remove a lot of wood in a hurry, but this can work to your disadvantage. One of the main problems with a belt sander is control. If the machine is tilted onto one edge of its pad even briefly, the resulting gash requires much sanding to remove. Always start and stop the machine while it is resting directly on the surface you want to sand. Use a belt sander for rough stock removal only—it's meant for shaping, not finishing.

Vibrating or random-orbit hand sanders are a better choice for fine sanding. They cut by rotating in

Opposite, from top:

Sanding can be broken down into four steps.

1. First, sand diagonally with coarse paper to remove milling marks.

2. Sand in opposite direction with finer sandpaper to remove first set of sanding scratches.

3. Using still finer sandpaper, remove previous set of scratches.

4. For final sanding, sand with the grain.

This page: Always read the back of your sandpaper. It will provide the information you need to make good sanding choices.

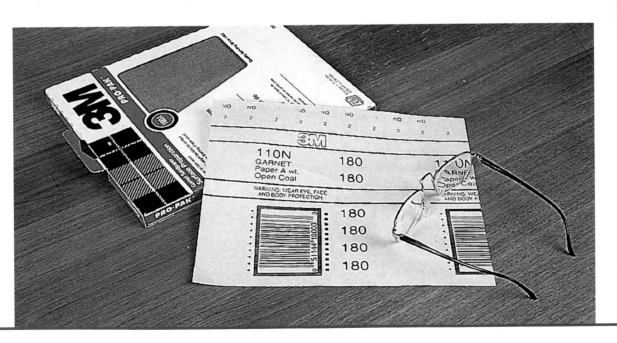

tiny circles, so the direction you move the machine is irrelevant; they always cut more or less across the grain. For that reason, they are great for all sanding steps except the final pass, which should be done by hand and with the grain. Use garnet paper when possible. The one problem associated with vibrating or random-orbit sanders is "pigtails," those small swirling scratches that show up only after you have stained or finished. The secret to avoiding pigtails is to lighten up and slow down—literally. Use a light hand on the sander so it abrades under its own weight. Bearing down only slows the speed of the head, causing pigtails and stressing the machine motor.

In general, switch to the orbital sander at about the 120-grit stage. Is it necessary to sand all the way to 600-grit to get an excellent finish? Absolutely not; most of the time you don't need to go past 320 grit. Going the extra mile with 400 and 600 grit is worthwhile only when you have a piece of wood that is highly figured, like crotch, burl, or bird's-eye.

"One of the most important aspects of finishes, I believe, is that they invite me to touch, to caress, and to take pleasure in the wood surface."

Sam Maloof (b. 1919)

SEALING THE WOOD

Once you have thoroughly sanded your project, your next consideration is whether to apply a sealer coat of finish. Actually, "sealer" is really the first coating applied to raw wood. While its use is always optional, it can be very helpful in some situations, performing some or all of the following functions:

- locking in contamination on the wood surface, such as grease, oil, wax, or sap and antioxidants that occur naturally in the wood;
- preventing spongy wood from excessively absorbing repeated coats of finish;
- reducing grain-raising under water-based finishes;
- acting as a tie or barrier coat to allow otherwise noncompatible finishes to go over one another;
- increasing adhesion of the topcoat to the substrate or stain;
- preparing an old finish for recoating with a different topcoat;

- making it easier to sand the first coat of finish;
- providing a superior moisture barrier.

When to use sealer

Strictly speaking, any finish that forms a film on wood can be used as a sealer. Some coatings are so good at this task on their own that they are called self-sealing finishes. Other finishes are not, and they benefit from special sealers. You can buy products formulated specifically as sealers. An excellent all-around choice, called SealCoat Universal Sanding Sealer, is a modified dewaxed shellac with a long shelf life. (Freshly mixed dewaxed shellac is an appropriate substitute.)

Shellac and oil-based finishes (including Danish oil, varnish, and polyurethane) work so well by themselves that they do not require any special sealer under them. Some finishers prefer to thin the first coat of these materials to make them dry quicker or sand easier, but that is strictly a personal choice.

Lacquer and water-based coatings, on the other hand, work better over sealer. The wood also plays a part. With dense woods, such as rock maple, you can usually omit the sealer. However, spongy or absorbent woods, like poplar, red alder, and most softwoods,

Opposite, top: Hand sanders are meant to be moved only about 1" per second. Moving the sander too fast or "scrubbing" will also cause pigtails.

Bottom left: Sandpaper comes in square sheets, stick-on disks backed with pressure sensitive adhesive (PSA) or hook-and-loop fasteners, belts, and even blocks and sponges.

Bottom right: A long-lived dewaxed shellac works for all sealing applications.

This page: Not every sort of topcoat finish benefits from a first coat of sealer. Oil and oil-based polyurethane do not, while water-based polyurethane definitely does.

can benefit greatly from sealer, especially under lacquer. The sealer coat envelopes the porous wood, preventing the first few coats of lacquer from being excessively absorbed.

Some problem woods, like rosewood and cocobolo, contain antioxidants that prevent certain finishes from curing. These need sealer under oil-based coatings but not necessarily under lacquer or shellac. Fortunately, it doesn't hurt to use the correct sealer. When in doubt, err on the side of caution and apply sealer first.

Applying sealer

Sealer can be wiped, brushed, or sprayed on. The problem is that after one coat, end grain and spongy areas may still be "hungry" and insufficiently sealed, while denser flat-grain areas are starting to build up too much coating. A good solution is to flood the sealer on liberally by hand, using a nylon abrasive pad as an applicator, then immediately wipe it off with paper shop towels while it is still wet. Wear gloves and work small areas at a time so the sealer doesn't dry before you wipe it off.

The advantage of this method is that it allows end grain to absorb as much sealer as it can but wipes any extra off flat-grain surfaces that tend to absorb less. Once the sealer is dry, the entire piece is uniformly sealed, and the next coat of finish will lay out similarly in all areas.

COLORING WOOD WITH STAIN

One decision you'll be confronted with in most projects is whether to color the wood. Part of the challenge is simply choosing an attractive color, but you will also need to consider how the wood will react to the stain. Hardwoods like oak or ash accept stain nicely right out of the can, but that is not the case for all hardwoods; maple and cherry often accept stain unevenly. Most softwoods—pine, cedar, spruce, hemlock, fir, cypress, larch, redwood, and

yew—can also cause problems when stain is applied. These woods are characterized by distinct alternating bands of earlywood and latewood that accept stain differently. The earlywood bands are softer and less dense than the latewood bands, and they are also lighter in color.

Stains are available in a variety of formulations. Common oil-based wood stain contains pigments that color the wood, sometimes mixed with dyes. Gel stains are handy for applying to vertical surfaces because they won't drip or splash.

There are also stain and varnish blends for a one-step finish that both colors the wood and applies a protective topcoat. While handy, this last type has an important drawback: Most projects require multiple coats of varnish, but stain/varnish blends get successively darker with each coat. And, unless care is taken while brushing, these blends are prone to streaking and can create darker areas where the finish is thicker, like in corners or the deeper recesses of moldings.

Applying stain couldn't be easier. Just flood it on the wood with a brush or soft cloth, allow the stain

to soak in for a couple of minutes, and wipe off the excess. Wear gloves, and test the stain on a piece of scrap wood that matches your project wood. You will instantly see how the stain will color the wood, as well as whether you will have to deal with several other common staining problems. Here are the typical challenges you may encounter:

• **Grain reversals:** One of the most common problems is due directly to the fact that the earlywood is spongier and absorbs more stain than latewood. Initially, the latewood bands are somewhat darker in color than the earlywood. Apply a fairly dark stain, and the two change positions as the earlywood sucks up stain and the latewood resists it. The result, called grain reversal, shows the formerly light bands quite dark and the dark grain lighter in comparison.

• **Excess stain absorption:** Apply a favorite stain for ash or maple to soft pine or spruce and you may be surprised. Since the earlywood stripes often make up the majority of the surface, the net result is a darker color than you anticipated. Stain also soaks into end grain more heavily than on the face and edge grain, resulting in a much darker color tone. Testing stain first on scrap samples of the softwood you use for your project will quickly show you what you will end up with.

Opposite: To apply sealer, flood it on liberally by hand, then wipe off the excess with shop towels. Wear gloves for this procedure.

Left: Wipe the stain off before it dries. Move quickly, but thoroughly rub the entire piece, working toward uniform coverage.

Above: Commercially available conditioners can help diminish splotching.

Right: Some woods are prone to splotching when colored with pigment stains, visible here as dark streaks or patches on the wood. From left: pine, poplar, and cherry.

Opposite: Aniline dyes are mixed prior to use by dissolving the powder in warm water. Foam brushes work best for application.

• **Splotching:** While heavier stain absorption is both predictable and acceptable, splotching, another common problem, is neither. Certain woods contain pockets of higher sap concentration. These are invisible in the raw wood, but when oil-based stains are applied, they show up as random puddles of splotchy color. They are very difficult to predict and are not at all attractive.

The reason these patches get darker is directly related to the solvents in the stain. The sap pockets soften with the same solvents used in oil-based stains, absorbing them in the process. As solvent is absorbed, dissolved stain is also absorbed, making those areas darker. This is problematic with oil-based stains containing dye as well as pigment, since dye is more easily absorbed than pigment. Consequently, some water-based stains, and even some entirely pigmented stains, are less prone to splotching.

Probably the easiest, and most common, fix for

these problems is wood conditioner. Most every manufacturer that makes oil-based stain also makes a wood conditioner designed to prevent splotching. Typically, oil-based wood conditioner is a mixture of common stain solvents and a small amount of clear resin.

When applying conditioner, also called stain controller, the instructions call for flooding it onto the raw, sanded wood, then wiping it all off. The important thing is to stain while the wood is still wet with conditioner. Allowing it to dry before staining decreases its effectiveness. Areas prone to splotching absorb the conditioner, but not excess stain. No more splotch! In essence, you have prestained the wood with colorless stain. The end result is that the colored stain will be less intense than if you had applied it to untreated wood. To get around this, choose a darker stain to begin with.

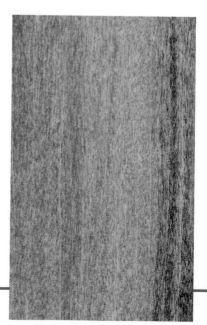

COLORING WOOD WITH DYES

If you don't mind grain reversal and want richer, darker staining, you can get that while avoiding splotching by using aniline dye instead of pigmented oil-based stain. Water-soluble dyes color richly and more uniformly and are not prey to splotching problems. That's because they contain no solvents to soften the sap pockets. However, be cautious with premixed, alcohol-based liquid dyes: They may contain a little solvent. These dyes are called NGR, for "non-grain raising." Powdered dyes that mix only with water are the best bet.

Applying aniline dye isn't difficult if you take a few precautions. Using a sponge and some warm distilled water, gently wet all the bare wood surfaces just enough to raise the grain before applying the dye. When dry, sand lightly with 220-grit paper, just enough to take all the fuzz off. Since dye is water-based, raising the grain beforehand and sanding it off will keep the dye from raising the grain again.

Mix the powdered dye in warm water according to the manufacturer's instructions. Mix and store your dye in plastic or glass containers. Don't use steel containers, because they will rust, changing the color of the dye. Let the mixture set for an hour, so that the dye dissolves completely before you apply it. Then add a little liquid dish soap—about one teaspoon for each quart of water—to your dye mixture. The soap helps break the surface tension of the water, allowing the dye to fill in all the grain. This is especially helpful when coloring oak or other open-pored woods.

Use a foam brush to flood the dye on the wood. Be sure to wear rubber gloves: Aniline dyes will stain your hands, and any oils or sweat on your skin will resuspend the dye and possibly change its color. After you have applied the dye, use a soft, clean, lint-free cotton cloth to wipe off the excess. Wipe off any fingerprints after you have set the piece down to dry.

Drying should take about an hour. Once the dye dries, use an oil-based varnish, shellac, or lacquer as a topcoat. Water-based varnish will reactivate the dye and smear it.

CHOOSING AND APPLYING TOPCOATS

There are numerous topcoats to choose from for your projects. Three of the most popular are polyurethane varnish, shellac, and lacquer. Each of these options has its own strengths and weaknesses when it comes to coloration, durability, and ease of application. To help you choose among them, it's important to have a good understanding of the characteristics of each type.

Polyurethane

If you're looking for the most durable finish you can apply with a brush, you can't beat polyurethane. Poly resists scratches, heat, water, solvents, and alkalis. Its main drawback, however, is the same as with all varnishes: It cures so slowly that dust has time to settle into the finish.

Like many finishes, polyurethane is named for its primary resin, though some cans labeled "polyurethane" also contain other resins. Resin is what remains behind to form a film layer once the solvent has evaporated. The resin defines the nature of the coating. In general, polyurethane or urethane resins (the terms may be used interchangeably) provide finishes with good durability, including resistance to heat, abrasion, chemicals, stains, and solvents. Polyurethane is tough enough for kitchen tables and cabinets, bathroom vanities, walls, doors, floors, all types of furniture projects. Woodworkers mainly use either oil-based or water-based polyurethanes. Both have good qualities, but they are different in many ways, giving rise to a heated debate over which is superior.

The primary differences between the two types

of polyurethane relate to how they are made. Oil-based, whose proper name is "oil-modified urethane," is produced by reacting common finishing oils, like linseed oil, with a chemical that causes the oil to form larger molecules. The result is something that looks and acts like oil-based varnish but is tougher. Polyurethane gel is simply a thicker version of the same thing in a suspended binder.

Water-based polyurethane, sometimes called waterborne, is an emulsion of resins in water and solvent. It dries fast and behaves more like lacquer than varnish.

Polyurethane is available in gloss, semigloss, and satin sheens. Stirring is essential for all but gloss polyurethane to keep the flatting agent mixed in the liquid. The effect of the flatting agent is cumulative, so that each additional coat dulls the surface more. To control the glossiness of your finish you may want to mix sheens, either between cans or coats.

Contrary to popular belief, polyurethane doesn't last forever, although it is more durable than most finishes. Polyurethane is vulnerable to extreme abrasion and will peel if water finds its way under the finish through cracks or open areas. For outdoor projects, reapply more coats whenever cracks begin to appear. Be sure the surface is clean and sanded lightly with 220-grit sandpaper to get a good bond before adding more coats.

If treated correctly, polyurethane can resist cracking for decades. More than anything else, this means keeping your finished piece out of direct sunlight. Strong light causes finishes to deteriorate faster than any other element, and polyurethane is especially vulnerable on projects left outdoors and exposed to sunlight.

Wiping on oil-based polyurethane will give you a thin, woody finish that is free from brush or spray marks, but water-based does not work well as a wipe-on. You can brush or spray both types of polyurethanes. Here are some guidelines to get you started.

One option for applying poly is to wipe it on, using either gel or liquid oil-based polyurethane straight from the can. Dip a fine nylon abrasive pad into the polyurethane and scrub it onto the surface of the wood. Wipe off all the excess before it dries. If you apply one coat per day, there is no need to sand between coats. Three coats will afford adequate

Opposite, left: Polyurethane is available in a number of forms: liquid, aerosol sprays, and the wipe-on polyurethane gel shown here.

Opposite, right: Pour your polyurethane into a clean container and add paint thinner if needed. After a coat is applied, tip off the excess with the brush held at 45°.

Left: Overapplying is one of the top problems with water-based finishes. To prevent this, use a foam paint pad.

Right: Sanding polyurethane between coats will remove dust nibs and other imperfections.

protection, but you can add more for a deeper-looking finish.

If you prefer to brush on the varnish, use a natural-bristle brush with oil-based polyurethane, and thin each coat about 10% or 15% with mineral spirits. Use a clean container to thin the mixture and hold it for brushing. Thinning helps create a smooth, bubble-free finish. Water-based poly requires synthetic bristle brushes, since natural bristles will splay and go limp in water. On flat surfaces, however, a paint pad works even better. It coats faster, creates fewer air bubbles, and allows you to apply thinner coats, which makes water-based coatings level better. Apply a minimum of three thin coats.

For the next two or three coats, brush the polyurethane (full strength or reduced 10%) in any direction, then hold your brush at a 45° angle and drag it lightly over the surface. This technique, called "tipping off," removes excess finish and straightens the brush lines. Applying polyurethane to a vertical surface should be done as thinly as possible so it won't sag or run. It helps to wipe your brush over the edge of a clean jar after each tipping-off stroke to squeeze out any excess finish. Continue to tip off until the finish stops sagging.

Allow each coat to cure overnight. If the weather is cold or damp, it may take longer. Test the finish by pushing your fingernail into an inconspicuous place—if it gives, you need to wait a while longer. To cut off dust nibs in the finish, lightly sand with 280-grit or finer sandpaper. If you have to wait more than a few days before you apply the next coat, it's wise to abrade the entire surface with 0000 steel wool. The fine scratches you make will give the next coat a better surface to hold on to.

Shellac

Shellac, also known as spirit varnish, was the favorite clear finish of 19th- and early 20th-century cabinetmakers. Its fast-drying properties were ideal for production furniture as well as interior woodwork. These days, modern coatings have made shellac the dinosaur of finishes, but there are still plenty of reasons to use it.

Shellac is made from the resinous secretion of the lac bug and processed into paper-thin sheets, which are broken into flakes that readily dissolve in denatured alcohol. Shellac's color falls anywhere from dark amber to clear—the darker the color the less refined the process. Darker tones are favored for use on dark woods, while bleached or blond shellac (clear) works best on light-colored woods.

Shellac has a mixed reputation for durability. On the downside, it is vulnerable to moisture damage. Most of us know that leaving a wet glass on a shellac finish will result in a white ring. Worse, spills from alcoholic drinks can severely damage the finish. In addition, direct sunlight and ammonia-based cleaners can also degrade, soften, or ruin the finish.

Shellac's short shelf life is another detraction. Any mixed material over six months old should be tested, even if the manufacturer claims the product remains usable for two or three years. Once brushed on a surface, old shellac can remain sticky for days, or it may appear dry to the touch but mar significantly under even slight pressure.

Shellac does, however, offer its share of benefits. When used appropriately, shellac finishes have lasted 100 to 150 years. If applied prior to paint or varnish, shellac seals in knots, silicone, and other blemishes like ink stains. As a thin wash coat, shellac is unsurpassed for sealing pine and other porous woods to prevent a splotchy or uneven appearance. Shellac dries to a hard, sandable surface in an hour or two, which allows finishers to get a jump on a project by using it for the first coat.

Unlike varnish, each coat of shellac melts into the underlying layers, eliminating any chance of between-layer failure, as is possible with polyurethane. Shellac is extremely clear—a benefit for highlighting the wood grain—and it doesn't darken significantly over time. Aside from imparting a warm, attractive tone to the wood, shellac brings out the depth of figured woods. It also polishes easily, and in moderate amounts the fumes are innocuous. If the finish gets scratched, it's also easy to repair by simply cleaning the surface and brushing on a few more coats. Provided the wood is in good condition, no more prep work is necessary.

Shellac is typically available from paint stores in a 3-pound cut; this means that 3 pounds of flakes were mixed with one gallon of alcohol. For greater mixing options, and to ensure freshness, buy shellac flakes (available from woodworking mail order suppliers) and mix them with denatured alcohol in any strength you desire. Proportions for different cuts are usually provided on the instructions that come with the shellac to make this process easier.

Always pour the amount you need in a separate container, and never return leftover material to the original container or you might contaminate

Bottom left: Shellac is available as dry flakes or buttons that are mixed with alcohol, or ready-to-use in a can.

Right, from top: Mixing shellac: Fill a jar half-full with dry shellac. Pour in denatured alcohol till full. Screw on the lid and shake the jar frequently for the next two hours or so, then leave it overnight. By morning it should be ready to use, but stir it to make sure all the shellac is dissolved. Remember to put a date on the jar and use it within six months.

the whole batch. For finish coats use shellac full-strength, but thin it for the first or sealer coats. Thinning proportions depend on the porosity of the wood; four or five parts alcohol to one part 3-pound-cut shellac is typical.

Shellac is sensitive to humidity and moisture, and on a damp day it might dry with a milky white haze called blushing. Blushing normally clears up when the air dries out. If it persists, try a quick pass of a blow dryer and thin your next coat. If the thinned coat blushes, give up until the weather is more favorable.

To apply shellac use a soft, natural-bristle brush. Load the brush liberally with material and flow it on in one direction going with the grain, making parallel paths across the surface. Shellac cannot be worked in or brushed out, so small brushes will hinder your progress. To prevent sags or runs as you are finishing furniture, try turning the piece so you are always working on a horizontal surface. It's a good idea to practice your technique on scrap wood first.

When you are finished, clean your brush with denatured alcohol and a final rinse of lacquer thinner, then wrap it in a cover made from a brown paper bag. This will preserve the brush's shape and keep out dust. One final note: Never contaminate your shellac or varnish brushes by using them in paint, and be sure to date any leftover shellac so you will know how old it is down the road.

Another application option is to apply shellac by hand using a simple pad. Turn a soft, lint-free cloth into an application pad by folding the corners into the center (an old T-shirt works well for this purpose). Repeat the process a couple of times until you have a round, full pad to work with. Dip it into the shellac and wipe the finish smoothly onto the surface. Padded shellac dries very quickly, so work in small areas, keeping the pad moving smoothly, and without overwiping. You can add a drop of mineral oil to the bottom of your pad to help it slide more easily.

Each coat of shellac is extremely thin, so build up several coats before smoothing them with an extra-fine sandpaper or an abrasive pad. Repeat this process a couple of times and let the finish cure overnight. Then wipe it down with a cloth dampened

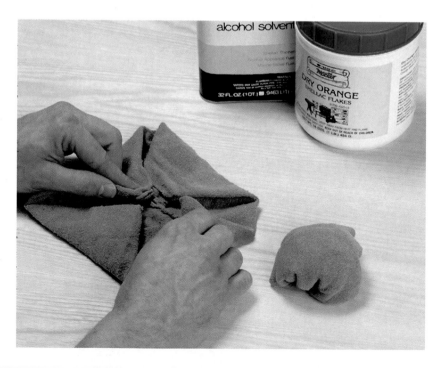

with naphtha (not alcohol!) to remove the mineral oil residue.

Shellac is also sold in aerosol cans. Spray it on in thin, overlapping coats to build up a durable film. Let each coat dry thoroughly before reapplying.

Lacquer

Lacquer finishes are not just for the pros, and you do not need fancy spray equipment or a dedicated spray booth to apply lacquer successfully. Brush-on formulations are quite "novice friendly." Brushing lacquer doesn't apply the same as ordinary varnish, but the technique is easy to master—and no finish dries faster. You may not have thought of lacquer as a brushable finish. In fact, it's usually sprayed because it cures too fast to be brushed. To make lacquer brushable, manufacturers slow the curing time by dissolving the lacquer in slower-evaporating solvents.

Another low-tech application option is to buy premixed aerosol lacquer and spray it on in several light overlapping coats.

Using lacquer has advantages and disadvantages. One the plus side, lacquer, even brushing lacquer, cures very fast. This reduces dust problems and allows you to apply two or three coats in a day. Another advantage is that unlike varnish, lacquer doesn't require sanding between coats. Each new coat of lacquer partially dissolves and fuses with the previous coat to make a perfect bond. You only have to sand to remove dust nibs or to level other flaws in the finish.

Lacquer's principal disadvantage is that it isn't as durable as varnish. Coarse objects will scratch it. Hot objects, such as coffee cups, will leave an imprint. Solvents, such as fingernail-polish remover, and strong alkalis, such as ammonia, will dissolve it. Therefore, on heavily used surfaces, such as tabletops, you still may prefer varnish. Lacquer also emits strong-smelling, flammable solvents as it cures. Be sure to wear a vapor respirator when working with lacquer, and apply it in a well-ventilated area.

Brushing lacquer comes in two sheens—gloss and semigloss. The semigloss is best for most situations and produces an

Opposite:
Turn a soft, lint-free cloth into a shellac application pad by folding the corners into the center. Repeat the process a couple of times until you have a round, full pad to work with.

Below left: Even without special spray equipment, you can still achieve a great lacquer finish with a brush-on formulation.

DEFT®

SEMI-GLOSS
CLEAR WOOD FINISH
DRIES IN 30 MINUTES
SEALS & FINISHES · INTERIOR
DANGER! FLAMMABLE. KEEP FROM HEAT OR FLAME. HARMFUL OR FATAL IF SWALLOWED — VAPOR HARMFUL. See cautions elsewhere on can.

attractive sheen without rubbing. The best applicator is a natural-bristle brush with flagged bristles. Flagged bristles are split on their ends so they feel soft and apply the finish smoothly. Don't use a sponge brush or the lacquer will dissolve it.

There are three tricks to brushing lacquer. First, apply the finish liberally in wet coats; second, move fast; and third, avoid brushing over areas that have begun to set up, even if you've missed a small spot. This differs from the way you brush polyurethane. With polyurethane you spread the finish over a large surface and then smooth it with long straight strokes running with the grain. With brushing lacquer you need to get each stroke pretty close to right the first time—no tipping off here.

For this reason it's important to practice applying brushing lacquer to scrap wood first. Once you've practiced, get started by brushing on your first coat of lacquer. There's no need to thin the lacquer unless the manufacturer recommends it, and with some brands you don't need to apply a separate sanding sealer first.

Let the lacquer cure for at least two hours. You'll notice that the surface feels rough; that is because, as with any finish, the first coat locks raised wood fibers in place. Sand the surface lightly with 280-grit or finer sandpaper just enough to make it feel smooth. Remove sanding dust with a brush, vacuum, or tack cloth, then brush on at least two full-strength coats, allowing a minimum of two hours' drying time between each coat. If you miss a place and the finish has begun to set up, don't go back and fill it in. You'll just cause more damage. Wait until the finish cures, sand the area smooth, then apply another coat. No matter what problems occur, you can always sand out the damage and apply another coat.

Clean your brush thoroughly with lacquer thinner in a well-ventilated area, then wash the brush with soap and water. Wrap the brush in heavy paper so the bristles dry straight, and store the brush in a drawer or hanging

from a hook. If lacquer hardens on the brush, just soak it in lacquer thinner to prepare it for use again.

RUBBING OUT A FINISH

As counterintuitive as it may seem, rubbing out a finish actually involves scratching your final topcoat to achieve various levels of sheen. Aside from producing millions of minute scratches, rubbing also removes trapped bits of microscopic dust and lint. Each successive grit rubs out the previous grit's scratches, in order to work toward a mirrorlike sheen.

Rubbing out works best with varnish and lacquer, because both in their raw form are high-gloss products. To achieve the clearest, smoothest, and hardest finish by rubbing out, you must start with a high-gloss product and then rub it out with abrasives.

One precaution applies to whatever degree of sheen you are after: Make sure the finish is completely cured before starting. Use your nose as a guide; if you smell the slightest hint of solvent remaining in the topcoat, it's not ready. Give varnish two weeks to a month to cure in dry weather. Lacquer will typically be ready in about a week.

Creating a satin sheen

To achieve a low-luster, velvety surface, use a felt sanding block, 400-grit wet/dry sandpaper, and mineral spirits as a lubricant to sand the final coat of high-gloss finish. Rub evenly and without bearing down forcefully.

When the initial gloss is removed, buff the surface briskly with 0000 steel wool and rubbing compound. Rub the corners and edges gingerly to prevent cutting through the finish. Rubbing compounds for woodworking are available from a variety of manufacturers, but automotive rubbing compound will also work. Then wipe away any remaining compound residue with a soft, dry cloth.

Building a high-gloss sheen

Building a high-gloss finish is a slightly different process. Start by abrading the surface with 400-grit wet/dry sandpaper and mineral spirits. Wet-sand the surface thoroughly so that no shiny spots remain.

The usual compounds for rubbing to a high-gloss finish are pumice stone (a lightweight volcanic ash), rottenstone (decomposed limestone), and rubbing oil (paraffin-based oil). All are available at paint stores or from woodworking suppliers. Start with a soft, dry felt pad to thoroughly rub the finish with pumice and oil. Clean the surface, and follow by rubbing with rottenstone and oil. The more you rub, the higher the sheen will become. A high-speed buffer outfitted with a wool bonnet can speed the process. Check your work carefully to find imperfections and in order to avoid burning through the edges and corners.

When you are satisfied with the sheen, wipe the surface clean with a very soft cloth. You should remember that a high-gloss finish is difficult to maintain. Even the slightest bit of damage will be clearly evident.

Finish up with wax

Top off your rubbed finish with a coat of paste wax and another round of buffing to give it a silky smooth feel. Rubbing out a finish takes time and lots of elbow grease.

However, a flawless finish is worth all the effort you invest, especially on a gorgeous piece of furniture you have built from scratch.

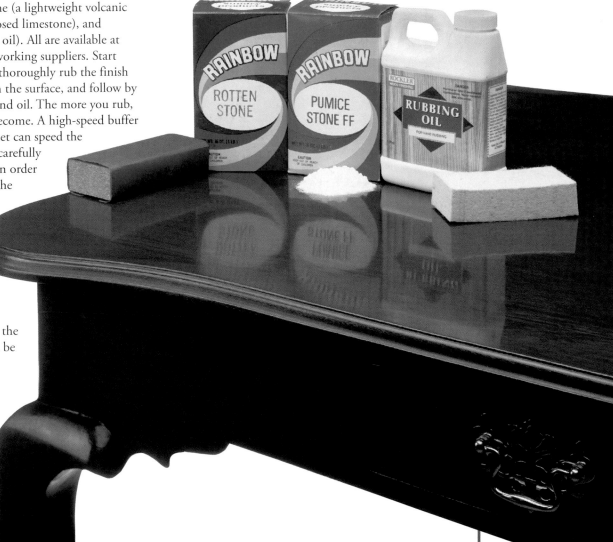

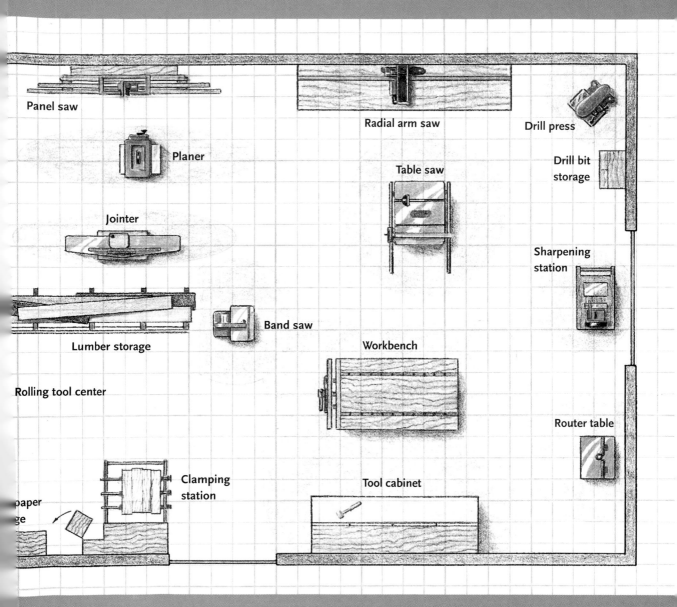

Panel saw

Radial arm saw

Drill press

Planer

Table saw

Drill bit
storage

Jointer

Sharpening
station

Lumber storage

Band saw

Workbench

Rolling tool center

Router table

paper
ge

Clamping
station

Tool cabinet

Set

San
stor

CHAPTER 16

Setting Up Shop

Setting Up Shop

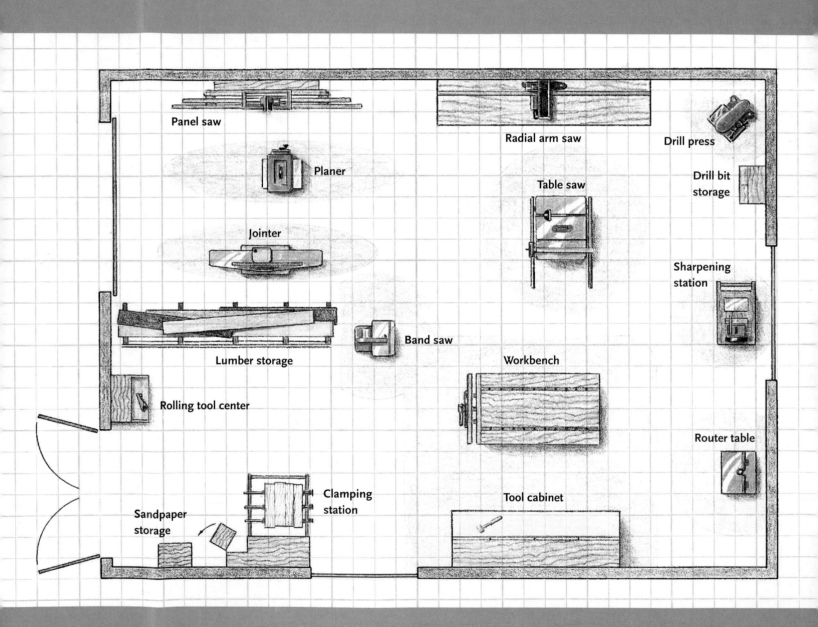

Panel saw

Radial arm saw

Drill press

Planer

Drill bit storage

Table saw

Jointer

Sharpening station

Lumber storage

Band saw

Workbench

Rolling tool center

Router table

Sandpaper storage

Clamping station

Tool cabinet

There are several unwritten rules that apply to buildings in general, and to workshops in particular. The first is that you will quickly fill whatever space you have. The second is that almost as soon as you move into a space, you will think of ways to improve it. If you cannot afford to build the workshop of your dreams all at once, don't give up. Dreams change, and you may be happier in the end with an incremental approach.

Almost every woodworker yearns for more elbow room and harbors a secret wish list of tools. But even an airplane hangar stocked with expensive woodworking equipment is no guarantee of an effective workspace. Indeed, a well-designed, pint-sized shop—whether it's stuffed in a basement, a garage, or a closet—can be a lot more pleasant and functional than a large, disorganized shop, especially if the extra area only provides room to spread out your mess.

There are a few core principles that can help make the process of planning a workshop less intimidating, the first of which is to personalize the layout.

PLANNING YOUR SHOP

Begin the layout process by reviewing critically and carefully the work you plan to do, the machinery you have or think you need, and, of course, your budget. Consider the way you work: What kinds of operations will you perform repeatedly or only occasionally? How much wood will you use, and is it primarily lumber or plywood? How can materials flow through the space most efficiently, from their arrival and storage to the completed project? Are there particular tasks, like finishing, that have special requirements and are best performed in a separate, dedicated area of your shop?

The best tool to use in planning your shop is a pencil—the more mistakes you address on paper, the fewer you will have to wrestle with on the shop floor. Make a list of every machine you own or plan to buy, and include a scaled diagram of its footprint and what you might call its "sphere of influence." That is the zone needed around each machine to accommodate not just the infeed and outflow, but the comfortable manipulation of any material that will normally occupy the area.

For example, as you review the path required to move a 4' x 8' sheet of plywood or a 10' board to the table saw, you may discover that your allotted space is simply too tight. You could move the machine or install removable doors in an obstructing wall to provide a pass-through for long boards. Or you might decide to create an intermediate "breakdown lane," in which materials can be ripped or crosscut to their approximate dimensions before they leave the storage area. That way you move smaller pieces around the shop, more safely and with a lot less effort and clutter.

In such a layout, lumber might enter the shop through a door, where it is immediately loaded into a storage rack. The rack flanks a miter saw or radial arm saw, which is used to cut the wood to rough length before other operations are performed. Directly across the corridor a band saw and a jointer can further reduce stock to workable dimensions before it enters the primary production area. Offcuts remain in the breakdown lane, where they are sorted, stored, or carted off through the same door the wood entered.

Plan your shop's workspace carefully, allowing as much room as needed for material movement around machinery.

A breakdown area in Kelly Mehler's Berea, Kentucky, shop allows him to start the machining process on materials as they enter the building.

Workshop triangles

A breakdown lane embodies one of the cardinal planning tools of any workspace designer: the work triangle. (The kitchen triangle—representing the relationship between sink, stove, and refrigerator—is the most common example.)

The traffic flow between a band saw, radial arm saw, and jointer defines a functional triangle, and it makes good sense to think about all your work areas in the same way, and not just those surrounding your machinery.

The most basic work triangle in the shop is defined by the relationship between the workbench, tool storage, and assembly areas. Their relative positions will vary widely, depending on the space available and the nature of your tools and work. Where the work is small and refined, the tools may be placed on the bench. Assembly stations are usually within easy reach, sometimes bolted right to the bench.

In a larger, multipurpose shop, hand tools might line the walls behind one bench, while a lower setup table is only a few feet away. For a wide variety of projects, this provides an ideal triangulation between hand-tool storage, workbench and vises, and an ample assembly area.

Work triangles are conceptual, so their geometry should not be taken literally. In a dedicated cabinet shop, a typical arrangement may include a radial arm saw and two miter saws placed in tandem on a long bench, with the radial arm saw permanently set to make 90° cuts, and the miter saws fixed at opposite 45° angles for slicing miters. With blades stored above and rolling scrap bins beneath the table, a workstation with this sort of arrangement is ideally suited for the repeated tasks performed in making frame-and-panel cabinets.

Sometimes the best work "triangle" is defined by a circle, with machinery arranged in a compact ring around a central dust collector. It is an effective, economical arrangement for a tight space, servicing a table saw, planer, jointer, belt sander, and other machines, oriented so that incoming and outgoing stock is fed at a tangent to the circle. Table heights can be staggered to allow work to pass unobstructed above or below the tables on adjacent machinery. Alternatively, you could arrange all machine tables at the same height to provide extended infeed and outfeed support for large stock.

Flexibility

From time to time, you can expect to encounter a project that calls for unusually long or bulky materials. It's often impossible to plan in advance for such occasions, but you can build flexibility into your layout to minimize disruption. This is especially important in small workshops, where available space is usually more limited and the range of projects may be much greater than in a full-time professional studio.

One of the best ways to incorporate flexibility into your shop is to arrange most of your large power tools around the perimeter of the workspace. Jointers and planers require only infeed and outfeed space, plus enough room on one side for the operator and a normal flow of material. The same holds true for the radial arm saw, miter saw, and band saw. The table saw is the one exception, because it requires ample space on all four sides. Its sphere of influence is by far the largest of any stationary tool, but the table saw's all-around capabilities also make it the most used machine in most shops. For maximum flexibility, mount the table saw on casters in the center of the shop floor, so that it can be easily transported as the need arises.

If your shop space is exceptionally small, you might consider putting all your machines on casters. That way, tools used only occasionally can be kept tucked into a corner with no consideration for operator or stock-feed areas, and wheeled out when

needed. Even a large tool like a lathe would occupy minimal space when not in use, freeing room for machines used more frequently.

When on wheels, long tools like lathes and jointers take up less working space when not left in a typical operating position. For example, a jointer needs a good bit of infeed and outfeed room when actually being used, so floor areas must be clear and open at each end of the machine. However, when not in use, a jointer can be left in generally the same spot but angled in such a way as to free up maneuvering space. Likewise, smaller machines can be wheeled out of the way into the jointer's unused infeed and outfeed areas.

SHOP LIGHTING CONSIDERATIONS

Lots of natural lighting can keep electric bills down but can also be a mixed blessing in the workshop. Strong highlights and shadows are hard on the eyes, and ultraviolet rays can affect the color of most wood species. A wet board may warp like a potato chip if left too long in direct sunlight. Soft, indirect illumination can be achieved by placing windows high on a south wall or where they will receive a northern exposure. Indirect northern light is especially desirable at the bench or in a finishing area.

When it comes to artificial light, fluorescent fixtures are generally inexpensive to install and operate and provide the best overall illumination. You may be happy with regular tubes, but full-spectrum fluorescent lamps offer accurate color rendition and can be well worth the extra cost. For true colors and good working comfort, look for lamps with a color rendering index (CRI) above 80. If you can afford the small investment, compact fluorescent bulbs use regular screw-in type light sockets and offer as much light as some incandescents at a fraction of the wattage.

Many woodworkers prefer incandescent bulbs, especially for task lighting. Clip-on lamps with large reflectors or student desk lamps with articulated shafts are highly adaptable. Halogen bulbs cost more than standard incandescents but are an excellent choice wherever stronger light and truer color rendition are desired. Keep in mind that halogen bulbs can create a lot of heat, so you probably don't want to mount them too close to working surfaces.

Whatever you choose, a comprehensive lighting plan will help you locate fixtures for the best unobstructed illumination at each tool or workstation.

MATERIAL STORAGE OPTIONS

Lumber is best stored off the floor and on a rack, especially if the floor is damp. A rack is also safer than standing boards on end against a wall, which can lead to a shop hazard if they are bumped and knocked over like 8' dominoes.

Lumber storage is an issue for any size workshop. What starts out long or wide ends up as much shorter offcuts that are sometimes too valuable to throw away. A good lumber rack needs to stow the large material so it is easy to load and unload, while also storing shorter pieces so they are easy to sort and see. Here are two options for full-duty lumber racks, plus a simpler bracket system. One of these styles is sure to suit your shop.

Mobile lumber rack

This mobile rack is designed to store all the essentials: full sheets of plywood and composites, partial sheets, long lengths of lumber, and short lengths. The rack is mounted on casters so it can be moved out of the way when necessary.

The key to the design is a wide and stable base platform, upon which the rack is built. The platform is a 2 x 4 frame topped off with a ½"-thick piece of plywood or oriented strand board (OSB) skin. Four 4" heavy-duty casters are attached to the bottom of the frame—two fixed casters at one end and a pair of swivel casters at the other. The rack steers somewhat like a car.

A 2 x 4 is attached vertically to the platform about halfway across each end. In front of these posts, a couple of bins with angled tops provide storage for short lengths of lumber and partial sheets. Behind the posts is a space for full sheets of plywood and other sheet goods. On top of this rear compartment is a rack for long lengths of lumber, pipe, and other awkward stock.

Stationary lumber rack

The key to the second lumber storage system is standard 1" inside-diameter (ID) black gas pipe. Three lengths of pipe run from floor to ceiling, each positioned 42" away from its neighbor.

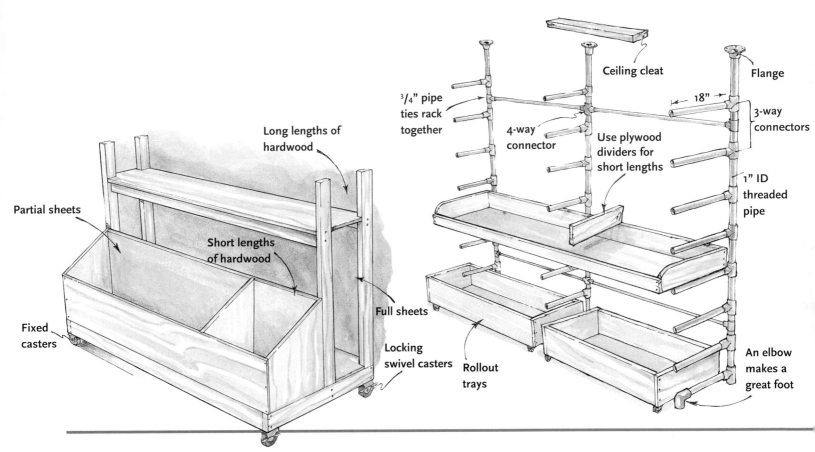

Long lengths of
hardwood

Partial sheets

Short lengths
of hardwood

Fixed
casters

Full sheets

Locking
swivel casters

Rollout
trays

¾" pipe
ties rack
together

Ceiling cleat

4-way
connector

Use plywood
dividers for
short lengths

Flange

18"

3-way
connectors

1" ID
threaded
pipe

An elbow
makes a
great foot

**Two wood-
storage
solutions**

These are not continuous lengths—T-shaped connectors are installed at various intervals along the pipe, including one at floor level. Tie these three uprights together with ¾" ID pipe at about 16" off the floor and the same distance from the ceiling. Anchor the rack using circular metal pipe flanges, screwing them to cleats between the ceiling joists.

To convert this skeleton into a rack, screw a 21"-long threaded pipe into each of the T-shaped connectors in each upright. Then, to provide a stable base, use short elbows to cap off the lowest piece of pipe and create feet for the unit. With the pipes in place, build the rest of the system with plywood.

Two plywood boxes measuring 9" x 30" x 40" roll in under the rack, each mounted on a set of four 1 ½" casters. These boxes hold short pieces of hardwood and softwood. Above them, two pairs of pipe arms support 8' lengths of thicker lumber.

Each of the next three sets of arms supports an 8' x 24" tray to hold stock measuring from 3' to 7' long, while the spaces above the trays are reserved for stock over 8'.

Three trays should be sufficient to manage all the medium-length stock in a serious hobby shop. These are made of ½" plywood, glued and screwed together. Round over a radius on the top front corner of each end piece to avoid catching yourself on a sharp corner or splintering the plywood.

Insert dividers in the trays if you wish to further organize wood by species, thickness, or other characteristics pertinent to your work.

Wall-mounted lumber rack

Here is an option for a space-saving, low-tech lumber rack that you can build easily in an afternoon. Metal L-brackets, available in most home centers, serve as shelf brackets here. You can also use them as connection points for continuous wood shelving. Look for brackets that are at least 7-gauge steel for maximum strength. Mount these brackets directly to the wall studs with lag screws if your shop walls have exposed studs. For drywall-sheathed walls, screw the brackets onto lengths of 2 x 2 lumber and bolt these to the wall studs instead. Make sure the lag screws are driven at least 2" into the studs, and use fender washers to help distribute the weight.

TOOL AND SUPPLY STORAGE

Nothing beats cabinets for storing finishing supplies, locking up tools, or stashing items that just can't be hung on the wall.

When it comes to shop-specific cabinetry, several manufacturers offer ready-made cabinets geared to total shop organization. Among the options are floor-standing wall lockers, wall-mounted upper cabinets, or rolling-base cabinets equipped with adjustable shelving or drawers. Cabinet construction can be steel beams and panels, wood, or laminated MDF or particleboard. Some commercially available shop cabinets feature built-in pegboard grids for even more storage and ventilation.

Some manufacturers offer integrated cabinet

systems that incorporate steel or wood workbenches with base cabinets stowed underneath the bench.

Other modular cabinets feature removable inserts on top—benchtop tools like miter saws, grinders, sanders, or a drill press can be mounted to the inserts to turn the cabinets into interchangeable tool workstations. The inserts slide into racks for storing the tools when not in use.

Wall organizers

Pegboard is probably the most widely used material when it comes to tool storage. Inexpensive, easy to cut and use, it's hard to beat. However, if you are tired of losing the hooks each time you pull a tool off the wall, try some of the new unbreakable, nylon pegboard hooks in numerous styles that lock in place with a pair of anchors and a push-in screw. The hooks can be removed with a screwdriver and used again and again.

One of the newest types of wall storage systems

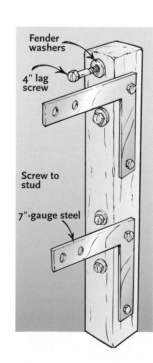

uses PVC panels with rows of L-shaped channels that hold specialized organizers. Similar to wall displays in retail stores, the panels come in a variety of sizes and colors and lock together to form larger panels with a seamless look. You can cut the panels with ordinary saws and mount them to walls with color-matched drywall screws. These wall panels are sold in bulk or packaged into kits with a selection of organizers. Accompanying bins, racks, and hooks are also sold separately, as are cabinets that mount on the L-channels.

For another wall storage option, consider magnetic bars that screw to wall studs or stick to the sides of metal cabinets. They are ideal for hanging any ferrous-metal tools, such as squares, rules, paint scrapers, and chisels. Nearly every woodworking supplier sells them, but you can also find them in kitchen stores.

Cord and air-hose winders

Extension cords can be a hazard when tangled underfoot. Keep them under control with cord winders, wall- or ceiling-mounted retractable reels, or low-cost and reusable cable clamps and hook-and-loop bow ties.

Air hoses for your pneumatic tools can also be a nuisance, unless you follow the lead of auto mechanics and switch to a retractable air-hose reel. These come with both hose and reel in a single wall- or ceiling-mount unit. They are not inexpensive, but sometimes convenience is worth every penny to eliminate a hassle. You can also buy a basic wind-up reel to stow the standard air hose you have now.

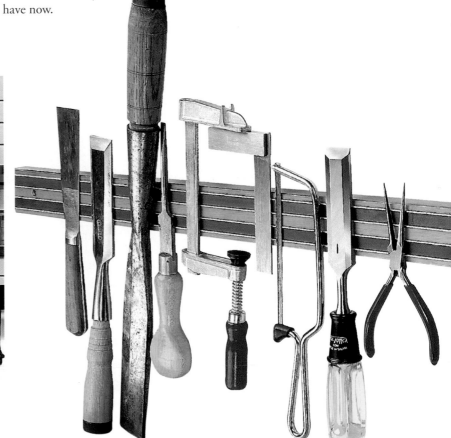

Storage boxes can keep router bits secure and nick-free.

Blade, bit, and clamp storage

The quickest way to chip carbide tips, next to dropping them, is to toss blades and bits in a drawer. Protect your investment and keep your router bits organized by making or buying a bit storage box. Wood boxes can be made or purchased and outfitted with perforated foam liners that can hold a variety of router bits. Woodworkers who have a lot of bits might consider a wall-mounted case with removable shelves drilled to hold bits securely.

Plastic cases for saw blades are inexpensive, and most have a wing nut to secure the blade, which fits into a shallow recess to protect the teeth. Blades can also be hung in a small cabinet, or slipped into a shop-made holder similar to a CD rack.

While the shop adage about never having too many clamps is true, sooner or later you need to organize them. A wall rack is easy to make for bar and pipe clamps by simply cutting slots into a board that acts as a shelf. Size the slots so that they fit the bar or pipe but are smaller than the clamping mechanisms. Mount the board just as you would a small shelf, slip the clamps into the slots, and slide them closed to hold them in place.

Small-part organizers

The black hole of shop storage has to be those cardboard boxes, drawers, or plastic baggies filled with endless varieties of leftover fasteners, plugs, dowel pins, biscuits, and other small parts. Plastic storage organizers are incredibly

inexpensive, come in a huge range in the number and size of drawers, and are available in any hardware store or home center. Many can be wall-mounted or stacked to form larger units. Identify the contents of each drawer by using hot-melt glue to attach a representative part to the front of the drawer. The hot-melt glue holds the part securely to the drawer front but snaps off easily should you decide to change the contents.

CARE OF SHOP MACHINERY

One of the first requirements in maintaining any machine is to clean it thoroughly—performing any kind of tune-up is a difficult and dirty job if machine components are caked in layers of dust. Of course, a general cleaning of machines after each use is always a good practice, but internal dust and debris can build up after a while even in the neatest of shops.

Different machines have different nooks and crannies where debris accumulates, even those

Every day (of use):

- ☐ Empty shop garbage cans and any open dust bins.
- ☐ Clean out rag storage cans; hang rags soaked with oil finish out to dry.
- ☐ Lubricate air-powered tools and/or refill reservoirs on automatic oilers.

Every week:

- ☐ Clean sawdust from shop floors and benches.
- ☐ Drain moisture from air compressor tanks, pipes, and manifold, and filter/moisture traps.
- ☐ Shake dust collector filter bags to remove excess dust cake (more often if necessary).
- ☐ Empty sawdust from dust collector bags or bins (more often if necessary).
- ☐ Empty shop vacuum and clean filter (more often if necessary).

Every month:

- ☐ Vacuum fine dust from tops of light fixtures and out of electrical outlets, switches, and junction boxes.
- ☐ Vacuum prefilters on air filtration devices.
- ☐ Clean out any tables or machines not connected to dust collection.
- ☐ Clean off built-up finish on spray guns, spray booth walls, etc.
- ☐ Check condition of air filter and oil level in air compressor (latter not required for oilless models).
- ☐ Test and reset ground-fault circuit interrupter (GFCI) outlets.

Twice a year:

- ☐ Inspect condition of machines and portable power tools; service as needed.
- ☐ Check fire extinguishers; recharge or replace as necessary.
- ☐ Change oil in air compressor pump (oilless compressors exempt).
- ☐ Treat metal surfaces on tools with rust-preventive spray or wax.
- ☐ Check compressed air system (tank, hoses, and fittings) for leaks.
- ☐ Check condition of filter bags/cartridges on dust collectors, air cleaners, and shop vacuums; replace as necessary.
- ☐ Inspect central dust collection system ductwork and hoses for air leaks or clogs.
- ☐ Check first-aid kit for completeness; refresh supplies as necessary.
- ☐ Check condition of glues and finishes; properly discard products that are old, dried out, or partially cured in container.
- ☐ Check shop for leaks or moisture that may ruin tools and stored lumber and supplies.

hooked up to central dust collection systems, but these general guidelines apply to all. Every door and panel should be opened, and accumulated debris vacuumed out. In areas where dust has caked, especially in gears or mountings, a stiff brush may be needed to loosen dust before vacuuming. For machines with lower compartments, such as cabinet saws and band saws, be sure to clean all the way to the bottom. Clean underneath the machine, being wary of debris other than sawdust—you may be surprised how many loose screws, nails, and other items have managed to hide there.

In the following sections, we will take a close look at maintaining and tuning the four main shop machines: table saw, band saw, planer, and jointer. And while their specific care will vary, consider a thorough cleaning inside and out to be an important part of maintaining and adjusting each of them. In fact, when tuning up any one of these pieces of equipment, a thorough cleaning should be the second step.

The first step is *always* unplugging them prior to any and all maintenance.

TABLE SAW MAINTENANCE

As the center of most shops, the table saw requires special attention when it comes to keeping it in good running order. All shop machines play a role in woodworking, but because the table saw is often the first machine used when processing lumber, proper performance of other machines depends on the table saw being accurate and reliable.

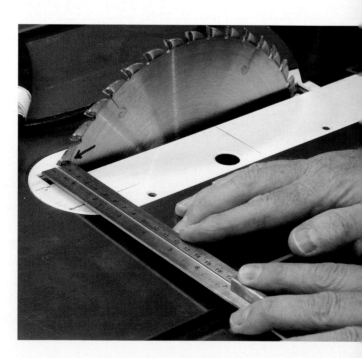

Blade alignment

The first item to check is the blade alignment. Because most cuts on a table saw register off the miter slots to maintain squareness, it is essential that the blade be perfectly parallel to the slots.

To determine blade alignment, set the blade at 90° and raise it to full height. Select a tooth at the front of the blade and mark its location on the plate. Now use a combination square to measure the exact distance from the side of the selected tooth and the closest edge of the miter slot. This is easiest if you loosen the square and use the miter slot itself as a registration point, extend the square's ruler until it just touches the side of the tooth, then lock the square. Rotate the blade by hand so the same tooth is now at the back, and slide the square down the miter slot to the tooth. If the distance is exactly the same, no adjustment is necessary.

If the distance is not the same, the blade must be aligned. For cabinet saws and some hybrid saws where the blade trunnions are attached to the cabinet, this is simply a matter of loosening the table and rotating it slightly until the blade is in line with the miter slot. For benchtop, contractor's, and hybrid saws with trunnions attached to the underside of the table, the trunnions must be loosened and adjusted accordingly. Table-mounted trunnions vary in configuration and bolt location, so check your owner's manual.

Fence alignment

For accurate rip cuts—and to prevent binding during cuts—the fence must also be aligned with the miter slot. Clamp a length of ¾" hardwood into the slot and slide the fence until it touches the wood. If the fence touches the wood along its full length, it is aligned and no adjustment is needed.

If the fence is not aligned, loosen it. Your fence is attached to its mount with a series of bolts; check your manual for their precise location. With the loosened fence held against the wood, retighten the bolts.

Blade angle

The adjustment wheel on the front of your saw likely has positive stops at 90° and 45°. Raise the blade to its full height and set the blade at these stops, then check the accuracy of the angles with a reliable square. If the angles are not accurate, you will need to reset the positive stops. Your saw's adjustment wheel will have a set-screw arrangement that locks in the stop angles. The location and configuration vary depending on the saw, so again use your owner's manual as a guide to locating and adjusting them. Set the blade close to the desired angle, loosen the set screw(s), and then set the saw to the correct angle using a reliable square as a guide. With the blade set correctly, retighten the set screw(s).

Since you already have your square out, this is also a good time to check that the splitter is square to the table and directly in line with the blade. Adjust as needed.

**Opposite:
Check blade alignment by measuring the distance between the blade and miter slot at both the front and back of the blade.**

Left: Loosen the fence, align with the miter slot, and retighten. Note how a piece of hardwood rests in the slot to act as a register.

Throat plate

A table saw's throat plate must be perfectly flush to the table surface. If it's too low, the workpiece will not receive adequate support during a cut; too high and the workpiece will catch on the plate and be lifted slightly off the table surface.

Remove the plate and clean any dust or debris from the mounting points (there will usually be four—one at each corner). Replace the plate and adjust each set screw in turn until the plate is flush with the surface.

Note that if the throat plate's set screws do not fit tightly, even the slightest vibration can cause them to move and quickly make the plate unflush. Some beeswax in the screw threads can tighten the fit.

Table surface

The cast-iron table on your saw—and on all your machines—should be smooth, clean of rust, and free of dried glue or other obstructions. If you use your table saw as an assembly table (many woodworkers do), check for glue frequently.

Scrape off all glue, dried finish, and debris; rust can be removed with steel wool or fine sandpaper. With the surface clean, a thorough going-over with fine steel wool will bring it to a nice shine. For further

protection, a coat of paste wax or a commercial cast-iron treatment compound can be applied as a last step.

BAND SAW MAINTENANCE

A band saw is a tremendously versatile and useful tool—but only if it's running well. Properly set up, it allows you to create poetry out of wood. Tuning up your band saw is not a huge undertaking.

Additional cleaning

You have already cleaned the machine (that's the second step for machinery maintenance, remember, right after unplugging it), but the band saw needs an extra cleaning step other machines do not require. Open both the top and lower blade covers and closely examine the surface of the tires covering the wheels. Sawdust has a habit of becoming trapped beneath the blade as it rotates, and the blade pressure tends to mash the sawdust into the rubber surface of the tires.

To clean the tires, first remove the blade. Then, spinning the wheels by hand, drag a stiff wire brush or some 100-grit sandpaper along the tire as it spins to remove the embedded debris. With the tires clean, give them a good inspection. If the rubber appears overly dry or shows any cracking, the tires should be replaced. With everything in order, replace the blade.

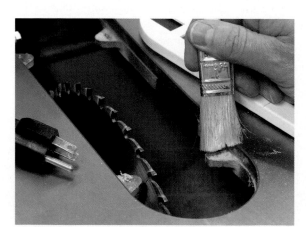

Thrust bearings

Most band saws have a system of thrust bearings—small metal wheels that the blade's back edge bumps into, keeping the blade from flexing backward during a cut. Their placement must be precise for the saw to function properly. Always check them whenever the blade has been replaced or adjusted, as they may no longer be in the correct position.

To adjust the bearings, first loosen the set screws that hold the guide blocks in place, and back the blocks out until they no longer touch the blade. Then back the thrust bearings off the rear of the blade about ¼". With everything out of the way, center the blade on the wheels by rotating the top wheel by hand as you adjust the machine's tracking control to shift the blade to the crown (top of the arch) of whichever wheel adjusts the tracking—usually the top wheel. This is a good time to reset blade tension if needed, according to the blade manufacturer's specifications.

With the blade properly centered, adjust the thrust bearings forward so they just barely touch the back edge of the blade. Ideally, when the saw is running, your blade will just tick the thrust bearings until you start to cut; the pressure of that action will drive the blade back to press against the bearings fully.

Guide blocks

While well-adjusted thrust bearings keep the blade from moving front to back, guide blocks control blade twisting and limit side-to-side movement. If your guide blocks are showing wear, replace them. Worn blocks ruin good saw blades. The best replacements are phenolic resin guides imbedded with graphite. They are superior to metal or wooden guide blocks in preventing wear and overheating.

The most important thing to remember in adjusting the guide blocks is that their position should change whenever you adjust or recenter the

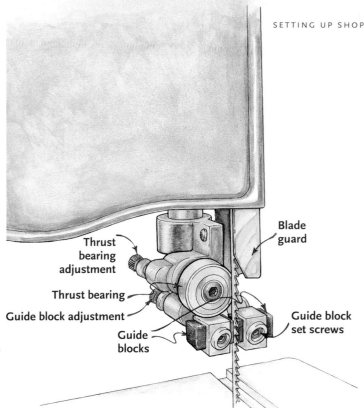

blade, and with the size of the saw blade you use. Set the blocks so they capture the sides of the saw blade, but they should not engage the saw teeth even when the blade is under cutting pressure. When the blocks are in the proper position, retighten the set screws.

PLANER MAINTENANCE

Today's planers—especially the benchtop variety—are fairly easy to maintain. Outside of regular cleaning, the main task is replacing cutter-head knives when needed.

Additional cleaning

As with band saws, planers require a few additional steps beyond your regular cleaning chores. The feed rollers can pick up a lot of wood chips and debris. When planing, these chips can press into the workpiece, sometimes leaving a small indentation. Rollers can also collect sticky pitch when milling boards, compounding the problem.

Clean the rollers periodically with a rag dipped into a bit of mineral spirits. For stubborn pitch or resin buildup, mineral spirits used with a Scotch-Brite pad will do the trick. Likewise, because lumber must slide smoothly across the table, the table surface should always be clean. A coat of paste wax will lower friction considerably.

Far left: Sawdust buildup beneath a table saw's throat plate can keep it from being flush with the table.

Middle: Remove sawdust buildup on band saw tires with a wire brush as shown here, or with a piece of sandpaper.

Above: A band saw's guide blocks and thrust bearings should be checked and adjusted frequently for proper blade guidance.

(Illustration labels: Thrust bearing adjustment; Thrust bearing; Guide block adjustment; Guide blocks; Blade guard; Guide block set screws)

Although planers and jointers cut wood in the same way with spinning knives, a jointer's cutter head is rigidly mounted beneath the workpiece, with workpiece thickness irrelevant to the machine's operation. Jointers and planers both use belts to drive the cutter head, but planers also have a chain system that raises and lowers the cutter head to accommodate workpiece thickness. These chains require a specific cleaning and lubrication schedule, which is set forth in the manual for a specific machine.

Always remember when cleaning a planer's table, belts, chains, or feed rollers that everything is located very close to the cutter head. Be extremely careful when cleaning; gloves are a good idea.

Replacing knives

Unlike jointers, most planers these days use double-edged disposable blades. Further, most planers' knives are indexed with slots or pin holes that allow the knives to be dropped into perfectly registered position for fast and easy replacement. Many manufacturers include a magnetic tool for handling and installing knives, making the process even easier.

The first step in changing knives is to expose the cutter head. Models vary, so check your manual to see how this is done on your machine. With the cutter head exposed, gib screws are loosened and tightened in much the same way as with a jointer. If

your machine has double-sided knives, they can just be reversed to the sharp side, simplifying installation. For single-edged knives, or double knives with both sides dull, remove them and replace with new blades.

Indexed knives are in proper alignment as soon as mounted and can usually be tightened down and put into service immediately. Nonindexed knives should be aligned according to the specific procedure outlined in the machine's manual.

JOINTER MAINTENANCE

A new jointer is usually well-tuned when it reaches your shop, but with use the knives become dull or nicked, and the tables may need adjustment. Before maintenance, refer to your owner's manual for specific location of components and how they adjust.

Installing knives

First, be aware that freshly sharpened jointer knives are unbelievably sharp. If you are comfortable working with gloves, by all means use them; if not, be extremely careful when handling knives. If by chance you should fumble a knife during handling, it's best to simply let it fall to the floor; you may need to have the knife resharpened, but you will lessen the chance of serious injury.

Remove the dull knives by loosening the holding screws or nuts (called gib screws), and thoroughly clean the mounting slots. If you own a newer machine, your

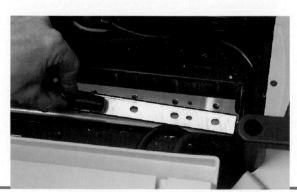

WORKBENCH PHILOSOPHY

Every shop needs a workbench, but the type of bench that appeals to you most may end up becoming a very personal choice.

Closely examined, the mundane physical objects in life—stair banisters, light switches, pots and pans—actually do have a significant history of design improvement and reflect a cultural philosophy arising from a method of work. And so it is with the workbenches of two well-known modern woodworkers, Frank Klausz and Ian Kirby.

The tradition that Klausz was raised in is simply a method of work refined by years of improvement. His European-style bench is perfectly suited to efficiently complement his woodworking techniques. An example is the tool tray: "It keeps my frequently used tools—hammer, ruler, sanding blocks, dust brush—at my fingertips. If I want to clear my bench quickly, I just push everything into the tray; at the end of the day, I put everything away and sweep any sawdust or shavings up the ramps at the ends of the tray."

Ask Kirby about the origins of his bench and he'll tell you, "Bench design and working methods go hand in hand. My bench design and the working methods I use were developed by the furniture makers of the English Arts and Crafts movement . . . and underscore the close relationship between design and methodology." The British Arts and Crafts tradition is based on the concept of beauty in simple and honest design. The right design, the right material, and the "rightful" or most efficient method of work. When you look at Kirby's bench, the essence of that philosophy is perfectly expressed.

"I learned all my woodworking skills on a bench like this, so naturally I feel the most comfortable with this design," says Kirby. "It works! I would not know how I could improve on it."

knives may be double-sided; if so, just flip them around to the sharp side and reinstall. Otherwise, set the old knives aside for resharpening and replace them with a sharp set.

Installing the new knives is fairly straightforward, but aligning them in the proper orientation takes a bit of time and finesse. A few newer machines are coming out with indexed knives—something planers have had for years—which allows knives to simply drop into the correct position, guided by indexing holes or slots. However, most machines do not have this feature, so you will likely have to align the knives yourself. The easiest way is with a magnetized installation fixture available from most woodworking suppliers. This fixture sticks to the outfeed table, with one end protruding over the cutter head, and pulls the loose knives up to the level of the outfeed table and holds them in place while you tighten the gib screws to lock the blades in place.

Test your knife installation by placing a straight stick on the outfeed table and then rotating the cutter head manually (use the pulley to avoid getting nicked by the sharp knives). The stick should move exactly the same distance with each knife, and on both sides of each knife. Repeat the process along the full length of each knife to make sure that all the cutters are in line.

Table adjustment

Once the knives are aligned and locked in place, fine-tune the height of the outfeed table. Joint the edges of two boards and examine the cut edges with a straightedge. If the rear of the boards show snipe (see page 113), the outfeed table is set too low.

Hold the jointed edges of the two boards together. If their centers touch and there are gaps at the ends, one or both of the tables are low near the cutter head. If the ends touch and there is a gap in the center, then one or both are high near the cutter head. Adjust only the infeed table (except in severe cases), then keep testing until the jointed edges rest against each other with no gaps.

Fence adjustment

The jointer fence should make a 90° cut when its gauge reads 90°. Use a square to make the initial fence setting, then make a test cut on a board and check it with the square. Adjust the fence as needed until the tool consistently makes 90° cuts. When it does, you can adjust the fence pointer to read 90°. Most jointers have a stop bolt that holds the fence at 90°. Even though this is a fairly reliable index, it is still a good idea to check your fence for square every time you change its setting, just to be sure it correctly dialed in at 90°.

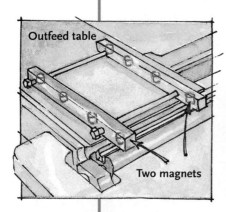

Outfeed table

Two magnets

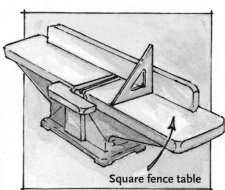

Square fence table

Projects

Shaker Sewing Stand

Hand sewing may be a largely forgotten skill these days, but the Shakers did it on a daily basis. Consequently, furniture intended to make sewing easier came in many forms, including this sewing stand.

This classic design was inspired by a sewing stand made in the Shaker community of Mount Lebanon, New York, around 1850. Many Shaker furniture items came from that area in the 19th century, their designs often emphasizing that simple things are the most beautiful. Practicality was important in their furniture designs as well, although in later years Shaker craftspeople relaxed their austere beliefs a little, especially in furniture made for outsiders.

An interesting characteristic of this sewing stand was that it was designed for use by two people at the same time. The drawer is shared and is constructed to pull in both directions.

Start with the pedestal

Since the three legs and the entire top assembly attach to the pedestal (piece 1), it is logical to turn this first. If you have to glue together two or more pieces to get the required size, carefully match the grain and wood color as closely as possible.

Turn the entire length to 3" in diameter and leave it at that size until after completing the three dovetail sockets at the lower end, which should be the headstock end when mounting it on the lathe. This way, the other end—or tailstock end—can later be turned to fit the 1½" hole in the upper assembly. It's also a little easier to clamp this piece when it's all the same size.

Making the dovetail sockets

As shown in the pedestal drawing on the next page, lay out the headstock end for the dovetail sockets using a protractor to keep them 120° apart. Draw a line to the center point to aid in determining the location of each of the router cuts. Using a ½" straight bit in a table-mounted router, make your first passes ¼" deep by 3" long. Use a stop block clamped to the fence of the router table to establish the length of cut.

To ensure that the dovetail sockets stay straight while you rout them, take

1. Turn the pedestal to a diameter of 3" and remove it from the lathe. Before completing the turning, form dovetail sockets for the legs, starting out on the router table.

2. Once the straight bit has done its work, use a sharp chisel to complete the dovetail walls and to flatten the areas that will later be covered by the ends of the legs.

Below: From the center of the pedestal, draw three lines 120° apart to help locate the mortises for the dovetail sockets. After routing the sockets, use a chisel to flatten the curvature of the pedestal around each socket.

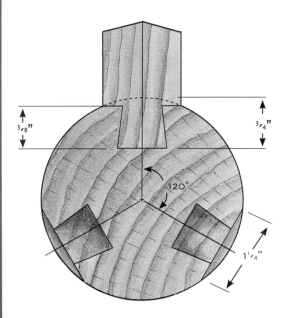

MATERIALS LIST T x W x L

1	Pedestal (1)	3" Dia. x 16³⁄₄"
2	Legs (3)	1¹⁄₄" x 5" x 14"
3	Drawer Box Bottom (1)	³⁄₄" x 17" x 13"
4	Drawer Box Sides (2)	³⁄₄" x 17" x 5"
5	Stabilizer (1)	³⁄₄" x 4" Dia.
6	Drawer Box Rails (2)	³⁄₄" x 2¹⁄₂" x 12"
7	Cleats (2)	³⁄₄" x ³⁄₄" x 15"
8	Drawer Fronts (2)	³⁄₄" x 3¹⁄₂" x 12"
9	Drawer Sides (2)	¹⁄₂" x 3¹⁄₂" x 16¹⁄₂"
10	Drawer Bottom (1)	¹⁄₄" x 11¹⁄₂" X 16"
11	Drawer Pulls (2)	1¹⁄₂" Dia. x 1"
12	Tabletop (1)	³⁄₄" x 19" x 24"

NOTE: Make pieces 3 and 4 from a single piece of glued-up lumber. To avoid exposed end grain, the grain in pieces 3, 4, and 6 should run around the opening at 90° to the table's drawer.

Opposite, top right: Sand the upper and lower edges of the three legs on an oscillating or drum sander or, in their absence, try clamping your belt sander upside down. Then use a 1/4" roundover bit (lower photo) to complete the machining.

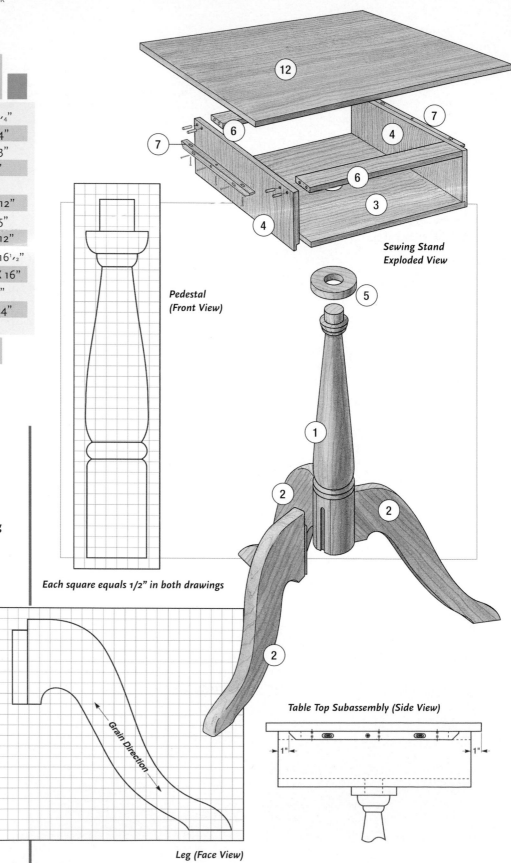

*Sewing Stand
Exploded View*

*Pedestal
(Front View)*

Each square equals 1/2" in both drawings

Table Top Subassembly (Side View)

Grain Direction

Leg (Face View)

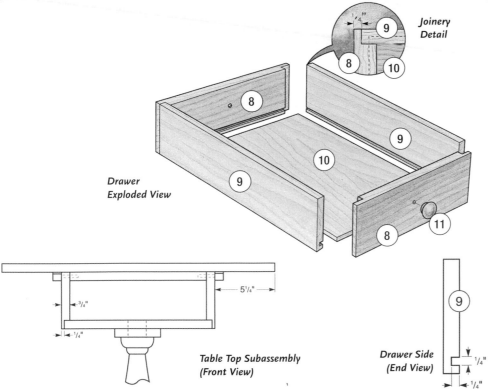

9 · ¼"

Joinery Detail

8 · **10**

8

9

10

9

Drawer Exploded View

8 · **11**

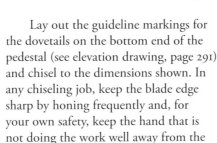

5¼"

¾"

¼"

Table Top Subassembly (Front View)

9

¼"

¼"

Drawer Side (End View)

a few moments to make a cradling jig with some scrap by cutting an arc into it that perfectly fits the 3" diameter of the pedestal. Face this with some double-stick tape. By pressing this jig against one side of the pedestal, you can easily hold the other side tight against the fence, preventing the pedestal from turning. After your first pass for each socket, successively increase the depth to ½", then to ¾" for your final passes.

Once you have reached the right depth, you are almost ready to complete the dovetail cuts with a sharp wood chisel. But first you will need to flatten the curvature of the pedestal around each dovetail socket. Do this by centering a 1¼" x 3½" piece of cardboard over the socket (representing one of the legs) and tracing around it with a pencil. By flattening this area, you ensure a tight fit of the leg against the pedestal. Use a sharp wood chisel, first making the cut across the top end 3½" from the bottom. Sandpaper, backed by a flat block, may be used for final flattening. When you are done with this task, the grooves should measure ⅝" deep.

Lay out the guideline markings for the dovetails on the bottom end of the pedestal (see elevation drawing, page 291) and chisel to the dimensions shown. In any chiseling job, keep the blade edge sharp by honing frequently and, for your own safety, keep the hand that is not doing the work well away from the business end of the chisel.

Shaping the legs

Use 1¼"-thick stock for the legs (pieces 2), choosing wood that is free of knots or blemishes. Use the scaled drawing to create a pattern and transfer it to your stock, paying careful attention to the grain direction. For the neatest and quickest sawing job, use a band saw, although it can also be done with a scroll saw or jigsaw. Sand the upper and lower edges until smooth, using the end of a belt sander or a drum sander. Follow up with a ¼" roundover bit.

Creating the leg's dovetails

If you plan to make the dovetail depth cuts by hand, start by marking the guidelines and clamping a straight piece

of scrap wood across the leg to guide the saw and protect the leg's surface from a wayward blade. Make the cuts ⁵⁄₁₆" deep, preferably with a backsaw.

However, you can probably do a neater and more accurate job on the table saw. Trace out two jigs, one for each side of the leg, to hold it in position during the cut, as shown in the photo series on page 295.

Using ¾" scrap stock, hold the scrap and one leg (the end you will be dovetailing) squarely against your table saw's rip fence and accurately transfer the leg's curves with a pencil.

On the table saw, set the blade to a depth of ⁵⁄₁₆", then make the shoulder cuts on each side of each leg to define the back of the tail. If you are short on experience with this type of joint, try shaping a complete dovetail on a piece of scrap stock first.

Consult the dimensions in the drawing on page 294 to complete your dovetails, testing the fit in the sockets as you go. To shape the dovetail to fit the pedestal socket, use a padded clamp to hold the leg firmly in place on a bench and

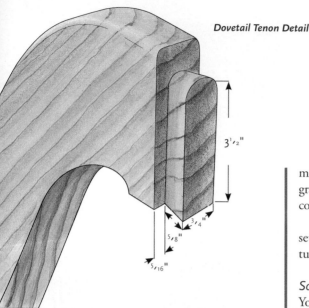

Dovetail Tenon Detail

3½"

¾"

⅝"

⁵⁄₁₆"

Above: The legs are joined to the pedestal with simple dovetails, as is traditional in Shaker-inspired furniture. The tops of the dovetails are rounded to match the router-formed sockets in the pedestal.

1, 2. To ensure straight shoulders on the tails, create two jigs to hold each leg exactly square as you form the shoulder of the dovetail. The curve in the leg is matched by the shape of the jig to hold the legs securely as they are being machined.

3. Once the shoulder cuts are made, use a chisel to shape the dovetails to fit the sockets in the pedestal perfectly. Chisel in the direction of the wood grain and use a padded clamp.

4. After the dovetail slots are completed, return the pedestal blank to the lathe to wrap up the turning process. Complete all but one sanding step on the lathe as well, saving a final pass to do by hand, sanding with the grain.

5. During the final glue-up of the legs to the pedestal, check for plumb with a carpenter's square to be sure there will be no tilt to the top.

make the chisel cuts in the direction of the grain, not across it. Round the tail's upper corners to match the shape of the socket.

After thoroughly sanding each leg, set them aside until after the pedestal turning is completed.

Some drawer frame details

You won't want to see end grain when looking at the sewing stand, so orient the grain of the drawer box bottom and sides (pieces 3 and 4) so it runs crosswise to the direction in which the drawer will slide. Glue up one 17" x 24" panel to create these three pieces, joining the edges with glue and biscuits, and then cut them each to size.

Form the rabbets on the sides (see drawings on previous page) and join them to the bottom with glue and 4d finishing nails. Now locate the center of the bottom piece and glue the stabilizer (piece 5) in place. Once the glue dries, drill the pedestal hole with a hole saw or expansion bit. As you can see from the drawings, the box rails (pieces 6) are held in place with two ⁵⁄₁₆" diameter x 1½" dowels at each end.

Before moving on to the drawer and pedestal, take a moment to form the two cleats (pieces 7) that attach the tabletop to the drawer box. Drill three holes in each direction on these two pieces (see the drawings on page 292), slotting the outside ones to allow for seasonal movement of the sides and top. Because round-head screws with washers were employed here, use a Forstner bit to set the screw heads below the surface.

Completing the pedestal

At this point you can return to the pedestal and bring it to final shape. Start by dry-fitting the legs and lightly marking their uppermost locations. Raise the first bead above that point, as shown in the drawing on page 292. Then move to the top end and turn it down to fit the hole in the center of the drawer box bottom. With the two ends done, follow the scaled drawing on page 292 to turn the pedestal's gently curving shape. Sand the pedestal while it's turning, ending with 220 grit or finer. When you are just about done, turn off the lathe and sand lengthwise by hand to remove any cross-grain scratches that may still show. Do not sand the upper tenon that fits into the drawer frame.

Attaching the legs

Before gluing the legs permanently in place, fit them into their sockets and set the assembly on a level table. While a variation might be almost invisible to the eye, the slightest error can magnify how much the table leans when complete, so use a square to check that the pedestal rises at exactly 90° from the surface. Mark the exact place where the upper edge of each leg meets the pedestal when it is vertical. If you have worked accurately to this point, each leg should be perfectly in line around the base of the column, with the pedestal rising perfectly plumb. If only slightly out-of-plumb, a bit of sanding on the underside of one of the feet may correct it. For a larger correction, use a sharp chisel to either slightly lengthen the dovetailed slot

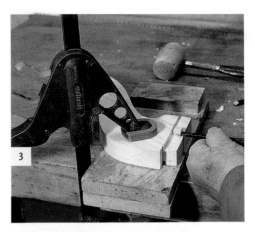

in the pedestal for that leg, or shorten the leg's dovetailed tenon—either fix will allow the leg to move upward, correcting the lean. The key is to make the adjustment very small so as not to overcorrect.

Glue the first leg and use a padded C-clamp and several heavy rubber bands to hold it tightly until dry. The goal is to apply equal pressure along the entire length of the glued joint. Use a wood chisel or knife to scrape away any fresh glue that squeezes out of the joint, then go over the surface with a wet cloth. After each joint dries, proceed to the next.

Making the drawer

The double-ended drawer (pieces 8 through 10) is made with rabbeted corner joints and a plywood bottom that slides into grooves before you attach the second front. Do not use glue to secure the drawer bottom. Center the drawer pulls (pieces 11) vertically and horizontally. Drill a hole for each and countersink it on the inside for the screw. Shaker-style drawer pulls may be made on the lathe or purchased locally, but try to match the wood species you used for the rest of the project. The Shakers frowned upon contrasting wood species used for the sake of ornamentation.

Final assembly

You are now ready to bring all the components together. Start by placing the pedestal on a level surface and applying glue to the top tenon. Press the drawer box in place, using your level to

ensure that it dries flat. While the glue dries, select some of your best boards with matching grain to glue up the tabletop (piece 12). Once the tabletop is glued and dried, trim its ends to size and sand the edges and top. Soften the edges with sandpaper, but only just enough to break the sharpness.

Finishing

Before attaching the tabletop, apply at least one coat of varnish to the inside of the drawer frame and to the underside of the tabletop to prevent uneven moisture absorption.

Stain your sewing stand, if you wish. After it dries, apply two or three coats of your favorite finish, sanding between coats. A bit of wax applied to the outside of the drawer will help it slide easily.

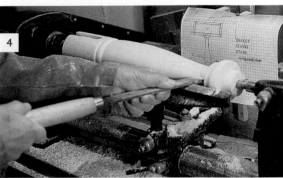

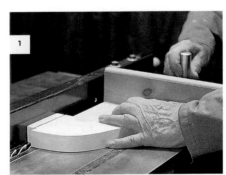

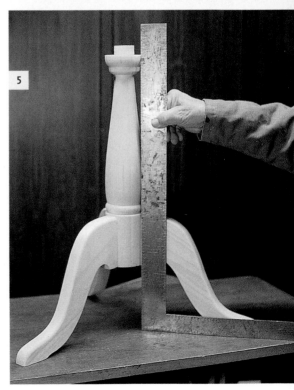

Chippendale Mirror

It is a special pleasure to recreate a piece from the mid-1700s, considered by many to be the high period of American cabinetmaking. The designs developed by Philadelphia furniture makers, who emulated the style of the English craftsman Thomas Chippendale, represent some of the most formal and graceful pieces of this period. While this mirror is far from the most ornate of Chippendale's creations, it does demonstrate the fluidity and flowery composition of his work.

Mahogany was the wood of choice for Philadelphia cabinetmakers, and the wood imported from Cuba was the most prized. Unfortunately, these trees are nearly extinct from overharvesting. Honduras mahogany is still quite common, so look for a piece with as much grain flair as you can find. Aniline dye stain can help re-create the deep red color of Cuban mahogany.

Machine the frame pieces

Begin by rough cutting the pieces for the mirror frame. Rip all the pieces for the frame (pieces 1–3), and follow by ripping the frame molding strips (pieces 4). Choose the faces that will show and arrange the four pieces of the frame as they will be joined, then joint the edge that you plan to orient toward the mirror.

Structurally, this project depends on mortise-and-tenon joints at each corner, with additional reinforcement achieved by gluing on the frame

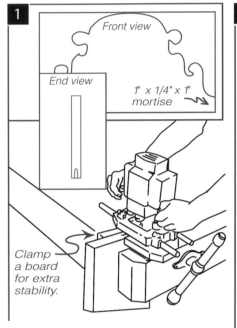

To add stability while routing the mortise, clamp the frame top in a vise alongside a scrap piece. Set your edge guide against the face of the top frame piece and rout the 1/4" x 1" x 1" mortise.

molding strips. The joints can be made very accurately with a router. Adjust a router equipped with a ¼" straight bit to cut a 1"-deep mortise in the edges of the top (piece 1) and bottom (piece 2), as shown in figure 1. Center this cut across the thickness of the material and cut the mortise 1" long. The frame sides (pieces 3) mate with the top and bottom along a 4" stretch, but the actual joint is only 1" long. Measure and mark a line 4" from the end of each side piece, as shown

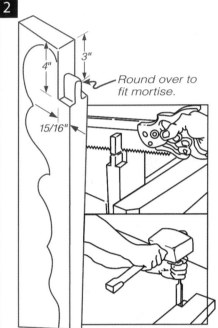

Mark out the tenons on the frame sides and rout the waste away with a 5/8" straight cutter. Remove the excess tenon and pare the shoulders square.

in figure 2. For this cut install a ⅝" straightedge guide in your router, and cut away swaths 1⅝6" wide by ¼" deep to create tenons 4" long at each end of the side pieces. Instead of cutting right up to the 4" line, leave a bit of wood and chisel up to the line for an accurate shoulder. These tenons should fit the mortises easily. Now that you have made these nice, long tenons, cut away 3" of them and round over the cut edge on the remaining tenon with a file to match

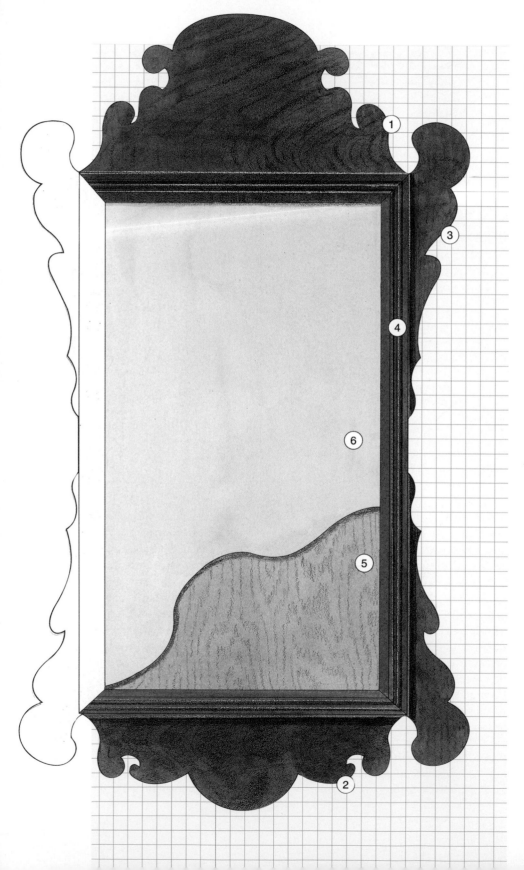

**One square
equals ¹⁄₂"**

the rounded mortise bottom. When
everything fits, glue the frame together.

Detailing the molding

Take the frame molding strips (pieces
4) and bevel one face at a 15° angle on
the table saw. With the ¾" edge on the
table and the 1⅜" side riding against the
fence, set your fence so that the blade
exits exactly at the top corner of the
molding strip. To get a smooth finish,
first take a heavy cut and follow this
with a light finish pass. One light pass
with a block plane is all that should be
necessary to remove any saw marks.

For a little more detail on the
frame molding strips, rout two grooves
down the length of each strip with
a small roundover bit. The two cuts
can be made on a router table to form
a nicely rounded bead between the
grooves, as shown in figure 3. The
center of the outside cut is ⅜" from
the outside edge, and the next cut is
carefully positioned to form the bead.
Practice on scrap wood to establish your
two fence positions for these cuts.

Cutting the frame perimeter

Go back to the frame, but treat it
gingerly at this point because the
small tenons at each corner can break
easily. Sand both faces to even out the
joints, and continue to sand to 120
grit. Transfer the decorative perimeter
design from the grid at left, and cut all
the curves using a saber saw with a fine
cutting blade.

The next step is tedious, but
there is no way around it. Refining the

MATERIALS LIST	T x W x L
1 Frame Top (1)	³/₄" x 10" x 19"
2 Frame Bottom (1)	³/₄" x 6³/₄" x 19"
3 Frame Sides (2)	³/₄" x 5" x 36"
4 Frame Molding Strips (4)	³/₄" x 1³/₈" x 34"
5 Plywood Back (1)	¹/₄" x 16" x 27⁷/₈" Plywood
6 Mirror (1)	³/₁₆" x 16" x 27⁷/₈"
7 Retaining Buttons (8)	Plastic
8 #6 Screws (8)	¹/₂" Roundhead
9 Hangers (2)	Brass
10 Wire	24"

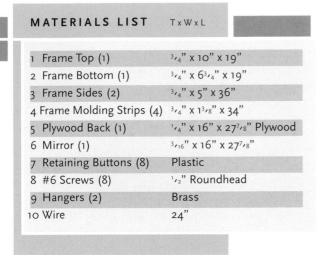

Create detail on molding strips with a small plunge rounding over bit.

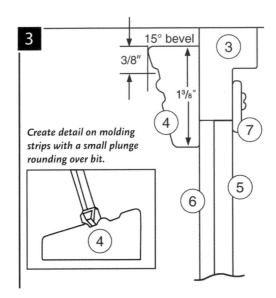

Two grooves are routed on each molding strip for added interest. Later, using a 7/8" Forstner bit, drill the holes on the back so the retaining buttons sit flush with the plywood backing.

outside edges takes a lot of patience, a sharp file, and plenty of 80-grit sandpaper. Use a delicate touch with the file and try to stroke it from the front face toward the back so that any chip-out will be hidden. Use the 80-grit sandpaper in the really tight places and to follow the filing, then sand to 120 grit.

Mitering your corners
The frame is now built, and the only major construction step left for the frame as a whole is to miter the ends of each molding strip and glue the strips to the frame. To make sure your molding pieces fit perfectly, lay the strips on the frame to mark your miters where these pieces intersect the corners of the mirror opening. Be sure to set the strips so 1" is on the frame and the rest is overhanging the opening, creating the ³/₈" rabbet that holds the mirror.

Cut a piece of ¼"-thick plywood (piece 5) to fit behind the mirror. Have a ³/₁₆"-thick mirror (piece 6) cut at a local glass company to fit this frame. The last step is to bore ⁷/₈"-diameter holes for the glass retaining buttons (pieces 7) that hold the mirror and plywood backing against the rabbet. Drill these holes in the frame to the depth of the plywood, using a Forstner bit to get clean, flat-bottomed holes. Now drill the pilot holes for the screws (pieces 8) that will fasten the glass retaining buttons.

Finishing up
Give your frame its final sanding to 150 grit. As described earlier, to help this piece look like the dark red Cuban mahogany that Chippendale probably would have used to build the frame, turn to aniline dye. Water-soluble aniline dye

will allow the grain to show through clearly, and red mahogany powder will provide the right amount of shading. Following the dying, you may need to lightly sand the wood to remove the raised grain. Avoid the edges of the frame, as it is very easy to sand through the tinted surface.

Try a semigloss tung oil for a built-up finish, applying six coats in all, and then wrap up with a coat of paste wax for a smooth, lustrous appearance. Insert the mirror, the plywood backing, and the retaining buttons. Secure two picture hangers (pieces 9) to the backside of the frame, stringing wire between the hangers.

I n all his designs, Gustav Stickley emphasized the relationship between beauty, simplicity, and function—ideals illustrated in this classic project. Its through-tenon joinery, matching wood plugs, triple slats, and gently curved lower rails lend an understated elegance. The center shelves are adjustable and should suit anyone's library or assortment of collectibles.

Mortise-and-tenon joinery

The key to building this bookcase is mortise-and-tenon joinery. All the cuts are square, so great results are just a matter of taking your time and laying out the joints with care.

Start by preparing stock for the stiles (pieces 1) according to the dimensions in the materials list on page 302. Use the elevation drawings to lay out pairs of upper and lower through mortises in the stiles. These mortises will house tenons cut on the ends of the rails (pieces 2 and 3). If you use quartersawn stock for the stiles, notice that the flake pattern appears only on two faces of the stile blanks. The other two faces are plain sawn. Keep the sides with the attractive flake patterns facing forward so they show prominently.

If you have access to a benchtop mortiser or mortising attachment for your drill press, cutting true, square mortises is easy work. However, you can also drill out the waste on a drill press, then clean up with a sharp chisel (as shown in the sidebar on next page). Whichever method you use, make a few test mortises first. Grain direction is a significant issue with wide-grained species such as white oak; a sharp cut along the grain can cause splitting, so work across the grain first whenever possible.

Once the eight through mortises are cut and cleaned up, mill a groove along the inside edge of each stile. Notice in the side panel assembly elevation that these grooves run from through mortise to through mortise and serve to capture the outer slats.

(continued on page 304)

Slatted Bookcase

TIPS ON MORTISE-AND-TENON JOINTS

The usual convention for cutting mortise-and-tenon joinery, like the through mortise and tenon joints in this project, is to mill the mortises first, then cut the tenons to fit. The reasoning here is simple: Your drill bit or mortising chisel automatically establishes the width of the mortise. It's easier to trim the tenons to fit the mortises than it is to tweak the width of the mortises.

If you bore your mortises with a drill press and Forstner bit, drill the ends of the mortise first, then make a series of side-by-side holes along the length of the mortise. Once these are cut, go back along the mortise and drill out the crescent-shaped waste areas that remain. Then shave the ends and walls of the mortise smooth and flat with sharp chisels. When the mortise extends all the way through the joint, as it does for the bookcase stiles, use a backup board beneath the workpiece to keep the drill bit from tearing out the bottom surface as it exits the wood.

Table saws make quick work of cutting tenons. If you cut the wide tenon cheeks with the workpiece on end, as shown here, secure the wood in a tenoning jig or support it against a tall auxiliary fence mounted to the rip fence. The workpiece should not rock or tip away from the fence as it passes through the blade, or a kickback could occur. Cut the short tenon cheeks with the workpiece held on edge against the saw table and backed up by the miter gauge.

Top: Scribe a line around the mortise with a sharp chisel or knife before you drill out the mortise waste. Scoring the wood fibers first will help minimize splintering. Once the primary waste is drilled out, smooth and square up the mortise with sharp chisels.

Bottom: You can cut the tenon cheeks in the rails with a standard saw blade by standing the rails on end and against a tall auxiliary fence mounted to the rip fence. Or mount the rails in a tenoning jig for even more stability.

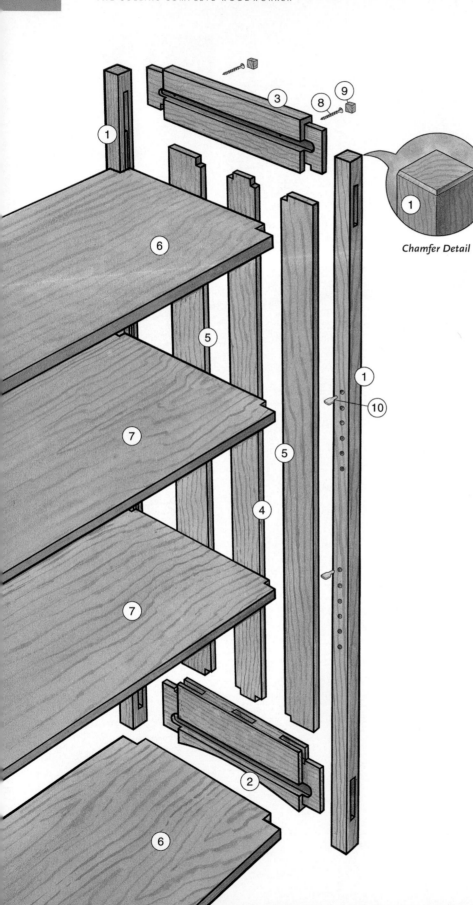

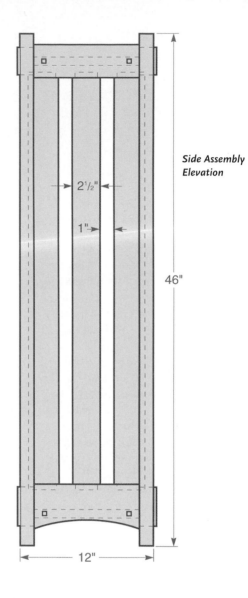

Chamfer Detail

Side Assembly Elevation

2¹⁄₂"

1"

46"

12"

MATERIALS LIST T x W x L

1	Stiles (4)	1¹⁄₄" x 1¹⁄₄" x 46"
2	Lower Rails (2)	³⁄₄" x 4" x 12¹⁄₂"
3	Upper Rails (2)	³⁄₄" x 3" x 12¹⁄₂"
4	Center Slats (2)	¹⁄₂" x 2¹⁄₂" x 37¹⁄₂"
5	Outer Slats (4)	¹⁄₂" x 2³⁄₄" x 37¹⁄₂"
6	Top & Bottom Shelves (2)	³⁄₄" x 11¹⁄₂" x 29"
7	Middle Shelves (2)	³⁄₄" x 11¹⁄₂" x 28¹⁄₂"
8	Screws (8)	#6 x 1¹⁄₄"
9	Plugs (8)	³⁄₈" x ³⁄₈" x ¹⁄₄"
10	Shelf Supports (8)	5mm Brass

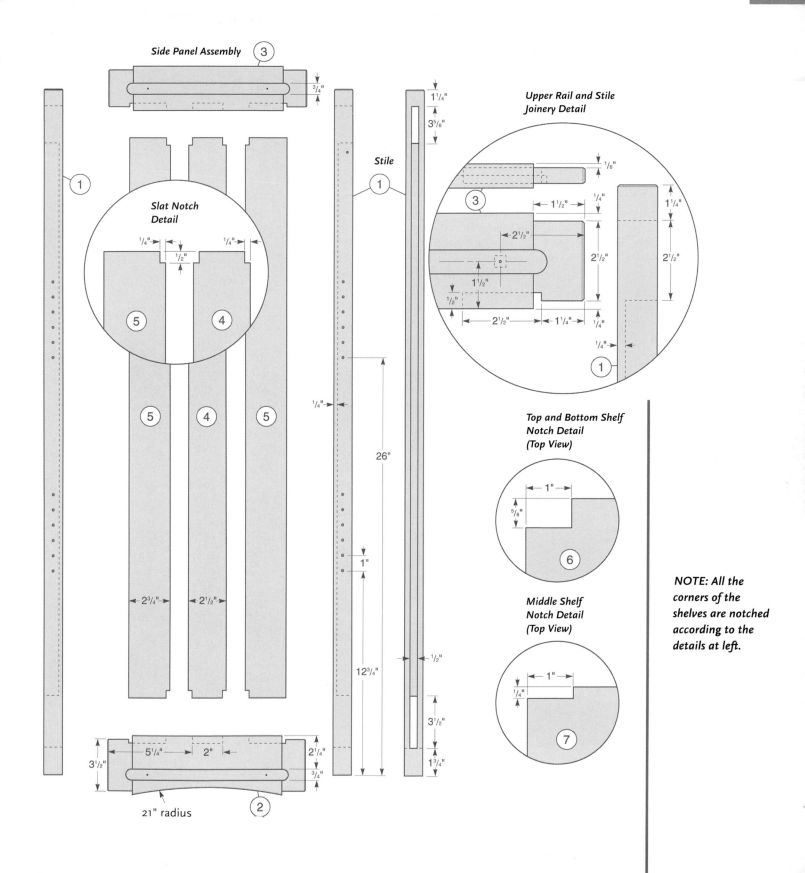

Side Panel Assembly ③

¾"

Slat Notch
Detail

¼" ½" ¼"

⑤ ④

Stile

① ①

1¼"

3⅝"

⑤ ④ ⑤

¼"

26"

2¾" 2½"

1"

12¾"

½"

3½"

3½"

5¼" 2" 2¼"

¾"

21" radius

②

Upper Rail and Stile
Joinery Detail

⅛"

③

1½" ¼"

2½"

2½" 1¼"

1½"

½"

2½" 1¼" ¼"

1¼"

2½"

¼"

①

Top and Bottom Shelf
Notch Detail
(Top View)

1"

⅝"

⑥

Middle Shelf
Notch Detail
(Top View)

1"

¼"

⑦

NOTE: All the
corners of the
shelves are notched
according to the
details at left.

The easiest way to mill the grooves is on the router table with a ½" straight bit raised to ¼". Test your setup on scrap stock, then use pencil marks on the router table fence and stock to start and stop the cuts at the mortises.

With the grooves completed, mill a chamfer around the top edges of the stiles using a router and ¼" chamfering bit or a block plane.

Rails and slats

The upper and lower rails (pieces 2 and 3) join all the fixed structural elements of the bookcase. Rip and crosscut the rail stock to size, then cut three mortises into the edges of the rails to house the outer and center slats (pieces 4 and 5). Use the side panel assembly elevation to find their locations.

Next, form tenons at the ends of the rails. See the upper rail and stile joinery detail on page 303 to lay out the tenons. Use your table saw and a tenoning jig to make the tenon cheeks by slicing off each side of the rails. This will reveal a notch in the tenons because of the mortises you cut earlier. Now lower your saw blade to ¼" and switch to the miter gauge to nibble away the edges of the rails and form the tenon shoulders. Chamfer the ends of the tenons as you did on the stiles.

Install a ¾" straight bit into the router. Use this setup to plow grooves on the inside of each rail (see figure 1 and the upper rail and stile joinery detail). These grooves will accept the ends of the top and bottom shelves, so make them ⅜" deep and 10 ½" long. It's all

right to leave the ends of the grooves rounded, as they will be hidden by the notched corners of the top and bottom shelves. On the bottom rails, lay out the 21" radius as shown in the elevation drawings. Use the band saw to cut these curved arches. Sand the edges to remove the saw marks while keeping the gentle curves identical.

Cut the slats to size (pieces 4 and 5) and notch the ends, following the slat notch detail drawing. The ends of the slats remain at full thickness and will fit into the stopped mortises you cut earlier in the edges of the rails.

Test fit the side assemblies by placing the notched ends of the slats into the rail mortises, then drive the stiles onto the slat and rail subassembly. When everything fits correctly, disassemble,

Plow grooves into the rails on your router table with a 3/4" straight bit. Clamp stops to the fence to control the length of the groove.

Drill pilot holes to hold the screws that will secure the fixed shelves. Reshape the tops of the holes with a 3/8" chisel to accept square plugs.

Use a depth gauge on your drill bit and a template to place the holes for your shelf supports. A piece of pegboard works great for drilling these rows of holes.

apply glue, and clamp the parts together. Keep the side assemblies perfectly square and flat until the glue cures, and scrape off any excess glue after it has set.

Shelves and supports

There are four shelves in this bookcase—two fixed shelves and two adjustable middle shelves (pieces 6 and 7). Cut them to size now. Note that the middle shelves are shorter than the fixed ones, because the latter fit into the mortises you made in the rails. The top and bottom shelves are glued in place and then secured with screws (pieces 8), whose heads will be hidden by square wooden plugs (pieces 9). Make the plugs by ripping strips from your ⅜" plug stock and crosscutting the strips into plugs. Predrill pilot holes through the rails, and then, with a chisel, cut ⅜" square mortises over the holes to receive the square plugs. Make these plug holes ¼" deep.

Notch the ends of all the shelves by gang cutting them in pairs using the table saw and miter gauge. See the elevation drawings to lay out the differing dimensions and shapes of the notches—those on the top and bottom shelves are deeper than the middle shelves. After checking the fit of the top and bottom shelves in the rails, apply glue in the rail mortises and insert the shelf tenons. Secure them with the screws, then glue the plugs in place.

Make four rows of shelf pin holes in the stiles of each side assembly for the two adjustable shelves. Refer to the elevation drawings again to determine the starting and stopping points of these rows. Drill the holes using a piece of pegboard as a template and with a sharp brad-point bit fitted with a depth collar. Clamp the template evenly in place on each stile before boring the holes.

Give all the project surfaces a thorough sanding up to 220 grit.

Stickley finish

Stickley developed a unique method of fuming white oak with ammonia to create a glowing aged and mellow color. You can mimic the unique look of the Stickley finish with a honey-colored gel stain to approximate the same fumed effect with much less fuss and danger. It is also convenient for staining vertical surfaces without the drippy mess. Just be sure to wipe all the excess gel out of nooks and crannies. Protect the wood with a few coats of satin varnish—the gel variety goes on smoothly and does not sag if you accidentally apply too much. It produces a rich luster that is very much in keeping with the Arts and Crafts tradition. The shelf supports (pieces 10) are the brass plug-in type; install them after the finish dries.

Matching the traditional fumed Stickley finish with less toxic alternatives is a challenge. Using a gel stain followed by a complementary gel varnish does the job quite handily.

The basic T-slot system opens up all sorts
of jig possibilities for holding a project
at the workbench while drilling, routing,
planing, sanding, or cutting.

T-Slot Workbench

Workbench Base (Side View)

1½"

5"

½" counterbore
with ³⁄₁₆" pilot hole

3½"

½" x ¾" rabbet

32¼"

3½"

9"

Workbench Base (End View)

24"

28¾"

21"

32¼"

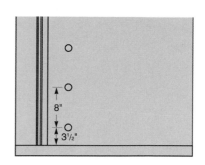

8"

3½"

Dog Hole Locations (Top View)

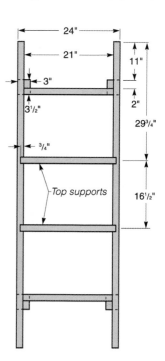

**Workbench Base
(Top View)**

24"

21"

11"

3"

2"

3½"

29¾"

¾"

Top supports

16½"

Below: Batten boards, which feature a curve of about 1/8" on their bottom edge, are used to apply pressure at the middle of a wide panel assembly during glue-up to hold it flat.

1/8"

A good workbench is the heart and soul of a shop, and every woodworker dreams of owning a classic European workbench. The beautiful maple top and elaborate shoulder vise symbolize the essence of fine craftsmanship, but the cost of building such a bench can be prohibitive to beginning woodworkers.

This workbench features a heavy, solid top, a metal T-track system, and an advanced, commercially available vise, but it should still cost less than $400 to build. The vise's two screws are connected by a bicycle chain that overcomes the racking problem commonly experienced with traditional vises. The chain drive can be quickly released to operate the screws independently, making it possible to cant the jaws a little when holding stock out near the edge of the bench. The T-track system is very flexible and lends itself to dozens of homemade jigs and accessories.

The first thing a bench should offer is a sturdy surface, and this one fills the bill. The hardboard top makes a sound work surface, and since it is screwed into place, it can be replaced when worn or damaged. The completed bench is heavy,

which is perfect for deadening the blows of a pounding mallet.

In addition to the basic bench, this project features an optional cabinet added to the leg structure to make good use of this otherwise empty space. An exploded view on page 311 will guide you through this addition if you want to include the cabinet.

Building the base

The base of the workstation is made with standard 2 x 4 stock, and most of the joinery is done with lap joints and screws. Almost all cuts were done with a table saw.

Begin by gluing up 2 x 4 stock for the legs (pieces 1) after cutting the pieces a couple inches longer than the material list lengths (see page 309). Use two pieces of lumber for each leg, spreading yellow glue on both mating surfaces to get a perfect bond, then clamp the pieces together. Clean off the excess glue from each lamination before it hardens.

Once the legs are removed from the clamps, cut all the base pieces to length. The side aprons (pieces 2) and top supports (pieces 3) give the top much of its rigidity and help keep the base from racking. The side stretchers

The clamp support jig steadies bar clamps on the bench tops while adjusting boards in a panel assembly. This allows a comfortable working height, and prevents clamps from tipping.

Clamp Support Jig

A T-square jig makes routing multiple dadoes fast and easy. Because it registers off the edge of the bench, it's also very accurate.

T-Square Jig

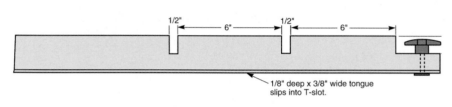

1/2"   6"   1/2"   6"

1/8" deep x 3/8" wide tongue slips into T-slot.

1/2"   4"   6"   1 3/4"

24"

Center the knob holes on T-slot track.   3/4"   14"

5"

(pieces 4), the end aprons (pieces 5), and end stretchers (pieces 6) complete the base, creating great stability and adding substantial weight to the bench.

Lay out the lap joint locations on the legs as shown in the lap joint detail on the opposite page. Keep in mind that all the leg joint positions are essentially the same, but as with all table legs, each one has to mirror the leg across from it. To cut the laps, install a ¾" dado blade in your table saw and raise the blade 1 ½". With the aid of your miter gauge

take several passes to remove the wood in each joint area.

Now lower the dado blade to ¾" and lay out the dadoes on the side aprons for joining with the top supports (see elevation at left). Cut each dado with a couple passes over the blade. Next, cut a rabbet ¾" wide by ½" deep along the top inside edge of each side stretcher. Stop the rabbets 1" from each end of the pieces. To protect your fence during these rabbeting cuts, be sure to clamp on a sacrificial wood face.

Before assembling the base, take care of two more small details that are easy to do now while other frame parts are not in the way. First, drill ½" counterbores with ³⁄₁₆" pilot holes in the bottom edge of the four aprons and two top supports. These holes will be used later for screwing down the bench top.

The second detail is trimming the angles on the ends of the side aprons, as shown in the illustration on page 307. The best tool for cutting the angles is a handheld circular saw, but a jigsaw will

work almost as well. After making the cuts, smooth the edges with a belt sander and 80-grit paper.

Assemble the workbench base in two stages: First glue and screw the side aprons and stretchers to the legs, then join these structures with the end aprons, end stretchers, and the top supports. Make sure that the two side stretcher rabbets face each other on the base assembly. Clean up any glue squeeze-out and sand the base to remove all the sharp edges.

If your shop floor is not perfectly level, install a leveling glide (pieces 7) in the bottom of each leg. To install these optional glides, flip the base upside down and drill a hole ½" diameter by 2" deep in the center of each leg bottom, then secure the threaded plates included in the package and screw in the levelers.

Moving up to the top
The top is basically a three-layer sandwich banded with thick maple rails.
Continued on page 310

T-slot track (rout 13/16" wide by 3/8" deep groove

Hardboard

3"

Side apron

End apron

Leg lamination

Gluing and screwing the top laminations creates a very solid work surface.

End View Detail

With two sets of toggle clamps, one set in line with T-slots and the other set at right angles to the slots, you can hold projects going across the bench or parallel with its length.

When sanding panels, regular clamps often get in the way. Cam dogs and an adjustable T-slot bar can make up the distance between bench dog holes.

Toggle Clamp Jig

1³/₄"
⁵/₈"
1/₈"
³/₈"

Cam Clamp Jig

Top view
1⁵/₁₆"
1/₄"
1⁵/₈"
1³/₄"
1/₂"
Side view

MATERIALS LIST T x W x L

#	Item	Dimensions
1	Legs (4)	3" x 3¹/₂" x 32¹/₄"
2	Side Aprons (2)	1¹/₂" x 3¹/₂" x 76"
3	Top Supports (2)	1¹/₂" x 3¹/₂" x 22¹/₂"
4	Side Stretchers (2)	1¹/₂" x 3¹/₂" x 54"
5	End Aprons (2)	1¹/₂" x 3¹/₂" x 21"
6	End Stretchers (2)	1¹/₂" x 3¹/₂" x 21"
7	Leveling Glides (1 set)	Heavy-duty
8	Top Panel (1)	³/₄" x 22" x 80"
9	Bottom Panel (1)	³/₄" x 18" x 80"
10	Hardboard (1)	¹/₄" x 22" x 80"
11	Maple Rails (2)	1³/₄" x 6" x 80"
12	End Cap (1)	1³/₄" x 1³/₄" x 30"
13	Inside Vise Jaw (1)	1³/₄" x 5³/₄" x 30"
14	Outside Vise Jaw (1)	2" x 5³/₄" x 30"
15	T-slot Tracks (4)	¹³/₃₂" x ¹³/₁₆" x 40"
16	Screws (30)	#6-1" panhead
17	Lag Bolts/Washers (3)	³/₈" x 2¹/₂"
18	Screws (15)	#12-2¹/₂"
19	Dog Heads (4)	¹/₂" x 2" x 2"
20	Dog Dowels (4)	1" Dia. x 1¹/₂" long

Lap Joint Detail

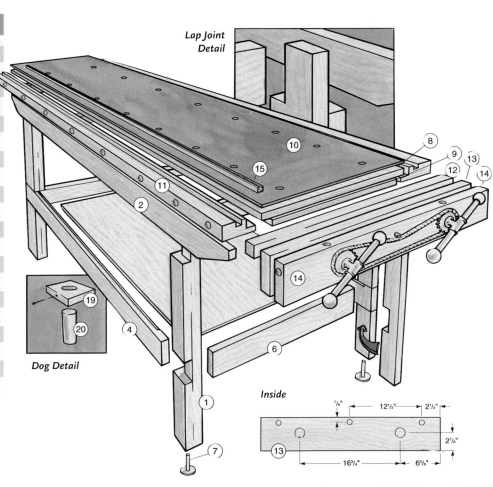

Dog Detail

Inside
⁷/₈" 12¹/₂" 2¹/₂"
2⁷/₈"
16³/₄" 6⁵/₈"

First, two panels of plywood (pieces 8 and 9) are laminated together to make the top stable and heavy, then above the plywood a layer of removable hardboard (piece 10) is added to take the dings and dents suffered by any workbench. When the hardboard becomes too scarred from working at the bench, remove it and use it as a template for making a new one. To complete the top assembly, attach maple rails (pieces 11) to the plywood, giving the top an attractive edge and a durable surface for anchoring the T-tracks (pieces 15).

Start building your top by cutting the two plywood panels to size and gluing them together. Use a brush or roller to spread yellow glue over both mating surfaces, then center the smaller panel on top of the larger one. Next, in order to keep them from slipping out of position, drive a brad into the assembly at each corner of the smaller panel. Clamping the plywood requires consistent pressure throughout the lamination, so cut several curved batten boards to apply pressure in the middle of the panels (see photo, page 307).

Rip and crosscut your maple to size for the rails, then drill 1 ½"-deep holes in one edge of each piece following the dog hole locations drawing on page 307. After drilling the 1" holes, install a ¾" dado blade in your table saw to cut a rabbet 1" deep by 2" wide in the other edge of each rail (see the exploded view drawing on previous page). Make several passes to complete each rabbet, being sure to clamp your protective wood face to the saw fence.

The maple rails should now be

glued and screwed to the upper plywood panel. Clamp the rails without glue to the plywood first and drill seven evenly spaced countersunk pilot holes through the plywood into each rail. This way, the glue will not cause the rails to slip out of alignment during clamping if you can drive the screws in at the same time.

When finished drilling, release the clamps, spread glue in the rail rabbets, and reclamp the assembly. With everything in place, drive the screws, then clean up any glue squeeze-out, especially along the inside edge of the rail.

The final piece to fit into the top is the tempered hardboard. Cut the sheet to fit between the rails as snugly as possible, then drill countersunk pilot holes along its edges for the screws that will hold it to the plywood.

T-tracks

One of the most important features on this bench is the T-track system. The efficient use of this bench revolves around jigs made with a T-bolt and a knob clamp. The T-bolt slides in a metal track that has been secured to the bench with screws, then the knob on the bolt is tightened to hold the jig in place. The aluminum track will last through a lifetime of constant use. The T-track, T-bolts, and knobs are available from most woodworking suppliers.

Installing the metal track requires a simple ¹³/₁₆"-wide by ⅜"-deep groove. Make sure the groove depth is accurate—too shallow and the track will stick up into the work surface; too deep and accessories will pull the track out of the groove.

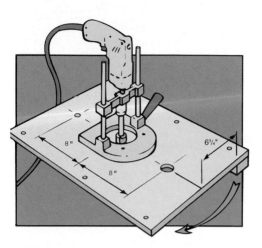

A drilling jig ensures accurate dog holes; just be sure to switch the fence for each row.

Lay out the track grooves on the maple rails as shown in the end view detail, page 308, then chuck a ½" straight bit in your router and attach a straightedge guide. Rout one ⅜"-deep pass for each track, then reset the edge guide to make a second pass, widening the grooves to ¹³/₁₆".

Since the track comes in 4' lengths, this bench requires four pieces to make up the two parallel tracks. To secure the tracks, set them into the grooves and drill ⁵/₃₂"-diameter holes every six inches. Next, drive a #6 x 1" panhead screw (pieces 16) into each hole. With a hacksaw, cut off any track that overhangs the end of the bench.

Benchtop details

Drilling bench dog holes in the top requires a great deal of accuracy. The simple jig shown above will help. The idea behind the jig is to use one dog hole to establish the position of the next hole. To ensure accuracy, it is a good idea to incorporate a portable drilling guide into the jig. Since the jig is guided by the

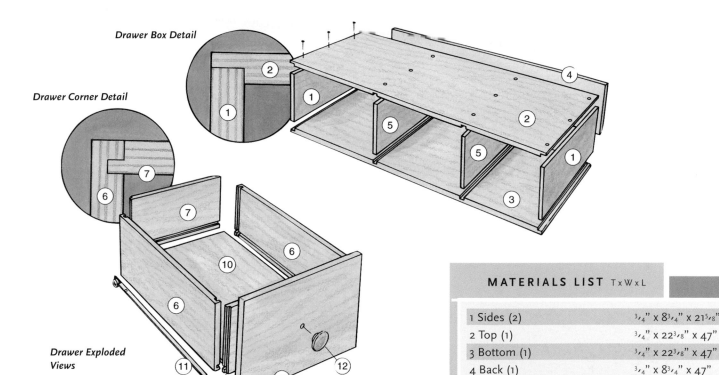

Drawer Box Detail

Drawer Corner Detail

Drawer Exploded Views

MATERIALS LIST TxWxL	
1 Sides (2)	$3/4$" x $83/4$" x $215/8$"
2 Top (1)	$3/4$" x $223/8$" x 47"
3 Bottom (1)	$3/4$" x $223/8$" x 47"
4 Back (1)	$3/4$" x $83/4$" x 47"
5 Dividers (2)	$3/4$" x $83/4$" x $215/8$"
6 Drawer Sides (6)	$3/4$" x 7" x $211/4$"
7 Drawer Backs (3)	$3/4$" x 7" x $127/8$"
8 Drawer Fronts (3)	$3/4$" x 7" x $127/8$"
9 Drawer Faces (3)	$3/4$" x $81/4$" x $151/8$"
10 Drawer Bottoms (3)	$1/4$" x $123/4$" x $201/4$"
11 Side Mount Slides (3 sets)	20" Blum
12 Knobs (3)	$11/2$" Dia.

maple rails, make two fence positions—one for the right-hand row of holes and one for the left.

Build the jig, then set it against the bench's top to drill the first hole as shown in the dog hole location drawing on page 307. Drill the hole, then use a center punch and the forward hole on the jig to locate the next hole.

Now move the jig forward until you can slip a 1" dowel through the rear jig hole and into the first bench hole. Lower the drill bit to the second hole location to make sure the bit spur goes right into the punch mark. Drill the second hole and use the center punch to mark the third hole. Continue this procedure for the rest of the dog holes. When you are done with the right-hand row, switch the fence and drill the left-hand row.

On the end of the bench top without the vise, the T-tracks are left open so fixtures and jigs can slip in and out. On the vise end of the bench, however, you

must install an end cap. Cut the end cap (piece 12) and the vise jaws (pieces 13 and 14) to size, then follow the inside jaw detail on page 309 to drill their mounting and vise screw holes. Clamp the end cap into position against the bench top and extend the pilot holes into the maple rails and the plywood lamination. Now secure the end cap to the bench with glue and screws (pieces 18), extend the pilot holes for the inside vise jaw, and secure it with lag bolts and washers (pieces 17).

Note that a Veritas twin-screw vise was used for this bench, but any commercially available vise can be used. Be sure to adjust mounting and screw holes accordingly to match the unit you purchase.

At this point, the benchtop and the base are ready for assembly. Square the top on the base, then clamp the two together. Now reach under the bench to extend the

pilot holes in the aprons and supports. Use #12 x 2½" screws (pieces 18) to secure the assembly.

Some final thoughts

Make the bench dogs (pieces 19 and 20) as shown in the dog detail drawing on page 21. If you do not plan to build the drawer cabinet, cut a plywood panel to fit between the side stretchers in the base for a storage shelf. If you plan to build the drawer cabinet, follow the drawings shown above.

Any number of jigs can be developed for the T-track system, including the four shown beginning on page 308.

Stickley-Inspired Leather-top Desk

Without sacrificing any of the charm or structural integrity of this Stickley-inspired design, modern methods and materials bring this white oak desk within the reach of almost any woodworker's skills.

This desk is a series of simple frame-and-panel subassemblies, joined with modern biscuits, hidden screws, and glue. The desk is designed with basic joinery; anyone with a little experience, a good router, and a table saw should have no problem building this modern Arts and Crafts piece.

Start with the back

The back of the desk is made up of two rails, two stiles, and three panels (pieces 1 through 4). Cut these and all the other parts to the dimensions shown in the materials list on the next page.

Chuck a ¼" bit in your table-mounted router, set the fence, and mill ½"-deep grooves in both edges of both stiles, plus the appropriate edges of the top and bottom rails according to the dimensions in the elevation drawings beginning on page 315. The groove cuts should be made in several passes, raising the bit about ⅛" each time to avoid tear-out and excessive wear on the router.

These stiles and rails have ¼"-wide tenons centered on their ends. Form them using a fine crosscut blade in the table saw coupled with the saw's miter gauge, and nibble away the waste in successive cuts.

The tenons at each end of the bottom rail are notched ¼" from the bottom. These cuts can be made on

a band saw, or by hand with a sharp backsaw. Dry-fit the frame together and check your joinery. When you are pleased with the fit, apply glue to the stile and rail joints (but not the plywood panels, as they need to float freely). Make sure the subassembly is flat and square as you clamp it up.

After the glue has cured, use a router and straightedge to plow a vertical ¼"-deep groove on the inside face of each stile. These grooves are a full 1¼" wide and will be used to join the interior frames to the back.

Building the interior frames

The interior frame subassemblies house the drawers and surround the desk owner's legs. Begin machining them at the router table by plowing a ½"-deep groove in each stile (pieces 5) and rail (pieces 6) at the locations shown on the elevation drawings. Then move to the table saw to mill tenons on the ends of each rail. These are relatively simple cuts, as no shoulder is required. Glue and clamp the two subassemblies together, again letting the panels (pieces 7) float freely.

Machining the legs

Use either solid or glued-up stock to make blanks for the legs (pieces 8). Either way, have the quartersawn grain showing on the front and back faces of each. After cutting the legs to size, taper their two outside faces, as shown in figure 1 at right.

Use a tapering jig and great care to slice the angles off the legs (See the desk

elevation front and side views for taper dimensions.).

Move back to the router table to mill the ½"-deep stopped grooves in each leg to accommodate the sides and back. Stopping the grooves in the right spot is simply a matter of matching up pencil marks on the leg and the router table fence. Wrap up the legs by using a router equipped with a ¼" straight bit to create the small mortises for the legs' decorative faux tenons (see the sidebar on page 317).

Figure 1: Tapering the outside faces of the legs adds an element of style to their blocky, rectangular shapes.

This project uses simple joinery and modern materials, like this white oak veneer plywood, to create an authentic Arts and Crafts appearance.

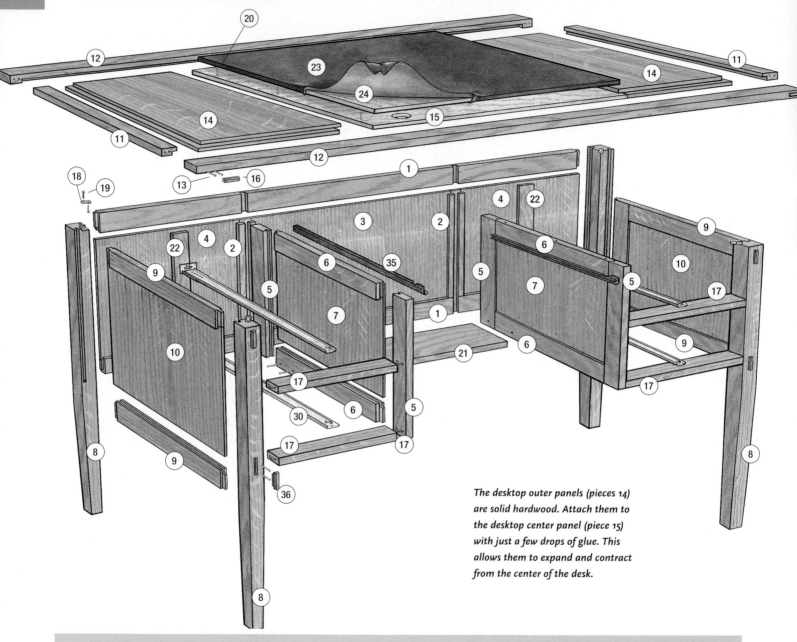

The desktop outer panels (pieces 14) are solid hardwood. Attach them to the desktop center panel (piece 15) with just a few drops of glue. This allows them to expand and contract from the center of the desk.

MATERIALS LIST T x W x L

1	Back Frame Rails (2)	$^{3}/_{4}$" x $2^{3}/_{4}$" x $49^{1}/_{4}$"
2	Back Frame Stiles (2)	$^{3}/_{4}$" x $2^{3}/_{4}$" x 8"
3	Back Frame Center Panel (1)	$^{1}/_{4}$" x 21" x 8"
4	Back Frame Side Panels (2)	$^{1}/_{4}$" x $12^{3}/_{8}$" x 8"
5	Interior Frame Stiles (4)	$1^{1}/_{4}$" x $2^{3}/_{4}$" x $12^{1}/_{2}$"
6	Interior Frame Rails (4)	$1^{1}/_{4}$" x $2^{3}/_{4}$" x $17^{1}/_{2}$"
7	Interior Frame Panels (2)	$^{1}/_{4}$" x $17^{1}/_{2}$" x 8"
8	Legs (4)	$2^{3}/_{4}$" x $2^{3}/_{4}$" x $28^{1}/_{2}$"
9	Exterior Frame Rails (4)	$^{3}/_{4}$" x $2^{3}/_{4}$" x $18^{1}/_{8}$"
10	Exterior Frame Panels (2)	$^{1}/_{4}$" x $18^{1}/_{8}$" x $9^{1}/_{2}$"
11	Desktop Sides (2)	$1^{1}/_{2}$" x 2" x 23"
12	Desktop Front & Back (2)	$1^{1}/_{2}$" x 2" x $56^{1}/_{2}$"
13	Large Screws (12)	#10 x 3"
14	Desktop Outer Panels (2)	$1^{1}/_{2}$" x 12" x 24"
15	Desktop Center Panel (1)	$^{3}/_{4}$" x 24" x $30^{1}/_{2}$"
16	Top Faux Tenons (4)	$^{1}/_{2}$" x $1^{1}/_{8}$" x $^{5}/_{8}$"
17	Drawer Dividers (4)	$1^{1}/_{4}$" x $2^{3}/_{4}$" x 12"
18	Tabletop Fasteners (4)	Steel
19	Tabletop Fastener Screws (8)	Steel
20	Tabletop Screws (12)	#8 x 2"
21	Leg Space Shelf (1)	$1^{1}/_{4}$" x 9" x $21^{3}/_{4}$"
22	Drawer Cleats (2)	$^{1}/_{4}$" x 3" x 7"
23	Leather (1)	25" x 31"
24	Leather Backer (1)	$^{3}/_{4}$" x $29^{1}/_{2}$" x 23"

**Leg Joinery Detail
(Top View)**

NOTE: *The tabletop fasteners are located on the top of each leg.*

½"

¼"

¼"

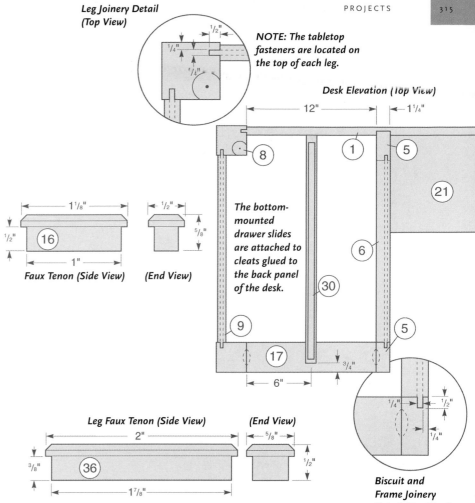

Desk Elevation (Top View)

12"

1¼"

8

1

5

21

6

30

9

5

17

6"

¾"

The bottom-mounted drawer slides are attached to cleats glued to the back panel of the desk.

**Biscuit and
Frame Joinery
Detail (Top View)**

¼"

½"

¼"

**Desk Elevation
(Front View)**

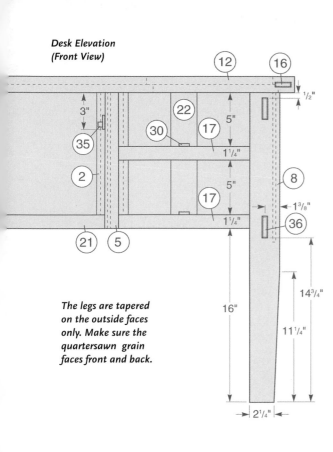

12

16

½"

3"

5"

22

30

17

35

1¼"

2

5"

8

17

1¾"

1¼"

36

21

5

14¾"

16"

11¼"

The legs are tapered on the outside faces only. Make sure the quartersawn grain faces front and back.

2¼"

Faux Tenon (Side View)

1⅛"

½"

½"

⅝"

16

1"

(End View)

Leg Faux Tenon (Side View)

2"

⅜"

36

1⅞"

(End View)

⅝"

½"

**Desk Elevation
(Side View)**

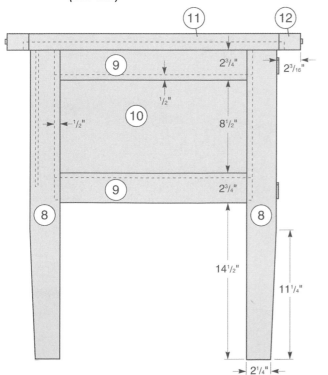

11

12

9

2¾"

2³⁄₁₆"

½"

10

8½"

½"

9

2¾"

8

8

14½"

11¼"

2¼"

Desk Elevation (Back View)

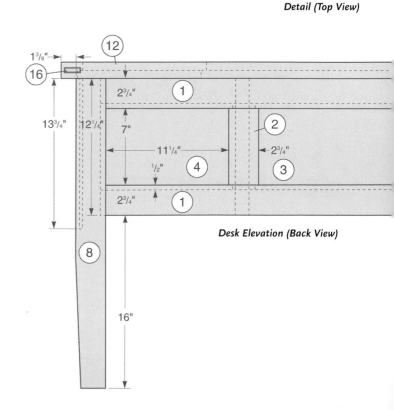

12

1³⁄₈"

16

2¾"

1

13¾"

12¼"

7"

2

11¼"

4

3

½"

2¾"

2¾"

1

8

16"

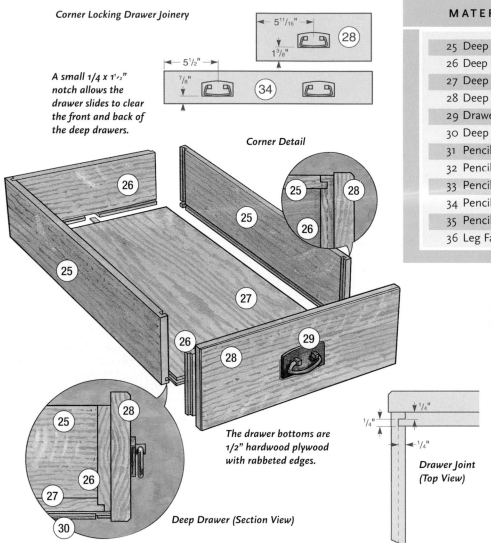

Corner Locking Drawer Joinery

← 5¹¹/₁₆" →

(28)

1³/₈"

A small 1/4 x 1¹/₂" notch allows the drawer slides to clear the front and back of the deep drawers.

← 5¹/₂" →

⁷/₈"

(34)

Corner Detail

(26)

(25) (28)

(25)

(25)

(26)

(26)

(27)

(26)

(29)

(28)

Deep Drawer (Section View)

(25) (28)

(26)

(27)

(30)

The drawer bottoms are 1/2" hardwood plywood with rabbeted edges.

¹/₄"

↓ ¹/₄"

¹/₄"

→ ¹/₄"

Drawer Joint (Top View)

MATERIALS LIST	T x W x L
25 Deep Drawer Sides (8)	¹/₂" x 4¹/₄" x 19³/₄"
26 Deep Drawer Fronts & Backs (8)	¹/₂" x 4¹/₄" x 10³/₄"
27 Deep Drawer Bottoms (4)	¹/₂" x 10³/₄" x 19¹/₈"
28 Deep Drawer Faces (4)	³/₄" x 4⁷/₈" x 11⁷/₈"
29 Drawer Pulls (6)	Mission style
30 Deep Drawer Slides (4)	21"
31 Pencil Drawer Sides (2)	¹/₂" x 2¹/₂" x 18"
32 Pencil Drawer Front & Back (2)	¹/₂" x 2¹/₂" x 20¹/₄"
33 Pencil Drawer Bottom (1)	¹/₂" x 20¹/₄" x 17¹/₂"
34 Pencil Drawer Face (1)	³/₄" x 3¹/₄" x 21⁵/₈"
35 Pencil Drawer Slides (1 pair)	18"
36 Leg Faux Tenons (4)	⁵/₈" x 2" x 1¹/₂"

The drawer fronts and backs (left inset) are rabbeted on their ends. Drawer sides (above right), have 1/4" dadoes milled across their ends. Both steps can be done on the same setup, as shown above. The 1/4" drawer bottom grooves are also formed on the same table saw setup.

Building the exterior frames
Cut and mill the four rails for the exterior frames (pieces 9), using the same techniques as you did for the interior frame rails; just notice that the lengths are different. Notch the tenons on the two bottom rails to create ¼" shoulders.

Test the tenons' fit in the legs, then cut the panels (pieces 10) to size. Glue and clamp the rails to the legs while slipping the panels in place without glue.

Building the top
Begin making the top by creating a

simple, butt-jointed frame with the front, back, and sides (pieces 11 and 12). Start by cutting the parts to size, then chop the small, shallow mortises for the faux tenons and screws on the long frame pieces. Drill each piece to properly accept the screws (pieces 13), then assemble the frame without glue. Turn the frame upside down and, using a bearing-guided rabbeting bit, mill a rabbet around the inside edge. Square the corners with a sharp chisel after routing.

Select solid hardwood stock with beautiful grain and figure for the two

outer desktop panels (pieces 14). Form rabbets on the edges of each panel. (Note that on three sides, this rabbet is milled on the top face, while on the fourth side it is milled on the bottom face.) Cut the center panel (piece 15) from ¾" plywood and, after drilling screw holes, attach it to the frame with screws only. Test fit the two outer panels to the center panel and frame. When all the parts fit together well, remove the screws and reassemble the top with glue and screws. Apply a couple drops of glue to the joint between the center panel and the inverted rabbet

Assemble the desktop frame and cut a rabbet in its bottom edge with a bearing-guided bit. Square the corners with a chisel.

Before final assembly, test fit the joints between pre-made subassemblies, such as the back subassembly and the legs.

on the outer panels. This will ensure both panels will expand and contract out from the center of the desk. Finally, glue the top faux tenons (pieces 16) in place.

Assembling the desk

Sand the subassemblies through 220 grit, and test fit all your joints. Then lay out and mill the eight biscuit slots for the drawer dividers (pieces 17). Glue and clamp the two interior frames in their dadoes in the back, then glue the subassembly into the stopped grooves in the legs (do not glue the panels in place during this process). Before the glue begins to set, install the drawer dividers with glue and biscuits. Make sure everything is square as you tighten the clamps. Once the glue dries, use a Forstner bit to create round mortises in the tops of the legs (see the leg joinery detail, page 315), then secure the tabletop fasteners (pieces 18) to the legs with screws (pieces 19).

To join the top and bottom subassemblies, start by placing the desktop on the lower desk assembly. From the underside, mark where the interior frames touch the desktop's center panel. Remove the top and drill pilot holes for screwing through the top into the interior fames, countersinking the holes from the upper face. Center the top on the desk body, then drive

your screws (pieces 20) down through the center panel into the pilot holes in the interior frame's top rails (pieces 6). Finish securing the frame by driving screws (pieces 19) up through the tabletop fasteners into pilot holes in its bottom face, then attach the leg space shelf (piece 21) with screws (pieces 13). Take a moment to glue the drawer cleats (pieces 22) to the plywood panels inside the drawer cavity (refer to the elevation drawings on page 315).

Drill a finger hole in the top's center panel to help lift the removable leather-covered panel, then cut the leather (piece 23) and its backer (piece 24) to shape and dry-fit them to the top of the desk. When the fit is right, attach the leather to the backer with spray adhesive.

Making the drawers

Refer to the drawings on page 316 to mill the joinery on the sides, fronts, and backs of the four deep drawers and the shallow pencil drawer (pieces 25 through 35). Assemble each box and sand smooth. Cut the drawer faces from attractive hardwood stock. Mount the drawer pulls with their bolt heads counterbored flush into the back of the drawer faces.

With the drawer boxes complete, install the drawer slides according to the manufacturer's instructions, then slide the drawers into their openings.

Use double-stick tape to temporarily position and mark the locations of the drawer faces, then screw the faces in place. Install the remaining faux tenons. Remove the drawer faces and hardware for finishing.

Wrap up this project by applying a light walnut oil stain, topped by at least three coats of clear satin varnish or lacquer. Sand between these coats with 400-grit paper. Reinstall the drawer faces and drawer pulls after the finish dries.

Glossary

gent's brace

air cleaner A ceiling or wall-mounted vacuum source with filtration that removes airborne dust from a shop; sometimes called an ambient air cleaner or air scrubber

air-dried Wood that has been cured by natural air drying

aliphatic resin The adhesive ingredient in yellow wood glue

Allen wrench A six-sided bar, usually L-shaped, used to turn screws with recessed hexagonal heads; sometimes called an Allen key

all-purpose blade Circular saw blade with a tooth configuration designed to perform both crosscutting and ripping operations; also called a combination blade

alternate top bevel (ATB) Teeth angled in alternated opposite directions on a saw blade

aluminum oxide A type of abrasive material used in sandpaper

aniline dye Water-soluble dye used for coloring wood

annual growth rings Rings visible in wood end grain separating earlywood from latewood; also called growth rings

antikickback pawl A table-saw attachment that allows cutting stock to move freely forward but whose teeth dig into the material to prevent it from ejecting backward toward the operator; also called antikickback spur

apron Rails around the base of a table to which the top and legs are joined

arbor The mounting shaft for a saw blade

ATB Alternate top bevel; teeth angled in alternated opposite directions on a saw blade

awl A sharp-pointed tool for piercing small holes in wood or other material

backsaw Handsaw with a thin rectangular blade that is stiffened with a reinforcing spine along its length on the side opposite the teeth; used primarily for mitering and cutting dovetails

band clamp A flexible strap connected to a ratcheting mechanism used to tighten it around irregularly shaped objects; also called a web clamp

band saw Powered saw that cuts by means of a thin metal blade running in a continuous loop around two or more large drive wheels, used for making tight-radius curved cuts or for resawing wood

bar clamp A clamp composed of a metal bar with a fixed jaw on one end paired to an adjustable jaw, usually tightened with a screw together with a ratchet mechanism

barrel hinge A jointed device used to connect two components such as a box and its lid and consisting of two small cylinders that are recessed into holes drilled into those components in order to make the connection nearly invisible

base plate The flat underside of a portable power tool; sometimes called a sole plate

batten A thin, flat board or strip of wood often used to cover the joint between two parallel boards or as a caul to apply even clamping pressure

beading tool A hand tool that creates a small, molded detail on the edge of a workpiece; can create single or multiple beads; also called scratch stock

bearing A wheel mounted on a router bit shank that guides a router bit through a cut; sometimes called a rub bearing. A bearing can also be mounted on a fixture or jig to guide a tool or workpiece through a cut.

belt sander Handheld electric sander using an abrasive belt; used for rapid stock removal and for leveling panels

bench dog A round or square peg fitted to matching holes in a workbench surface; used as a stop to hold a workpiece in place

bench grinder A machine consisting of a motor and a shaft with a spinning wheel on one or both ends. Most commonly the wheel is an abrasive disk used to sharpen tools, but it can also be a wire wheel for cleaning or a cloth wheel for buffing.

bench knife A handled cutting and marking tool with a generally short, pointed blade, sharpened only on one side

bench plane Flat-bottomed hand tool consisting of a sharp blade called an iron and a mating cover called a chip breaker, which protrude through a slot in the tool's sole plate, used to smooth and flatten wooden stock. Other common features are a handle at the rear of the tool, a knob for grasping the front of the tool, and a mechanism to adjust the depth and position of the blade.

benchtop A description applied to a woodworking machine designed without its own stand and intended for use on a table or bench surface; benchtop machines are often considered portable

bevel An angle measurement; can apply to lumber cuts, or to the angle of the cutting edge on chisels and other tools

bird's-eye A type of wood figuring that resembles dots or small eyes; most commonly found in maple

biscuit Small, flat, football-shaped pieces of compressed wood glued into slots on opposing workpieces to align and strengthen joints

biscuit joiner Portable power tool used to cut slots for biscuits; sometimes called a plate joiner

bit Any cutter designed to work while spinning, such as a router bit or drill bit; bits are mounted in a tool's chuck or collet

blade guard A protective shield covering the portion of a table saw blade or other cutter that protrudes through a table top, or a similar shield on a portable power tool

blade plate The flat disk that forms the body of a circular saw blade

blade rim The periphery of a circular saw blade where the teeth are located

blade stabilizer Thin plates that mount on the sides of a saw blade to help minimize vibration

blank A square or rectangular piece of wood intended for carving or turning

blast gate On a dust collection system, a sliding door mounted in ductwork that allows airflow to be opened or restricted depending on need

block plane A small utility plane usually used one-handed

blushing Milky discoloration of a wood finish caused when moisture is trapped in the curing finish

board foot A measurement of lumber equal to a board 1' long, 1' wide, and 1" thick; usually abbreviated bf when combined with a numeral

book match The pattern created when adjoining pieces of veneer or resawn wood are opened like a book, resulting in grain that is mirror-imaged

bore The hole in a circular saw blade, sized to fit the saw arbor

bow Wood defect where a board bends from end to end along its flat axis

box joint A corner joint made of interlocking square cuts on the ends of workpieces

box nail A wire nail with a sharp point and flat head similar to a common nail but with a thinner shaft and a slightly dulled point to prevent splitting thin wood

brace Sometimes called bit and brace, a manual drilling tool consisting of an articulated crank-style handle and a chuck into which an auger bit is mounted

brad A nail with a very small head designed to be driven flat with, or slightly below, the surface

brad point A wood boring bit similar to a twist drill but with a sharp spur at its point to lead the shaft into the hole

bridle joint A connection between two woodworking components similar to a tongue-and-groove joint but made on the narrow rather than the wide dimension of the material

British Standard Whitworth (BSW) Specification for the number and spacing of threads on screws and bolts, devised by 19th-century British engineer Joseph Whitworth

bullnose The rounded-over edge of a piece of material used as a finish detail; also, a hand plane or router bit used to create such an edge in wood

burl A rounded, often gnarled, protrusion on a tree trunk usually the result of disease; the highly figured wood cut from such a growth, often used for veneer

burnish To firmly rub a surface in order to polish it or to adhere a glued surface treatment, often done with a rounded tool. Also, to treat the edge of a cutting tool to slightly roll the edge after sharpening.

bushing In woodturning, small metal tubes used as guides to turn pen parts to the correct diameter for a finished pen

butterfly hinge Type of butt hinge with its plates cut in a decorative winglike pattern

butt hinge Hinge consisting of two rectangular plates connected by a pin used to attach a door to a fixed component

butt joint Joint formed by placing two flat mating surfaces squarely against each other

butt matched The pattern created when two resawn pieces of wood are arranged end to end, resulting in grain that is mirror-imaged along the shorter dimension

cabinet saw Heavy-duty professional table saw, generally equipped with a large cast-iron top, accurate fence, and powerful motor and blade mounted on a trunnion assembly attached directly to the cabinet, not the tabletop, facilitating precision adjustment

cabinet scraper A flat piece of metal used to smooth a wood surface

caliper Compasslike hand tool for measuring inside and outside diameters

cap iron The metal structure on a plane that holds the cutting iron in place; its curved edge creates the curled shaving common to hand planing

carbide An extremely hard alloy used to create extra sharp and durable cutting surfaces on blades, bits, and other tools

carcass The basic structure of a cabinet or other generally rectangular construct; sometimes spelled carcase

carving in the round A fully three-dimensional style of carving, as in sculpture

case-hardened lumber Wood that has been improperly kiln dried such that the outer portion is dry but the inner portion retains moisture, resulting in internal stresses that cause the material to deform in an undesirable way

casework Cabinets or other generally rectangular constructs

casing Wooden trim around wall openings

caul A piece of material, often scrap wood, placed between clamp and workpiece to provide even clamping pressure and prevent marring of the surface

C-clamp A clamp in a shape resembling the letter C and with a screw mechanism to tighten onto the workpiece

CFM Cubic feet per minute, generally used to measure airflow

chamfer A 45° bevel cut to ease the sharp edge of a workpiece

check Cracks in a piece of lumber

cheek The wide face of a tenon

chip carving Style of carving in which numerous small pyramid-shaped bits of wood are removed from a workpiece by means of a series of shallow knife cuts

chuck A cylindrical metal apparatus on a drill or other tool that can be tightened to hold a bit

clear Description for a piece of lumber that is free of defects

cleat A strip of wood or other material used to support or reinforce the surface to which it is attached

closed coat Type of sandpaper in which the abrasive grains are tightly distributed, used when clogging of the paper is not an issue

close-grained Any wood with narrow, inconspicuous growth rings, small pores, and a smooth surface texture, such as maple, cherry, and poplar

clutch Apparatus on an electric drill that can control the amount of torque applied to a bit

coarse-grained Any wood with wide, conspicuous growth rings, large pores, and a grainy surface texture, such as oak, ash, and walnut; also called open-grained

coated abrasives Products such as sandpaper in which gritty material is adhered to a flexible backing

collet The mounting collar of a router or rotary tool that holds a bit

color rendering index A measure of how well a fluorescent light accurately renders true color, an important factor when gauging finishing and wood color; often abbreviated CRI on packaging

combination blade A circular saw blade with a tooth configuration designed to perform both crosscutting and ripping operations; sometimes called an all-purpose blade

combination machine A stationary woodworking machine, usually European-made, that combines a table saw, jointer, planer, and/or other machines into a single unit; sometimes called simply combo machine

common The lowest grade of lumber, further broken down into #1, #2, and #3

common nail A fastener made from steel wire with a sharpened point on one end and a flat head on the other, generally available untreated (bright) or coated with zinc for rust resistance (galvanized)

compound miter A cut angled to both the edge and face of a board

compression wood A condition of lumber in which the tree was subject to mechanical stress, most often occurring below the stress point

mechanical compressor Device that creates and stores compressed air to power pneumatic tools

contractor's saw A sturdy but somewhat portable table saw, often equipped with a cast-iron top and extension

wings, an accurate fence, and a fairly powerful motor that can operate on standard house current, enabling it to be transported to a job site

cope To cut a piece of wood so that it exactly matches the profile of another workpiece

cope-and-stick Joinery where complementary profiles, sometimes very intricate in shape, are glued together

corner clamp Clamp designed to hold corner joinery at 90°

counterbore A cylindrical depression drilled into the surface of a workpiece in order to recess a screw or bolt head or nut

countersink A conical depression drilled into the surface of a workpiece in order to recess a screw head

cove A concave edge profile

crook Wood defect where a board bends from side to side along its flat axis

crossbearer A wooden caul, occasionally convex shaped, used to apply even clamping pressure to a glued-up assembly; sometimes called a batten

crosscut To cut wood across the grain

crosscut blade Table-saw or handsaw blade designed for cutting across the grain

crotch lumber Wood obtained from the intersection of two major limbs of a tree, often yielding a desirable grain pattern

crowning A deformed condition in lumber in which the edges bend away from the center, resulting in a convex shape

cupping A deformed condition in lumber in which the edges bend away from the center, resulting in a concave shape

curly A desirable rippled grain pattern in certain woods; often referred to as tiger, and sometimes called fiddleback

cutoff The waste resulting from cutting a piece of lumber; sometimes call an offcut

cutoff blade For wood, a circular saw blade designed especially for crosscutting; for metal, a circular saw blade with an abrasive surface in place of cutting teeth

cutoff saw A powered crosscutting or miter saw, with models available for wood and for metal; sometimes called a chop saw

cutter The sharpened component of a tool that makes contact with and slices, surfaces, trims, or otherwise shapes the workpiece

cutter head The spinning drum in which the knives (blades) of a powered wood surfacing tool such as a jointer or planer are mounted

cyanoacrylic A fast-bonding glue; sometimes called "super" glue, or simply CA glue

cyclone A type of dust collector that directs airflow in a circular motion to separate dust particles by size

---

d The abbreviation used to indicate the nail specification "pennyweight" (see *penny*); for example, 10d finish nails

dado A rectangular groove cut across the grain

dado head (or cutter) System of individual saw blades that are stacked to create dadoes of specific sizes; used in a table saw or radial arm saw

Danish oil A type of penetrating wood finish, generally either clear or with a darker tint

dead-blow mallet Striking tool with loose lead shot contained within its head to concentrate all its energy into a single, nonbouncing blow, and a soft face to prevent marring the workpiece

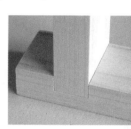

dado joint

deck screw A coarse-threaded wood fastener, similar to a drywall screw but with a thicker, less brittle shaft

denatured alcohol Clear, colorless liquid used as a cleaner and solvent, as well as a fast-drying vehicle for finishes such as shellac

detent A preset adjustment on a tool, usually set for common angles such as 45° or 90°; also called a positive stop

dewaxed shellac A natural wood finish derived from excretions of the lac beetle and further processed to separate out its naturally occurring wax component in order to prevent the cured finish from interfering with the bonding ability of subsequent finish coats

D-handle Part of a tool, shaped like the capital letter D, that allows the user to firmly grasp it

dial indicator An instrument for measuring short distances to very precise tolerances; sometimes called a dial gauge

diamond dresser A rough scraping tool

used to clean debris from the surface of a grinding wheel

dimensional lumber Wood building material cut to standard sizes, both in width and thickness, such as a 2 x 4, and sold in various lengths

direct drive A motor shaft attached directly to a cutter or blade; sometimes called in-line

disk sander A powered surfacing tool, either handheld or stationary, that operates by spinning a circular abrasive disk

double-stick tape Tape with adhesive on both sides, often used to temporarily attach components and jigs; sometimes called carpet tape

dovetail

dovetail Attractive and very strong joint formed by mating one or more angled, fan-shaped "pins" to correspondingly sized and shaped notches, called "tails." The joinery can be visible from both sides (through), from only one side (half blind), or invisible (blind).

dowel A cylindrical length of wood, often used as a pin to reinforce a joint

dowel center A metal disk that slips into a dowel hole to mark drilling position on a mating workpiece

downdraft table A flat, perforated surface attached to a vacuum source used to remove dust during sanding

Dozuki Thin-bladed Japanese saw that cuts on the pull stroke

drawer slide A system of tracks and rollers that attaches to the outsides of a drawer box and the insides of the drawer opening enabling the drawer to be opened and closed and maintain its alignment within the carcass; also called a drawer glide

drawknife A chairmaking tool with a straight blade with perpendicular wooden handles

driver bit A screwdriver tip that is installed in a drill in place of a drill bit to facilitate powered screw driving

dry fit To test-fit components without glue or fasteners

drying oil When used on wood, any oil-based finish that penetrates the surface and hardens when exposed to air; linseed and tung oil are drying oils

drywall screw Coarse-threaded wood fastener commonly used as an all-purpose wood screw, similar to a deck screw but with a thinner, more brittle shaft

drum sander Surfacing machine consisting of a spinning cylinder wrapped with a flexible abrasive sheet. Machines with smaller vertical cylinders are used for sanding curved surfaces and contours; machines with larger horizontal cylinders, sometimes called wide-belt sanders, are generally equipped with a conveyor belt and are often used to size pieces and panels to precise thickness.

dual bevel Describes a miter saw that can cut both left and right bevels

dust collector A system of ducts and hoses connected to a vacuum device for the removal of sawdust, wood chips, and other debris generated during woodworking operations

dust nibs Tiny specks of airborne particles that settle on a workpiece before the finish has dried, leaving a rough texture on the surface that must be sanded away before the next coat is applied

dust port An accessory attached to a power tool to connect it to a dust collection system

earlywood Young, flexible timber that forms early in the spring and lies directly beneath the bark; also called springwood

edge band To apply a decorative veneer or other treatment to the exposed edges of plywood or other undesirable wood surface

edge-banding tape Narrow, thin material, generally either wood veneer or plastic laminate, sold in rolls and used to conceal the exposed edges of plywood or other unattractive surfaces. Often supplied with pressure-sensitive or heat-activated adhesive applied to the back.

edge-belt sander Surfacing machine consisting of an abrasive belt that both oscillates vertically and revolves and is mounted perpendicular to a horizontal table to achieve precise 90° edges; often combined in a single machine with a spindle sander

edge grain Boards cut from the tree such that the growth rings run perpendicular to the face and parallel to the edges; also called vertical grain. Quartersawn wood displays edge grain.

elbow In a dust collection system, an angled connector joining two air ducts end grain Growth-ring pattern of wood as seen in cross section relative to the tree

epoxy An adhesive capable of joining dissimilar materials and sometimes of filling voids, usually consisting of two parts, a resin and a hardener, which must be mixed together to activate

equilibrium moisture content When a board's moisture content equals that of the surrounding air

extension table An accessory, often constructed of cast iron or pressed steel, designed to increase the effective width of a table saw or other power tool; sometimes called a wing

face The outward (visible) surface of a cabinet or other piece of furniture or of a piece of wood

face frame The front of a cabinet consisting of vertical stiles and horizontal rails, to which the doors and drawers are attached

faceplate A metal disk used to attach wood blanks to a lathe for turning bowls or similar projects that cannot be secured simultaneously by the headstock and tailstock

FAS "Firsts and seconds"; the highest grade of hardwood lumber, at least 83% clear of defects; followed by selects and no. 1 common

feather board Comblike accessory with flexible teeth that is attached to a cutting tool in order to hold the workpiece tight to the bit or blade and allowing it to move only in the direction of the cut, thus preventing kickback

feed rate The speed at which material is fed into a woodworking machine

feeler gauge Measuring tool consisting of several precisely sized strips of steel designed to achieve an accurate measurement of small gaps. Although commonly an automotive tool, it finds many applications in the wood shop.

fence Fixture attached to a stationary machine or tool that guides the workpiece in a straight line against the tool, or guides a portable tool in a straight line against a workpiece

fiddleback An attractive rippled grain pattern in wood often seen on the backs of violins; also referred to as curly or tiger

figure A desirable pattern that sometimes occurs in a wood grain

filler Material used to pack, stuff, or shim generally unseen voids or gaps

film finish Transparent outer protective surface of a piece of furniture or cabinetry that has been treated with a product such as lacquer or varnish

finger joint A method of connecting pieces of wood, either perpendicularly or end to end, by means of interlocking parallel cuts; sometimes used to describe a box joint

finial Decorative cap most often placed atop a thin vertical object such as a newel post, flagpole, weathervane, or hinge pin

firsts and seconds (FAS) The highest grade of hardwood lumber, at least 83% clear of defects; followed by selects and no. 1 common

fishtail A type of chisel used in wood carving, named for the shape of its blade

fixed-base A type of router in which the bit must be set at a single depth that is not adjustable during the cutting process

fixture An auxiliary device secured to a tool to guide workpieces through the tool in a consistent and repeatable fashion

flat sawn Lumber cut in parallel slices from a log so that the grain pattern is partially or entirely parallel to the face of the board; also called plain sawn

flattening agent A chemical compound added to wood finish to reduce gloss; sometimes called flatting agent

flat-top tooth Circular-saw tooth with 0° of bevel ground in the top, most often used for ripping wood; also called flat-top grind

flint A low-grade abrasive used in inexpensive sandpaper

flitch A thin slice of wood shaved or peeled from a log, most often made into veneer

flush-trim bit Straight-sided cutter for use in a router, normally with an integral guide bearing that follows the shape of a pattern or workpiece, resulting in a cut that exactly conforms to that shape

Forstner bit A drill bit used for making flat-bottomed holes, often in larger diameters than standard twist drills make

frameless cabinet Cabinet in which the top, bottom, sides, and sometimes fixed shelves form the structure without the need for a face frame; if doors are

cherry wood grain

present they are attached directly to the sides by means of special hinges

framing lumber Lumber used primarily in the building trades, usually a nominal 2" thick (2 x 4, 2 x 6, etc.)

framing nail A large common nail or spike most often used in building construction

framing nailer A portable tool, most often powered by compressed air, used to drive large nails in building construction

fret saw A thin-bladed cutting tool similar to a coping saw but with a deeper frame; used to make the same types of cuts as a powered scroll saw

fretwork Intricate decorative patterns cut from flat stock with a fret saw or scroll saw; often called gingerbread

friction polish Any finish that is cured by heat generated through friction; commonly used in woodturning applications

frog Angled section of a hand plane body that supports the blade

full-extension slide Type of drawer glide designed to bear the weight of a drawer box pulled all the way out of its opening

garnet A medium-grade abrasive (a step above flint) used as the grit in sandpaper

gingerbread Intricate decorative patterns cut from flat stock with a fret saw or scroll saw; often called fretwork

gib screws Screws used to hold blades in place in a cutter head

glue line A smooth, flat surface on the edge of a board, suitable for joining to a similarly prepared board with no gaps; the appearance created by such a joint

gouge A chisel having a curved cutting edge

grain The pattern in wood resulting from the arrangement of the tree's growth rings

grain reversal In staining, when pigment adheres more thickly to the lighter areas of wood and not to denser dark areas, resulting in the reversal of light and dark grain areas

green Freshly cut timber that has not yet been dried

green woodturning The practice of using uncured wood for turning blanks

grit The abrasive material adhered to a backing to produce sandpaper and similar abrasive products

groove Rectangular channel cut in the direction of the grain, usually along the long dimension of a board; similar to a dado, which is cut across the grain

growth ring A pattern of alternating light and dark wood created by seasonal changes during a single year of a tree's life cycle

guard Any device designed to prevent hands from coming into contact with a cutting edge

guide blocks On a band saw, small metal, ceramic or phenolic blocks that mount on each side of the blade to keep it from twisting and flexing from side-to-side during cuts

guide collar A metal bushing attached to the base plate of a router through which the bit protrudes and which follows a pattern to produce a precisely shaped cut

gullet The deep spaces between teeth on a saw blade

half-blind dovetail Dovetails that are visible only on one side

hand screw A type of clamp with jaws that are tightened by twisting opposing threaded shafts

handwheel An adjustment wheel on a piece of woodworking machinery

hardboard A thin, hard-surfaced building material made from compressed wood fibers; often referred to as Masonite, a well-known brand name of hardboard

hardwood Any lumber from a deciduous tree

haunched mortise-and-tenon Like a standard mortise-and-tenon joint except the tenon has an additional stub or shoulder on the top that fits into a matching recess in the mortise

heartwood Lumber taken from the center, dead portion of a tree

hide glue Adhesive made from collagen extracted from the skins of animals

high-speed steel (HSS) Heat-resistant metal alloy used to make cutting tools

hinge mortise A small recess cut in a

door or frame to facilitate the flush mounting of a hinge

hole saw A circular cutting tool mounted in a drill with a pilot bit in the center and teeth around the perimeter, designed to create larger-diameter holes than are generally practical with standard drill bits

hollow grind A concave appearance of a bevel formed on a grinding wheel

hollow vessel A generally vase-shaped woodturning, often with an opening that is smaller than the diameter of the turning

hollowing tool A small-ended scraper, sometimes with a curved shaft, designed for making hollow vessels on a lathe

hone A small stone used to give a fine edge to cutting tools

honing guide A jig designed to hold a chisel or plane iron at the correct angle for sharpening

hook The amount of forward (positive) or backward (negative) lean of a tooth on a circular saw blade relative to the blade's circumference

hot-melt glue A cylindrical plastic adhesive that is heated to melting temperature in a special glue gun/applicator and bonds nearly instantly upon cooling to room temperature

HSS High-speed steel; a heat-resistant metal alloy used to make cutting tools

hybrid table saw A power tool that is similar in power and cost to a contractor's saw but sharing many design features of a cabinet saw, such as motor and blade mounting configuration

impact driver Power tool similar to an electric drill that combines rotary drilling motion with a back-and-forth tapping motion to secure screws, nuts, and bolts more efficiently

infeed The side of a stationary tool from which the workpiece is fed into a cutter

induction motor A heavy-duty electrical motor of the type found on most stationary woodworking machinery

insert A removable, often replaceable, part of a tool such as the throat plate on a table saw

insert cutter An accessory for a saw, router, shaper, molding machine, or other cutting tool, consisting of a heavy circular base into which two or more matching knives can be installed to

create detailed profiles in wood. Knives with different patterns can be installed in the same base, helping to control tooling costs.

iron The cutting blade of a hand plane

jig An auxiliary device most often secured to a workpiece to guide it through a tool (or a tool through the workpiece), or to make multiple measurements in a consistent and repeatable fashion

jointer A machine that mills a straight, flat surface on lumber

kerf The thickness of a saw blade; also the cut made by that blade

kickback A highly dangerous situation in which a spinning blade snags a workpiece and hurls it back at the operator at high velocity

kiln A heated container or small building used to dry lumber

knife The replaceable cutting edge in a woodworking tool; also called a cutter or a blade

knife hinge A door-mounting device that opens and closes by means of a stack of interlocking flat metal bars, rather than a pin as in a standard hinge

knot Defect in lumber created where a branch was attached to the tree

lac bug Insect (*Laccifera lacca*) whose secreted resinous shell is used for the creation of shellac finish

lacquer A clear, fast-drying, solvent-based wood finish

lag screw A large, heavy-duty fastener most often used to anchor heavy components directly into a structure's wood framing; also called a lag bolt

laminate (n.) A thin plastic layer attached to sheet material to create a smooth, colorful, and durable surface

laminate (v.) (1) to attach laminate to sheet material; (2) the process of gluing up a larger workpiece from several smaller pieces

laminate trimmer A small router used primarily to trim the overhanging edge of applied laminate

lap joint A method of connecting two pieces of wood of equal thickness by removing half the material from the top surface of one piece and half from the bottom surface of the other and securing the two mating surfaces with glue or fasteners

palm sander

lapping plate A smooth, perfectly flat plate of any hard material used for sharpening

latewood Harder wood that is produced during the latter part of the growing season; also called summerwood

leg set An optional stand that converts a bench-based tool into a floor-standing machine

linseed oil A substance extracted from the seeds of the flax plant and used as a wood finish; available both boiled (referred to as BLO) and raw

live center One of two mounting points on a lathe for spindle turning, it spins on its own bearings and is installed at the nondriven, tailstock end

loose knot A knot that is detached from the surrounding wood, but frequently held in place within a board by its shape

loose side The rough side of a piece of veneer

luthier Woodworker who specializes in making stringed instruments

machine screw Threaded fastener similar to a small bolt but with a slotted or Phillips head like a screw, used with a nut or in a tapped hole; sometimes called a stove bolt

mallet A generally wooden, large-headed striking tool

mandrel A mounting rod used to turn hollow cylindrical blanks on a lathe, as for pen parts

marking gauge A device that uses a knife or other sharp point to transfer measured lines to a workpiece

marquetry Technique using veneer of contrasting woods cut into pieces and arranged to form a pattern

medium-density fiberboard (MDF) An engineered wood product made from compressed wood fibers, sawdust, resins, and waxes and generally available in 4' x 8' sheets

milk paint A milk-based (casein) furniture paint

mineral spirits A standard solvent for oil-based paint and varnishes; also called paint thinner

Mission Furniture style with predominantly straight lines and minimal ornamentation

miter box A tool used for cutting moldings and other narrow stock at precise angles, particularly 45° to achieve mitered corners; can be manual, used in conjunction with a backsaw, or powered with its own circular saw blade

miter gauge An accessory with an adjustable fence enabling angled cuts; has a rectangular runner on the underside that allows it to be used on any woodworking machine equipped with a miter slot

miter joint A joint created by joining two pieces of wood cut at complementary angles

miter slot A shallow slot on a woodworking machine that guides a miter gauge or other device equipped with a runner sized to fit to the slot

miter square A square used to measure or mark angles

moisture content The amount of water contained in a piece of lumber

molding A length of wood into which a decorative profile has been milled, often used as transition between two walls or surfaces

Morse taper (MT) A standard for mounting shafts used on drill presses, chuck components, and lathe centers manufactured with a slightly conical shape to facilitate quick bit changes and accurate centering

mortise A generally rectangular cavity cut into a framing member to accept a mating tenon or a piece of hardware, such as a hinge

mortise-and-tenon A strong form of joinery in which a generally rectangular stub (tenon) cut on one piece of stock is inserted into a matching cavity (mortise) cut into another and secured with glue or pegs

mortiser A machine similar to a drill press but with a hollow, square chisel surrounding the drill bit, used to cut square or rectangular cavities, known as mortises, in wood

mullion A thin divider strip used to separate panes of glass or mirror within a multiple arrangement; sometimes called a muntin

nail set A metal tool similar to a punch used to recess the heads of finishing nails below the surface

mortiser

natural-edge turning A woodturning, usually a bowl or goblet, that features remnants of bark along the rim

nondrying oil When used on wood, any oil-based finish that penetrates the surface but does not harden when exposed to air; mineral oil and most vegetable oils are nondrying

newel The upright post at the top or bottom of a staircase into which the banister assembly is mounted

NGR A non-grain-raising wood finish

ogee An S-shaped decorative molding or edge profile consisting of a concave arc flowing into a convex arc; sometimes called a Roman ogee

one-by (1-by) Dimensional lumber nominally 1" thick

one-off A one-of-a-kind project, usually a piece of furniture made to a customer's specifications

open coat Type of sandpaper that has abrasive grains spaced to cover only 50–70% of its surface in order to prevent clogging

open-grained Any wood with wide, conspicuous growth ring, large pores, and a grainy surface texture, such as oak, ash, and walnut; also called coarse-grained

open time The amount of time that glue can be exposed to the air and still be workable; also called working life or pot life

orbital An eccentric, somewhat circular motion used by some powered cutting and sanding tools

oriented strand board Type of building panel similar to plywood, made up of small, flat wood chips glued together to form large sheets; often abbreviated OSB

oscillating drum sander A powered surfacing tool in which an abrasive cylinder simultaneously rotates and moves up and down for sanding complex shapes

outboard turning To pivot a lathe's headstock away from the lathe bed, increasing the machine's capacity for turning large bowls

outfeed The side of a cutting tool where the processed material exits

overlay door A cabinet door that completely covers the front face of the box

painter's tape Adhesive paper tape (usually blue) used to mask areas adjacent to surfaces being painted and then be easily removed without leaving any residue

paint thinner A standard solvent for oil-based paint and varnishes; also called mineral spirits

palm sander A small, handheld power tool used to smooth wooden surfaces

panel A flat rectangle of wood often constructed by gluing several boards together side by side

panel saw A woodworking machine used for cutting large sheets of material to a more manageable size

particleboard A building or substrate material made by compressing tiny wood chips with adhesive and forming them into sheets

parting tool A chisel with a V-shaped cutting edge; also called a V-tool

pawl The toothed component in a ratchet or a table saw's antikickback device

pegboard A sheet of hardboard perforated with evenly spaced holes, most often used as a mounting surface for specialized brackets and hangers

pen lathe A very small lathe, usually weighing less than 12 pounds, used for small turnings such as pens and jewelry

penny The specification designating sizes of nails; also called pennyweight. Abbreviated with the letter d; for example, 10d finish nails.

Phillips A type of screw invented by Henry Phillips in the 1930s, with a cross-shaped indentation in the head; also the cross-shaped screwdriver head used to turn it

piano hinge A long, narrow hinge with attachment points at short-spaced intervals and a connecting pin running its entire length

pigment The component in paint, stain, or other finish that provides the color

pigtail scratches The curlicue scratches sometimes caused by handheld electric sanders; sometimes called swirling

pilaster A flat, pillar-shaped detail added to the upper portion of furniture for decoration

pilot bearing A bearing mounted on a bit that guides the bit during a cut

pin In a dovetail joint, that portion of the wood that fits between the tails

pin nailer A powered tool that drives tiny, sharp, nearly invisible pins into small moldings and other thin furniture components to provide mechanical fastening to supplement gluing

pin router A power tool with a router bit protruding from a horizontal surface similar to a router table but with an overhead locating pin that follows a pattern to guide the material over the bit in order to create multiple identical pieces

pipe clamp A clamp made by attaching a fixed jaw on one end of a length of steel pipe and an adjustable jaw at the other end

pitch For lumber, refers to thick sap or resin deposits in the wood

pitch In saw blades, refers to the number of teeth per inch

pith The central core of a log or tree branch

pivot block A guide used for resawing that allows the workpiece to be pivoted to follow a cut line; sometimes called a point fence

pivot hinge A type of hinge that enables a door or window to swing open around a single point

plain sawn The most common type of cut lumber; shows pronounced growth rings running almost parallel to the board's face

platen A flat plate or caul often part of an assembly used to adhere veneer to a substrate

plug A round piece of wood glued in place over a countersunk screw to hide the screw head

plunge router A router with the motor mounted on spring-loaded columns

plywood Wood sheet made of individual layers of thinner wood, glued together with the grain of each layer running 90° to the adjoining layers

polyurethane A type of flexible plastic used in sheeting, expanding foam insulation, and glues; often called simply poly

polyvinyl acetate The adhesive ingredient in white glue; often called PVA glue

positive stop A preset adjustment on a tool, usually set for common angles such as 45° or 90°; also called a detent

pot life The amount of time that glue can be exposed to the air and still be workable; also called working life or open time

pneumatic Air-powered; used to describe air-driven tools

pocket hole An elliptical slot bored at an angle in the face of a board, through which a screw is driven to secure that board to an adjacent piece of wood; sometimes called screw pocket

primary wood The main wood used in project construction that is generally seen, such as tops, sides, doors, and drawer fronts

proud Protruding slightly above the wood's surface

PSA Pressure sensitive adhesive; a peel-off backing on some sanding disks

psi Pounds per square inch

pumice A porous volcanic stone formed from cooled lava used to make a mild abrasive

push stick An accessory used to push a workpiece through a cutting edge, keeping hands a safe distance away

PVA polyvinyl acetate; adhesive ingredient in white glue

quartersawn Lumber cut with growth rings almost parallel to the board's edges

Queen Anne English furniture design based on the Baroque style developed during the reign of Queen Anne, 1702–14

rabbet A shelflike joint sized to match the workpiece that fits into it; European form is "rebate"

rack A twisting action of a frame that can loosen joints

rail The horizontal component of a frame

raised grain A lifting of grain on the surface of a board usually caused by the application of water or a water-based finish

raised panel A construction in which the thinned edges of a wooden panel are inserted into a channel formed on the inside edges of the stiles and rails; the panel used in such construction

reaction wood A condition of lumber in which the tree was subject to mechanical stress during its growth; see "compression wood" and "tension wood"

rake The angle of a cutting surface relative to the center line of the tool

raker The flat-topped tooth in a alternate top bevel (ATB) circular saw blade that cleans out the material at the bottom of the cut to flatten it

random orbit The eccentric, swirling motion of a tool such as a disk sander designed to minimize the visible pattern of sanding scratches

ray flecking A desirable pattern on the surface of quartersawn lumber

reciprocating A back-and-forth motion as with the blade of a reciprocating saw

relief carving Carving style that is partially three-dimensional as seen from the front

relief cut A kerf cut on the hidden side of a board used to relieve internal stress on the visible side to prevent splitting or cracking

resaw To cut wood into thinner multiple, often matching, pieces

resin Thick sap or pitch deposits sometimes found in lumber

rift sawn A variation of quartersawn lumber sawn at 30° to 60° to the board's surface, producing vertical grain but no ray flecking

right side The side of a board that will be visible in the finished piece; the smooth side of a sheet of veneer

rip To cut wood with the grain

rip blade Table saw or handsaw blade designed for cutting with the grain

riving knife A thin piece of metal behind a saw blade that prevents wood from touching the rear of the blade and possibly causing a kickback; unlike a splitter, which is fixed, a riving knife moves to always keep the same orientation with the saw blade

Robertson head A type of square-drive screw

rotary cut Veneer cut by "peeling" thin layers off a turning log

rotary tool Small handheld electric tool that spins a variety of cutting, grinding, sanding, polishing, and other specialty tips; often used for hobby crafts

rottenstone An extremely fine, gritty abrasive used for polishing

roughing gouge A large gouge used to remove a lot of material quickly

rough sawn Unsurfaced cut lumber

rough turn To bring a rough blank into a balanced, round shape on the lathe

roundover A convex edge profile

router Power tool used primarily for cutting edge profiles and mortises

rubbing compound Mild abrasive used to remove oxidization from the topmost layers of finish, thereby restoring its shine

rubbing out a finish The process of using ultrafine abrasives to produce a highly polished surface

runout The degree to which a rotating tool wobbles as it spins; an undesirable characteristic

S2S Lumber that has been surfaced on two sides

S4S Lumber that has been surfaced on all four sides

sacrificial fence A temporary fence attached to a main fence that is often damaged during the cutting process, then discarded

sanding drum A spinning cylinder wrapped with a flexible abrasive sheet

sapwood Lumber taken from the outer, living portion of a tree

sawyer A person who operates a saw; commonly used to describe someone who works in a sawmill

scarf joint An angled joint used to join wood end to end

scorp Drawknife with a curved blade used for hollowing bowls and chair seats

scraper A lathe chisel having a flat but rounded cutting edge

scuff sand Light sanding given to wood finishes between multiple coats to improve adhesion of successive coats

scroller One who uses a scroll saw

sealer coat The first application of finish, designed to seal wood pores and fibers

scroll saw

secondary bevel An additional sharpening step performed on the cutting edge of a blade, chisel, or plane iron that creates a bevel a few degrees off from the primary bevel

secondary wood Wood used in project construction that is generally not seen, such as drawer boxes and interior cabinet shelves

select The second-highest grade of hardwood lumber, which is at least 83% clear on one face

self-indexing Cutter knives in a woodworking machine that are notched or otherwise indexed so that they automatically seat in the correct position

self-sealing finishes Any wood finish that seals the wood on the first coat

set To drive a fastener, usually a nail, slightly below the wood surface

set screw A small screw commonly used to adjust a machine component, such as the level of the throat plate on a table saw, or the guide blocks on a band saw

shank The portion of a bit or other cutter that mounts into a machine

shaper A heavy-duty woodworking machine similar to a router designed to mill profiles on workpiece edges

shaving horse A combination bench and seat for carving; a movable end piece is held with the foot to clamp a workpiece in place, freeing both hands

sheen Description of the amount of gloss in a wood finish.

sheet goods Plywood, MDF, or other materials usually sold in sheets, with 4' x 8' being the most common size

sheet-metal screw A sharp-pointed, self-tapping threaded fastener most often used to attach pieces of thin metal to each other or some other material

shellac A clear wood finish made from alcohol and the shell of the lac beetle

shim Thin piece of wood or metal slipped into a gap to tighten it

shooting The act of putting a straight edge on a workpiece

shooting board A perfectly straight piece of wood used as a guide for planing or cutting

shoulder On a wooden workpiece, the area that surrounds or abuts a projection; for example, the end of a board from which a tenon projects

shoulder On a saw blade, a raised portion of metal behind each tooth

crosscut sled

that adds strength to the blade and helps prevent kickback

silicon carbide A very hard, uniform, fast-cutting abrasive material used in high-quality sandpapers and on the cutting edges of tools

skew A straight chisel with an angled cutting edge

skip To run a rough-sawn board through a planer just enough to reveal the wood's characteristics

skip tooth A saw blade with regularly spaced gaps between teeth

sled Device to guide a workpiece squarely and safely through the cutting edge of a woodworking machine, usually a table saw

sliding bevel An adjustable square used to measure or mark angles; sometimes called a bevel gauge

sliding dovetail A form of joinery similar to a dado but with angled rather than vertical sides and a mating piece with grooves cut along its width at a corresponding angle

sliding table On a table saw, a movable portion of the table used to feed a workpiece squarely through the blade

slip match A veneer pattern created by aligning successive pieces side by side vertically but offsetting them horizontally

slip stone A generally handheld stone used to hone the inside curve of a gouge's cutting edge

slot mortiser A horizontal boring machine that cuts elongated slots

slurry Pastelike mix of sawdust, abrasive, and liquid as the result of wet sanding

snipe A slight concave that can occur on the ends of boards during milling

sole The bottom of a woodworking tool; often called the base

solid surface A very hard plastic material used for countertops

soft start An electronic control for an electric motor that eases the motor up to full speed when turned on

softwood Any lumber from a conifer

Soss hinge A fully concealed knife-style hinge in which one side is mortised into the door and the other side is mortised into the door frame

spade bit Drill bit with a wide, spade-shaped cutting edge used to drill large-diameter holes

spalted Lumber where natural decay has caused unique and attractive grain patterns

specific gravity A measurement of the density of wood

spindle In woodturning, a cylindrical turning on the lathe

spindle In machinery, the mounting post of a power tool

spindle sander Machine with a round, oscillating sanding drum that protrudes at 90° through a metal work table

spline A thin strip of wood set into opposing slots of wood being joined; when used on the outside corner of a miter joint, it is called a miter key

split point Type of drill bit with pilot point at the tip for accurate hole location

splitter A thin piece of metal or plastic behind a saw blade that prevents wood from touching the rear of the blade and possibly causing a kickback

splotching An area on wood surface where stain has been absorbed unevenly; also called blotching

spokeshave A hand tool with a thin blade used to create rounded workpieces

spoon gouge A wood-carving tool in which the end of the blade is bent to reach otherwise inaccessible areas

spring clamp Spring-loaded clamp resembling a large clothespin

spur center Star-shaped center mounted to a lathe's headstock that engages and turns the workpiece

square A hand tool used to measure, confirm, and mark 90° angles

square drive A screw head with a cube-shaped recess; also, the four-sided tool used to drive it

squeeze-out Excess glue that oozes out of a joint after clamping pressure is applied

stain controller Solution applied to wood prior to staining to prevent uneven stain absorption; sometimes called wood conditioner

starve To use insufficient glue, or to clamp so tightly that too much glue is squeezed out of a joint

stearates Chemical compounds whose uses include drying agents in paints and sanding agents in lacquers

stepped point A raised point on the tip of drill bit that helps center the bit when drilling

sticker To separate drying lumber with thin wooden slats to allow air circulation between the boards

stile The vertical component of a frame

stop block A small, generally square piece of wood fixed at a specific distance from a saw blade and used as an index to cut multiple boards of exactly equal length

stopped Any cut that does not go all the way through a workpiece; for example, a stopped mortise

story stick A piece of wood used to record dimensions for a project

stove bolt A threaded fastener with a slotted or Phillips head like a screw, used with a nut or in a tapped hole; occasionally called a machine screw

straight chisel Chisel with a straight cutting edge

straight-lined Stock consisting of rough boards with one straight edge

strap hinge A variation of a butt hinge with a rectangular vertical plate affixed to the door frame but a long, narrow metal bar attached across the width of a door or gate

stretcher A horizontal component that connects table or chair legs, used to strengthen construction

substrate Thicker wood or other material used as a foundation beneath veneer

summerwood Harder wood that is produced during the latter part of the growing season; also called latewood

surfaced Lumber that has been planed smooth

swarf Fine metal shavings or filings removed by a cutting tool; the metallic equivalent of sawdust

sweep Description of the curve used on the cutting edge of a gouge

swing A lathe's maximum diameter capacity, expressed as double the distance from the headstock's center of rotation to the lathe bed

swing match A veneer pattern in which alternate adjacent strips of veneer are turned end for end

swirling The curlicue scratches sometimes caused by handheld electric sanders; also called pigtail scratches

---

tack cloth A sticky cloth used to remove dust from freshly sanded wood before staining or finishing

tack time The time it takes glue to begin to hold

tail The cutout portion of a dovetail joint, designed to accept a matching pin

tailstock The apparatus on the unpowered side of a lathe that holds a workpiece for spindle turning

taper Any cut that gradually decreases a workpiece's dimension toward its end

T-bolt Bolt with a T-shaped head, designed to slide into a slot before being tightened; often used for temporary tightening or attachment of jigs, fixtures, and fences

tear-out Splintering caused on the underside or end of a workpiece when a saw blade, router bit, or other cutter exits the wood

TEFC Totally enclosed fan-cooled; describes a sealed motor with an internal impeller designed to lower the operating temperature

tempering Process of using heat to harden a blade or knife to better accept a sharpened edge

template A pattern used to guide a router or other cutting tool

tenon The stub cut on the end of a workpiece intended to be inserted and secured into a matching cavity, or mortise, cut into another workpiece

tensioning Describes the amount of tautness applied to a band saw blade by adjusting the upper support wheel

tension wood A condition of lumber in which the tree was subject to mechanical stress, most often occurring in deciduous trees above the stress point

threaded insert A small metal cylinder threaded both inside and out, designed to be screwed into a workpiece and left there as an anchoring point for a bolt or other fastener

through Any cut that goes completely through a workpiece, such as a through mortise

thrust bearings Metals wheels mounted behind a band saw blade that support the blade during cuts to prevent flexing

tiger figuring A type of wood figuring that resembles a tiger's stripes

tipping off The practice of smoothing out a wet finish by holding the brush at 45° to the surface as it is swept the length of a workpiece

T-nut T-shaped mounting hardware driven into a workpiece and left there as an anchoring point for a bolt or other fastener

toe-nail To drive nails at an angle to the workpiece

toggle clamp A clamp with set open and closed positions, usually adjustable to a specific dimension

tongue-and-groove A variation on a mortise-and-tenon joint, formed by mating a groove cut along the length of a board's edge with a tenon formed along the mating piece

tool rest A horizontal metal bar on a lathe that holds a chisel steady while cutting

torque A measure of the amount of force used to rotate a shaft

Torx head Type of screw head that resembles a star pattern

TPI Teeth per inch

treenware Carved woodenware, such as eating or cooking utensils

triple chip Flat-top teeth on a saw blade that have been chamfered 45° on the corners of the cutting edge

trunnion Metal mounting brackets that hold a motor

try square A hand tool used to measure, confirm, and mark right angles

T-slot A slot of metal or wood in an inverted T shape, used as a guide for accessories

tung oil An oil finish made from tung nuts; the term is often used generically to describe any penetrating oil finish

tungsten carbide An alloy of tungsten and carbon used to harden edges

turn between centers Spindle turning on the lathe with the workpiece held between the headstock and tailstock

twist Lumber defect where the board is twisted along its length

twist bit Drill bit featuring a recessed spiral cut along the length of the bit

two-by (2-by) Dimensional lumber nominally 2" thick

UHMW Ultrahigh molecular weight plastic; commonly used to create sliding jigs

universal motor A small electrical motor with a high power-to-weight ratio, used primarily on portable woodworking tools

urethane A plastic binder used in a coating that cures very hard, imparting high durability to finished wood

vacuum press A plastic bag that holds a glued-up veneered workpiece and that, once air has been evacuated, presses the veneer in place until dry

vapor respirator A facemask used to protect against dust inhalation

varnish Any of a number of hard-curing film finishes used on wood

veiner A small gouge used to carve thin grooves or lines

veneer An extremely thin sheet of wood, generally adhered to a thicker piece of secondary wood called a substrate

veneer-core plywood Plywood made by gluing multiple sheets of veneer with grain alternating at 90° in each layer

veneer press Method of clamping an entire sheet of veneer to a substrate. Small veneer presses may have a handwheel and screw that tightens as a single unit on a workpiece; large presses consist of multiple clamps that spread pressure through a system of cauls and platens.

veneer roller A roller used to smooth freshly glued veneer to its substrate

veneer tape Thin, removable paper tape applied to the face side of veneer to join separate pieces together while they are being glued to a substrate; it is removed after the glue has dried

V-tool A chisel with a V-shaped cutting edge; also called a parting tool

---

wane A natural edge on lumber, often with bark still attached

warp Any defect in lumber that deforms a board's shape

washboarding Describes the ridges formed when veneer is improperly glued to its substrate

wash coat A very thin coat of finish, often used as a seal coat

water stone A flat abrasive stone used for sharpening cutting edges; lubricated with water in use

ways The bed rails on a lathe

web clamp A flexible strap connected to a ratcheting mechanism used to tighten

it around irregularly shaped objects; also called a band clamp

white glue Wood glue based on polyvinyl acetate with woodworking properties similar to yellow glue but offering a longer working time; sometimes called PVA glue

wide-belt sander A stationary sanding machine that uses a sanding belt larger than 12" in width

winding sticks Perfectly straight pieces of wood set on a board in pairs to determine the amount of twist by sighting along the board's length and noting the difference in orientation between the two sticks

wire edge The thin burr that forms on a cutting edge during sharpening

witness lines A shape or series of lines drawn over multiple workpieces to indicate assembly orientation; sometimes called witness marks

wobble dado A dado cutter composed of a single blade that is angled to widen the cut made as the blade spins

wood conditioner Solution applied to wood prior to staining to prevent uneven stain absorption; sometimes called stain controller

woodcut A type of relief carving where an image is created by removing waste below the surface of the wood

working life The amount of time that glue can be exposed to the air and still be workable; also called open time or pot life

worm drive A driveshaft with a spiral groove that transfers rotation at a 90° angle to the motor; used most commonly in circular saws

wormy Wood with channels and tunnels caused by insect damage; often an attractive and desirable trait

---

x Signifies "by" when used to connect two dimensions, such as 8" x 10"

---

yellow glue Common woodworking glue based on aliphatic resin

---

zero-clearance insert A plate mounted into a saw table that surrounds the blade such that there is virtually no clearance at the sides of the blade, used to minimize tear-out

wood wane

Resources

BOOKS AND DVDS
There are literally thousands of fine books on woodworking; here are just a few.

Getting Started in Woodworking
by Aimé Ontario Fraser
Taunton Press, 2003

Sam Maloof, Woodworker
by Sam Maloof
Oxford University Press, 1989

Setting Up Shop
by Sandor Nagyszalanczy
Taunton Press, 2000

Bill Hylton's Power-Tool Joinery
by Bill Hylton
Popular Woodworking Books, 2005

The Accurate Router
by Ian Kirby
Cambium Press, 1998

Wood Finishing Basics on DVD
by Michael Dresdner
Taunton Press, 2004

EDUCATION
From evening and weekend classes for adults, to organizations promoting and aiding woodworking education in public schools, here's a sampling of contacts.

Wood Education and
Resource Center
301 Hardwood Lane
Princeton, WV 24740
(304) 487-1510.
www.na.fs.fed.us/werc

WoodIndustryEd.org
c/o AWFS
5733 Rickenbacker Road
Commerce, CA 90040
(800) 946-2937
education@awfs.org

WoodLINKS USA
11826 Seven Pine Drive
Holland, MI 49424
www.woodlinks.com

Woodworker's Journal eZine
www.woodworkersjournal.com/ezine/schools.cfm
(Includes a state-by-state list of woodworking schools and classes.)

MATERIALS AND SUPPLIES
Rockler Woodworking and
Hardware
4365 Willow Drive
Medina, MN 55340
(800) 279-4441
www.rockler.com

Van Dyke's Restorers
P.O. Box 278
39771 S. D. Hwy. 34
Woonsocket, SD 57385
(800) 787-3355
www.vandykesrestorers.com

Woodfinder
P.O. Box 493
Springtown, PA 18081
(877) 933-4637
www.woodfinder.com

ONLINE SITES
These sites feature a variety of collected information, including archives, tool reviews, technique articles, and more. Most also have an interactive forum or user information exchange.

Woodworking.com
(Woodworking portal site)
www.woodworking.com

WoodCentral
(Woodworking forum)
www.woodcentral.com

Women in Woodworking
(For the growing number of women woodworkers)
www.womeninwoodworking.com

WoodWorkWeb
www.woodworkweb.com

Woodworker's Journal
www.woodworkersjournal.com

ORGANIZATIONS
There are hundreds of organizations dedicated to a variety of woodworking disciplines, with chapters and locations in all 50 states. These will get you started.

American Association of
Woodturners
222 Landmark Center
75 W. 5th Street
St. Paul, MN 55102
(651) 484-9094
www.woodturner.org

The Furniture Society
111 Grovewood Road
Asheville, NC 28804
(828) 255-1950
www.furnituresociety.org

National Wood Carvers
Association
P.O. Box 43218
Cincinnati, OH 45243
(513) 561-0627
www.chipchats.org

Scrollsaw Association
of the World
768 Rifle Road
Sylvania, GA 30467
(912) 829-5708
www.saw-online.com

SHOWS AND EVENTS
Throughout the year, dozens of woodworking events occur each week, from furniture shows and competitions, to tool exhibitions and swap meets.

Association of Woodworking &
Furnishings Suppliers
5733 Rickenbacker Road
Commerce, CA 90040
(800) 946-2937
www.awfs.org

Fine Furnishings
Providence Show
KL Communications
4 Halidon Terrace
Newport, RI 02840
(401) 841-9201
www.finefurnishingsshow.com

International Woodworking
Machinery & Furniture
Supply Fair
3520 Piedmont Road N.E., Suite 350
Atlanta GA 30305
(404) 693-8333
www.iwfatlanta.com

Philadelphia Furniture
& Furnishings Show
162 N. Third Street
Philadelphia, PA 19106
(215) 440-0718
www.pffshow.com

The WoodWorks Shows
3 Links Productions
P.O. Box 665
New Hope, PA 18938
(215) 862-7157
www.woodworksevents.com

Walnut music stand, by Wendell Castle

Index

Picture Credits

With the exception of the images credited below, all photographs and illustrations are from Woodworker's Journal *or courtesy of Rockler Woodworking and Hardware.*

FRONT COVER Getty/Photodisc Blue

CHAPTER 1: A Brief History of Woodworking and Furniture Styles

xvi Johann Helgason/Shutterstock. **2** *Cabinet_* c. 1675, André-Charles Boulle Oak with various other sorts of wood, 189 x 129 x 59.3 cm, Rijksmuseum, Amsterdam **3** Winterthur Museum, Delaware **4t** "Portrait of Daniel Marot" by Jacob Gole, after James Parmentier line engraving, late 17th century 10¾ in. x 7¾ in. (272 mm x 196 mm) plate size; 13⅛ in. x 9 in. (332 mm x 228 mm) paper size, Rijksmuseum, Amsterdam, given by the daughter of compiler William Fleming MD, Mary Elizabeth Stopford, 1931-06-25 **4b** courtesy of Sotheby's **5.** Winterthur Museum, Delaware, Accession 55.784 **6t** Peale, Charles *Portrait of Benjamin Randolph* Philadelphia Museum of Art: Gift of Mr. And Mrs. Timothy Johnes Westbrook, 1990 **6l** Winterthur Museum, Delaware. **6b** Winterthur Museum, Delaware **7l** National Museum of American History, Behring Center, Smithsonian Institution (2000-3214). **7r** Philadelphia Museum of Art: Purchased with museum funds, 1929 **8** Duncan Phyfe Room, Winterthur Museum, Delaware **9tl** Winterthur Museum, Delaware **9tm** Winterthur Museum, Delaware **9tr** Winterthur Museum, Delaware, Accession 57.882.1 **9b** Winterthur Museum, Delaware, Accession 57.599.1 **9br** Winterthur Museum, Delaware, Accession 57.775 **10** Winterthur Museum, Delaware, Accession 57.68 **11** Winterthur Museum, Delaware, **11b** Winterthur Museum, Delaware, Accession 57.914 **12.** Winterthur Museum, Delaware, Accession 57.912 **13** Baltimore Museum of Art. **14l** Courtesy of Hancock Shaker Village, Pittsfield, Massachusetts, photo by P. Rochleau. **14b** Faith and Deming Andrews Collection **15t** Shaker Museum and Library, Old Chatham and New Lebanon New York **15b** Faith and Deming Andrews Collection **17t** © Christie's Images New York, Accession 139P1072 **17b** © Christie's Images New York, Accession 139P1082 **18** Virginia Museum of Fine Arts, Richmond. The Mary Morton Parsons Fund for American Decorative Arts. **19** Rago Arts and Auction Center, Lambertville, NJ **20t** The Art Institute of Chicago, Bessie Bennett Fund **20b** Art Institute of Chicago **20r** The Craftsman Farms Foundation, Parsippany, New Jersey, courtesy of L. and J.G. Stickley Co. **21** Philadelphia Museum of Art **22tl** The Craftsman Farms Foundation, Parsippany, New Jersey, courtesy of L. and J.G. Stickley Co **22c** Virginia Museum of Fine Arts, Richmond. The Adolph D. and Wilkins C. Williams fund. **22b** The Craftsman Farms Foundation, Parsippany, New Jersey, Courtesy of L. and JG. Stickley Co.. **23** The Craftsman Farms Foundation, Parsippany, New Jersey, courtesy of L. and J.G. Stickley Co. **24bl** Virginia Museum of Fine Arts, Richmond. The Sydney and Frances Lewis Art Nouveau Fund. **24bc** Virginia Museum of Fine Arts, Richmond. Gift of Sydney and Frances Lewis. **24br** The Gamble House, Pasadena, California, USA/ The Bridgeman Art Library, photo by Mark Fiennes **26bl** courtesy of Sam Maloof (photo by Tim Rue) **26** Maloof, 1997.88©1980. Sam Maloof, *Rocker* 1980, 44¾ x 45¾ x 26¾ in. (113.7 x 116.2 x 67.9 cm) Smithsonian American Art Museum, gift,of Roger and Frances Kennedy (1997.88). **27t** courtesy of James Krenov (photo by Kevin Shea) **27b** courtesy of James Krenov (photography: *Sister Kevin Shea. 003, 004* Bengt Carlen **27br** Osgood, 1990.53©1989. Jere Osgood. *Cylinder-Front Desk* 1989. 45⅞ x 43¼ x 29 in (116.5 x 109.9 x 73.7 cm.) Smithsonian American Art Museum, gift of the James Renwick Alliance and museum purchase made possible by the Smithsonian Institution Collections Acquisition Program (1990.53) **27tr** photo courtesy of Jere Osgood. **28l** photo courtesy of A.J. Hamler **28c** photo courtesy of Soomi Amagasu, George Nakashima, Woodworker, S.A. **29tr** *Conoid Bench* 1977 George Nakashima walnut and hickory 31⅛ x 84½ x 35⅝ in. (79.1 x 214.6 x 90.5 cm) Smithsonian American Art Museum, gift of Dr. and Mrs. Warren D. Brill (1991.121) **29br** *Coffee Table* 195 Wendell Castle, American walnut and padauk 23⅜ x 63½ x 31 in. (59.4 x 161.3 x 78.8 cm) Smithsonian American Art Museum, gift of the Ruhe family in memory of Dr. Lehman Ruhe (1993.24) **29b** © Wendell Castle, Inc. (photo by George Kamper)

CHAPTER 2: The Nature of Hardwood

30 photo courtesy of John English **37b** photo courtesy of John English **39–52** illustrations by Phoebe Chui and Pleum Nithiruedee Chenaphun **39–51, 52l, 53–55** wood grain photos courtesy of Paul Hinds, woodpics@hobbithous.inc.com **52r** photo courtesy of A.J. Hamler

CHAPTER 3: A Safe and Comfortable Workshop

58 Fogstock LLC/ Index Open

CHAPTER 5: Portable Power Tools

94b photo courtesy A.J. Hamler

CHAPTER 8: Techniques for Making Project Parts

142 photo courtesy Dana Van Pelt **144**(all) photos courtesy A.J. Hamler

CHAPTER 9: Joining Wood.

158 Photos.com. **162–163**(all) photos courtesy A.J. Hamler **174b** photo courtesy A.J. Hamler

CHAPTER 10: Veneering Basics

176 photo courtesy of Glenn Cormier **180l** photo courtesy A.J. Hamler

CHAPTER 11: Carving and Scrolling

188 photo courtesy of John Garton **192l** photo courtesy of Wayne Barton **192b** photo courtesy of Wayne Shinlever

CHAPTER 14: Hardware

234 photo courtesy of A.J. Hamler **236** photo courtesy of Shapiro-Gordon family archive **238bl** photo courtesy of A.J. Hamler

CHAPTER 15: Sanding and Finishing

260b photos courtesy of A.J. Hamler

CHAPTER 16: Setting Up Shop

282 photo courtesy of A.J. Hamler **283** photo courtesy of A.J. Hamler **284** photo courtesy of A.J. Hamler **286l** photo courtesy of A.J. Hamler

319 photo courtesy A.J. Hamler **326** *Music Stand*, 1975, Wendell Castle. Walnut 42⅛ x 26⅜ x 19¼ in. (107.0 x 67.0 x 49.0 cm). Smithsonian American Art Museum purchase (1975.168)

Thanks as well to these woodworking companies for supplying photos used in this book.

Amana Tool

Black & Decker Corp.

Bosch Tool Corp.

CMT Utensili

Delta Machinery

DeWalt

Ecogate

Forrest Manufacturing Co.

Freud Inc.

Grizzly Industrial Inc.

Hitachi

Kreg Tool Co.

Laguna Tools Inc.

Makita U.S.A.

Oneida Air Systems

Porter-Cable Corp.

Ridgid Tool Co.

Ryobi

Sears Brands (Craftsman)

Steel City Tool Works

3M

Tormek AB

Trend Machinery Co.

WMH Tool Group